Ageing and Spirituality across Faiths and Cultures

Ageing and Spirituality across Faiths and Cultures

Edited by Elizabeth MacKinlay

Jessica Kingsley Publishers
London and Philadelphia

First published in 2010
by Jessica Kingsley Publishers
116 Pentonville Road
London N1 9JB, UK
and
400 Market Street, Suite 400
Philadelphia, PA 19106, USA

www.jkp.com

Copyright © Jessica Kingsley Publishers 2010

The chapters of this book have been peer-reviewed, and fulfil the criteria
for original research as set out by the Australian Government Department
of Innovation, Industry, Science and Research (DIISR).

Library of Congress Cataloging in Publication Data
A CIP catalog record for this book is available from the Library of Congress

British Library Cataloguing in Publication Data
A CIP catalogue record for this book is available from the British Library

ISBN 978 1 84905 006 7

Printed and bound in Great Britain by
MPG Books Limited

Contents

Acknowledgements

I acknowledge the commitment and valuable contribution of each of the authors to this book. I also acknowledge the valuable secretarial work of Ellen Kennedy and the support of Merrie Hepworth for editorial assistance and reading and checking the manuscript.

Preface

This book began its formation in the process of the fourth national conference on ageing and spirituality hosted by the Centre for Ageing and Pastoral Studies (CAPS) in August 2008. This conference took place in Australia; however, the issues raised have implications for the ageing of populations and spiritual and pastoral care internationally. Demographics raise the importance of this topic of ageing people in the context of faiths and cultures, but beneath the demographics of ageing lie critical factors of what it means to be human and how people of different cultures and faith relate to each other, especially in later life.

The conference that was the starting point for this book set out to explore and examine ageing in the context of faiths and cultures that make up Western societies in the early twenty-first century. We based our explorations on hearing from the major faiths that currently have ageing populations in Western societies.

The aims of this conference were to bring researchers, practitioners and older people together to share and examine issues of faiths and cultures within the context of ageing and spirituality. Theological and ethical issues of ageing, religion and spirituality in different faiths and cultural communities have been examined in the essays within this book. Authors have examined ways of integrating key issues of diverse faiths and cultures related to ageing and spirituality identified during the conference. In addressing these aims, emphasis has been given to the types of cultures commonly experienced by older people, in both community and residential care, and implications and challenges for policy and community development.

During the three days of the conference we explored and examined issues of faiths and cultures in the context of growing older in societies with a diversity of faiths and cultures. These issues touch each of us personally; they touch us in our growing older, in our practice of care, and in the development of policies that drive the provision of appropriate care for older people. The complexity of the composition of the current cohort of older people is amply shown in Chapter 3, by Seebus and Peut, on the cultural and religious diversity of older Australians, based on research of the Australian Institute of Health and Welfare.

The book contains chapters written by authors from the major faiths, about the cultures, traditions and faiths of their older people. Authors come from a wide range of backgrounds and cultures, with chapters written by both academics and practitioners. Issues of culture and faith diversity raise important issues of inclusion versus exclusion, of respect for others, of learning about others and being open to the differences that we find. We have choices in the ways that we approach each other in a community.

In this book Rachael Kohn ponders the richness of experiences of ageing, in Chapter 4, 'The Ageing Spirit'. Elizabeth MacKinlay (Chapter 5) addresses the topic of pastoral and spiritual care provided from a Christian perspective, while Rosalie Hudson (Chapter 11) provides an Eastern Orthodox perspective on ageing and dementia care. A practice-orientated chapter on holistic care in a Greek Orthodox aged care facility is provided by Robyn Simmonds and Nicholas Stavropoulos (Chapter 12), while Gabrielle Brian reflects on the ageing journey of older religious sisters, in their final life vocation (Chapter 15).

Christian and Muslim perspectives on ageing are the subject of Chapter 2, by James Haire, introducing other faith perspectives into the mix. A chapter on Muslim faith and ageing is co-authored by Mohamad Abdalla and Ikebal Mohammed Adam Patel (Chapter 8), while a Jewish perspective is provided by Jeffrey Cohen (Chapter 6). Chapter 9, on ageing and Buddhism, is written by Subhana Barzaghi. A chapter focusing on dying in Buddhist and Hindu cultures is jointly written by Amy Rayner and Purushottama Bilimoria (Chapter 10).

Understanding the complexities of ageing, culture and spirituality is important so that we might attempt to honour and sensitively provide opportunities for growth and flourishing in later life, as well as to provide care for people from a diversity of faiths and cultures, not only our own. In Chapter 7, issues of Indigenous ageing pertaining to culture and spirituality are addressed with great sensitivity by Dennis McDermott. Dennis uses poetry to engage the heart of these issues. A life-course perspective for understanding Indigenous ageing is suggested, acknowledging the importance of a whole of life view. The importance of cultural competence is advocated.

Ann Harrington's chapter (Chapter 13) is on the well-being of older people, focusing on spiritual well-being, while in Chapter 14 Tracey McDonald writes on care of a large subsection, and perhaps subculture, of ageing: the issues of ageing veterans. Elizabeth Pringle, writing from her role with the Aged Care Standards and Accreditation Agency, responsible for education and standards of aged care in Australia, explains the standards in relation to specific requirements of spirituality and culture (Chapter 16).

These are very practical issues that those who work in residential aged care work and grapple with on a daily basis.

The final chapter of the book, by Elizabeth MacKinlay, takes up the process and outcomes of a search conference held to carry forward the concepts, goals and challenges facing practitioners of ageing and spiritual and pastoral care, focusing on standards, education and research needs of this emerging field.

A book such as this collection of essays on faith and cultures in later life can only attempt to open the conversation, and highlight some of the issues in this important field. It was with this in mind that these essays were drawn together as a beginning to the conversation.

CHAPTER 1

Ageing and Spirituality: Living and Being in Multifaith and Multicultural Communities

Elizabeth MacKinlay

In this collection of essays we are seeking to understand more clearly the faiths that underlie the beliefs, practices and values of older people from the various faiths and cultures that comprise Western societies. There are certain commonalities within the journey of ageing, across faiths and cultures; there are also differences.

Ageing comprises a variety of perspectives, depending on the definition of the beginning of being 'old'. If the definition of being 'old' is 65 years, in current Western societies, then the years of being old until death can be around three decades or more. Within that chronological perspective of ageing are many variations. First, those who are ageing 'well'; they may continue to hold jobs and continue to contribute in the workplace until into their seventies, some even later. Can it really be said that they are 'old'? Still some of their peers, even only in their sixties, may live with chronic illnesses and disabilities, preventing full engagement with life. Are these people 'old'?

There has been much focus on positive ageing in recent decades with the 'successful ageing' paradigm, led by Rowe and Kahn (1997). This paradigm has certain value in current societies, to encourage healthy and active ageing, and to reduce use of scarce health resources. It also has the disadvantage of casting a judgement over the later years, suggesting that if some older people age successfully, then others must age unsuccessfully; that is, some may fail the test.

The importance of culture

But what is meant by culture, especially when put into the context of ageing? It is necessary first to explore the dimensions of culture.

Culture is the way that a group of people define meaning in their being. Geertz (1975), taking an anthropological view, describes a concept of culture as:

> an historically transmitted pattern of meanings embodied in symbols, a system of inherited conceptions expressed in symbolic forms by means of which men communicate, perpetuate, and develop the knowledge about and attitudes to life. (p.89)

This is a very inclusive view of culture and within the context of this description it can be said that meaning permeates all that a community is. It can be said that the symbols used by a culture name or point to the meanings held by that culture; they provide for the group a common understanding of their identity. Thus culture can be the vehicle for holding and affirming understandings held by the group, including values and beliefs, while it also presents a view of identity of *this* community in comparison with any other community.

The view set out by Geertz makes it possible to see connections between both the secular and the sacred, and further, 'the secular can be imbued with sacred power by the people' of that group, or culture (MacKinlay 2001, p.91). Cultures may change over time and the symbols and rituals that support the cultures also change. New cultures may form within the larger society – for instance, the ageing population of veterans from World War II, ageing veterans from the Korean, and now from the Vietnam wars form cohesive cultures within the Australian society. Chapter 14 in this book is written from the perspective of care for ageing veterans.

Questions of Indigenous culture, spirituality and ageing are taken up by Dennis McDermott in Chapter 7. As McDermott writes, Indigenous cultures and spirituality are complex. He uses the term 'cultural ease' to describe a needed attribute for those Indigenous health practitioners to be effective providers of care. This attribute is the ability to work in 'right relationship' with others, and 'to foreground the humility, flexibility and self-reflexivity required for culturally competent and culturally safe practice' (page 106).

A culture of ageing?

Erik Erikson (1997, p.114) wrote in 1987 that since we lack 'a culturally viable ideal of old age, our civilization does not really harbor a concept of the whole of life'. It may be that he was considering a concept of ageing within the whole of Western society, rather than a subculture of ageing, and in this context, he saw no evidence of such a culture within the whole of the lifespan. What I want to explore here is the possibility of a culture of later life.

It can be asked, in societies that have increasing proportions of older adults, is there an identifiable culture of ageing? Indeed, it can be asked, *should* there be a culture of ageing? Do cultures simply evolve, can they be intentionally formed, or is it a combination of both? Until recently, it seems there has been little thought given to the development of cultures of ageing, except perhaps in the provision of villages for retirement of older people. But a culture of ageing – might that be a useful way of considering the later part of the lifespan?

When Erikson first set out his eight-stage version of the life cycle, he had not considered the addition of a further stage that would account for further changes that might take in the later years of the life cycle. It was as Erik and his wife Joan grew still older themselves that they further considered the addition of a further stage. Joan notes that in original stages of development, each of the stages was expressed by the 'syntonic quotient' first, followed by the dystonic – for instance, trust versus basic mistrust. Here trust is the syntonic or positive adjustment, while dystonic represents the mal-adjustive aspect. In childhood development, the syntonic was seen as the most likely emphasis; in other words, the emphasis was on positive development and growth. Balance between the syntonic and dystonic was always seen as important. Now, through the eyes of the author, writing in her nineties, she sees that the syntonic and dystonic have been reversed, as she acknowledges that increasing disabilities and illnesses more often accompany life. Thus she has reversed the order of expressing the stages, for example in frailty, the dominant aspect may become despair versus integrity, rather than integrity versus despair. The ninth stage, which is a coming together of all the previous life stages, can be set out as follows: first, basic mistrust versus trust; with the outcome of *hope*. The second stage becomes shame and doubt versus autonomy: *will*. The third stage becomes guilt versus initiative: *purpose*. The fourth is inferiority versus industry: *competence*. The fifth will be identity confusion versus identity: *fidelity*. The sixth, isolation versus intimacy: *love*; the seventh, stagnation versus generativity: *care*. The eighth stage becomes despair and disgust versus integrity, with the outcome of *wisdom*.

Joan Erikson, writing of this more recently acknowledged ninth stage of the life cycle, and the struggle that is implicit within all the preceding life stages, goes on to say:

> Lacking a culturally viable ideal of old age, our civilization does not harbor a concept of the whole of life. As a result, our society does not truly know

how to integrate elders into its primary patterns and conventions or into its vital functioning. Rather than be included, aged individuals are often ostracized, neglected, and overlooked; elders are seen no longer as bearers of wisdom but as embodiments of shame. (Erikson 1997, p.114)

Is this still so?

What kind of culture embraces ageing? I would suggest it must be an inclusive culture that honours all ages. To do this, we must be willing to explore and examine not only the earlier stages of the life cycle, but the later years as well. In this exploration, we must be open to the life struggles, the richness of the faiths and cultures that constitute the fabric of the wider society, and to ageing itself.

The conference that was the starting point for this book set out to explore and examine ageing in the context of faiths and cultures that make up Western societies. It was based on growing community realisations of the increasing numbers of ageing people of different cultures and faiths. Our explorations were based on hearing from the major faiths that currently have ageing populations, acknowledging that Christianity remains the most common religion of older people in many Western societies. In the UK 72 per cent of people stated their religion as Christian (ONS 2001); in the USA 47.4 per cent said they were Christian church adherents (US Census Bureau 2009)[1]; in Australia, 64 per cent according to recent figures (ABS 2006). Authors included in this book, from the major faith groups, of Judaism, Islam, Buddhism and Hinduism, have written about the cultures and faith of their older people. It is important to hear the voices of the people who are part of the whole and rich fabric of Western societies in the early twenty-first century. It is only on hearing the voices that we might begin to honour and sensitively provide care for older people from a diversity of faiths and cultures, not only our own.

To those who are not defined as 'old', old may seem at best to be a homogeneous collection of people with little further to contribute to society, and at worst, a drain on resources that could be spent on other priorities of life. However, Erikson's question of finding a 'culturally viable ideal of old age' may not be possible at all. Once the later years of life are examined more carefully, it becomes clear that there is great diversity among older people. To construct a culture of ageing may be neither possible nor of any practical value, either to older people, or indeed to any age groups. However, it is important to identify particular subgroups, and perhaps subcultures of older people where care needs might become more urgent and more difficult to fulfil. It may be in these subgroups of ageing people that particular cultures exist. Examples are not hard to find; the growing numbers of older people who live with dementia could be said to constitute one very vulnerable group. In fact, if the definition of culture, as cited earlier (Geertz 1975), depends on the identity of the group being formed, through common understanding of the group members, then in the case of dementia, it might be argued by some that a culture may only exist by definition of others, not the group members, as they no longer hold agency. Can it be argued that a culture of dementia exists within residential aged care? On what basis can it exist, and if it does, how can people who have dementia be empowered to have a voice in their own culture, to build an inclusive culture that supports them in their vulnerability?

Another group, which can be further subdivided, consists of those whose culture and/or faith identifies them as a minority group within the mainstream Western society, such as immigrant groups, particularly those who lack language skills needed to function effectively within the dominant culture.

Many post-World War II immigrants suffered greatly during the war years and came to their new countries with little means of support and, particularly the women, with little understanding of the English language. Chapter 3, written by Seebus and Peut, gives an excellent picture of the cultural and faith backgrounds of such immigrants coming to Australia.

Another complication that comes with increasing age is frailty, and this, when overlaid by being a member of a minority cultural and faith group, can become a serious isolating factor.

Ageing, frailty and culture

Preserving the culture of people who are becoming increasingly frail in later life is a particular challenge for those who provide their care. It is a responsibility of carers to support and affirm the culture of frail and otherwise disabled older people. Frail older people need the presence of familiar symbols, language and rituals to support their continuing identity as members of the particular culture and subculture. The importance of culture to elderly people is recognised in the Aged Care and Accreditation Agency Guidelines for residential aged care in Australia. These standards are described by Pringle in Chapter 16 of this book.

The importance of religious symbols to support meaning is also important for many older people. In this book, the major faiths of people who are ageing are considered, including the symbols and rituals that support these people. While it is widely recognised that religious symbols are important for adherents of particular religions, it is helpful to consider the ways in which these religious symbols may be of value. Geertz (1975) notes that for those who accept the usefulness of religious symbols, these:

provide a cosmic guarantee not only for their ability to comprehend the world, but also, comprehending it, to give a precision to their feeling, a definition to their emotions which enables them, morosely or joyfully, grimly or cavalierly, to endure it. (p.104)

With increased individualism in the postmodern society, the significance of symbols and ritual may be in danger of being lost, or weakened. It is hard for individuals to live into, or draw meaning from their symbols in isolation, and particularly to engage with the meaning of rituals, as these, in essence, belong to communities, not individuals. The way that society's weak and vulnerable people are supported can be seen as evidence of the cohesiveness of a culture. A healthy culture will have symbols that resonate with the people; they will support the emotional life of the group, pointing the way to what is held as important within that group or culture. People who are frail need others who will support and affirm them in their adherence to ways of worship, including the appropriate use of rituals, symbols and culture that are familiar and meaningful.

Individualism and community: Inclusive or isolating?

Much emphasis is currently given to supporting and affirming people (not only older people) in their individualism and autonomy. Yet the nature of ageing, which for many is accompanied by increasing disability and frailty, renders the exercise of autonomy increasingly difficult. It seems that not only is it important to uphold the individual, but it is important, too, to affirm the community, whether this is the community of a particular culture, or the community of faith of particular individuals. Perhaps this is even more so when a particular community has few members, and these are becoming elderly. Meaning is held in connectedness between people, and may be threatened by loss of relationships in later life, especially in the context of dementia and frailty. Further, frailty makes for enormous shifts in power, which compromises the ability of individuals to remain autonomous in achieving their needs, whether these are physical, mental, emotional or spiritual. At a very practical level, isolation and loneliness await many frail older people who have lost their ability to drive and move easily around their communities. These people lose the ability to access their needs for daily activities, and even their access to meaningful community. Meaningful community provides the basis for human flourishing and connectedness.

The importance of communities of faith is emphasised in Swinton's work (2007) where he describes the role of healing and re-membering in strengthening communities. Re-membering means to bring together again. This involves using groups in much the same way that the early church functioned, in times of great 'tribulation, to share fellowship, joy, pain, and hope' (Swinton 2007, p.124). Issues of past hurt, guilt and grief can be supported through practice of lament in small groups. Lament, modelled on the Biblical practices of lament, can work to support the members in expressing their grief and hurt in secure and safe places, thus moving towards resolution and healing, so that the group members can grow into healing and mutual support, and flourish.

Religions and ageing in the early twenty-first century

In relation to the Australian experience, much that is of relevance to the proportion of older people in each major *religious* group is covered in more depth in Seebus and Peut (Chapter 3). Religion itself needs to be understood in relation to both spirituality and the secular society, its values and ways of being a community. Koenig, McCullough and Larson (2001, p.18) define religion as:

> an organized system of beliefs, practices, rituals, and symbols designed
>
> (a) to facilitate closeness to the sacred or transcendent (God, higher power, or ultimate truth/reality), and
>
> (b) to foster an understanding of one's relationship and responsibility to others in living together in a community.

The major religions in Western countries are the three Abrahamic faiths (Christianity, Islam and Judaism), Buddhism and Hinduism. According to Greeley (1982) other groups within societies can also become religions; for example, humanism, or feminism. In comparison to religion as defined above, spirituality can be understood as a more individual response to what each person finds meaningful, as mediated through relationship, environment and the arts (and religious practices for those who practise a religion). Relationship in spirituality can be whatever the person wants it to be. Thus for people who work out their spirituality through religion (and in particular for the Abrahamic faiths), their relationship will be with God, sometimes termed the 'vertical' relationship. The so-called horizontal dimension of the spiritual then is worked out through relationship with others.

Pluralism and its place in Western societies in the twenty-first century

Are we really talking about pluralism? What does genuine pluralism look like? It is certainly not 'being like everyone else'; rather, as Hauerwas (1988, p.250) describes it, genuine pluralism is about sustaining our differences, as Christians, or people of other particular faiths and cultures. Genuine pluralism honours differences. It is only through the honouring of the cultures and belief systems of others that real pluralism can exist. The aim of pluralism is not to produce a sameness across a society; therefore moves to reduce the diversity of cultures and beliefs and their practices are to do dishonour to all.

Real pluralism seeks to allow people to practise their religion and culture according to their understandings and needs. Bouma (2006) uses the image from the tower of Babel (Genesis 11: 1–9) to show that 'God is relationship, and relationship requires difference, diversity and otherness' (Bouma 2006, p.120). This concept is contextualised by Bouma in his statement: 'The challenge for the twenty-first century is to understand, practise and extend the inclusivity of God's love across lifestyles, across religious forms and across divisions and differences not yet apparent to us' (2006, p.121). It seems that there is a growing awareness of this across Western societies, as people acknowledge their own religious beliefs and at the same time accept that there is a variety of ways of working out one's religion, even within the one faith. On the other side of this openness to others are the fundamentalist religious groups that claim exclusivity for their own beliefs (Bouma 2006). Cultural diversity is seen by Bouma to be as important for cultural vitality and sustainability 'as biodiversity is to life itself' (2006, p.121). He points out that few purity-seeking religious organisations persist, and likewise, that secular exclusivist organisations like Mao's Cultural Revolution did great damage and did not endure.

When I approached speakers inviting them to participate in the conference on which this book is based, a number of them stated they could only give one view, or one perspective of being Indigenous, or being Jewish, or being Buddhist; or 'I can give only one view of being Christian'. We acknowledged this diversity in the conference by including Orthodox Christianity as well as Western Christianity, recognising also that there are many different denominations even within these.

Types of cultures and ageing

Perhaps what we mean here is more correctly defined as subcultures. Older veterans form a particular subculture. The aged care industry forms another. There are many more, including the subcultures of older people from non-English-speaking backgrounds and the whole group now called CALD (culturally and linguistically diverse). The current cohorts of people in their ninth decade contain many who immigrated from Europe at the end of World War II. Older people are also divided into groups by their disabilities, in order to separate them from others; for example, impaired mobility, sensory losses and mental incapacity, to name some of the more important subgroupings.

We also know that there are numbers of people of different ages who do not profess any kind of religious faith, and yet they may be providing care for others for whom faith is important. Further, these people without a religious faith may need spiritual care themselves. Any of us, regardless of our own faith perspective, may need to provide spiritual care to others of very different backgrounds and beliefs.

In the current cohort of people over 65 years of age, many have had some experiences of organised religion, at least in their childhood. However, there are some of these older people who may have been hurt by the church in the past, and who have rejected their religious belief system. It is important that pastoral and spiritual care is given with sensitivity and respect for the recipients of care, while maintaining the integrity of the carers.

The provision of care to older people

Care must be culturally and religiously sensitive. This assumes that those who provide care will have a strong knowledge base of older people's culture and spirituality. There is a growing body of knowledge about the spiritual needs of older people; it can now be argued that the spirituality of ageing forms a special area of study in its own right (Atchley 2009). Yet, ageing is not only about caring for weak and vulnerable older people, for, as Atchley suggests, two major dimensions of ageing and spirituality are becoming a sage and 'serving from spirit' (2009, p.xii). Thus, even in frailty, elderly people may care for each other, and expressions of wisdom of the sage may be seen among them. It is often far easier for elderly people to continue to give to others while they remain within the wider community, than it is following admission to an aged care facility. Ways of engaging with older people within aged care facilities, that honour their ability to still 'be' authentic human beings, who should be supported in their continuing life journeys towards later-life flourishing, require important focus. There is still a need to affirm ministry by, to and with older adults. As frailty increases, so does the need for interdependency; for example, an elderly person may require physical support and care, but still be able to engage in an effective prayer ministry.

Providers of spiritual and pastoral care

The terms 'spiritual' and 'pastoral' care are often used interchangeably; however, there are subtle differences in meaning. Spiritual care seems to be as it says – care of the spirit. This care, at one level, may be delivered by anyone who is in relationship with another person. However, the depths of the spiritual dimension can be touched by skilled pastoral practitioners, working in relationship with others. For example, spiritual advisors or spiritual directors accompany people on an ever deepening spiritual journey of guidance and spiritual growth. Spiritual care may also be provided by health care professionals, but with caution. Spiritual care cannot be delivered as a 'dose', like a medicine or treatment. *Relationship* lies at the heart of spiritual care and makes the provision of spiritual care a privileged place of presence, one with another.

In later life, and especially in frailty, dementia and palliative care, other health care practitioners may be the ones present at a time of spiritual need. These practitioners need to be spiritually sensitive and skilled communicators, particularly in their readiness to listen. Spiritual care is sufficiently well researched and developed now to be able to incorporate the required skills into professional and vocational preparation of practitioners. An important component of education in this field is the raising of practitioners' sensitivity to the spirituality of the people they are caring for, with all its variations according to culture and religion.

Pastoral care includes all of the above; however, it differs from spiritual care in that these practitioners have their whole focus on care of the spirit and emotional needs of those they care for. They could be said to be the 'specialists' of this field. This is indeed a privileged role. Chaplains also provide pastoral and spiritual care, and in addition, chaplains are the providers of religious care. Issues of education, standards and the future of role development in pastoral and spiritual care are taken up in the final chapter of this book.

Pastoral and spiritual care across faiths and cultures

Specific chapters of this book provide examples of the diversity of religious and spiritual needs and care of older people within Western societies in the early years of the twenty-first century. As this book had its beginnings in a conference held in Australia, many of the contributors take Australian diversity as their basis. However, their arguments can be, and are, equally applied to other Western countries. Christian, Jewish, Islamic, Buddhist and Hindu practices in faith and care of older adults make up the main part of this book. One chapter is written from an Australian Indigenous perspective of ageing and spirituality. Other chapters provide demographic information on ageing in Australia, the perspective of setting and oversight of standards for the provision of aged care, and a view of the particular subculture of ageing veterans and their care. A journey with a group of ageing religious sisters provides insight into yet another aspect of the diversity of ageing and spirituality.

Conclusion

Sometimes the spiritual seems hard to express and the words of prose do not seem able justly to portray the truth and depth of human being. In this context McDermott (Chapter 7) uses poetry in his expression of Indigenous spirituality and ageing. It is pertinent that poetry is a mode of communication of the depths, as seen for example in Killick's (1997) collection of poetry collected while listening to people living with dementia. Another example of deep concepts more readily communicated through poetry is the poem written by Barbara Noon:

> Sometimes I picture myself like a candle.
> I used to be a candle about eight feet tall –
> burning bright.
> Now every day I lose a little bit of me.
> Someday the candle will be
> very small.
> But the flame will be
> just as bright.
>
> (Noon 2003, printed with permission)

The poem needs little explanation, as the reader can easily grasp the profundity of what is being expressed. On first reading there is an element of surprise for the reader, who may not previously have thought of dementia and the concept of spirituality in this way.

There is a sense of journey and discovery in the many aspects of ageing set in the diversity of religion and cultures that exist within current Western societies. Vulnerability exists side by side with human flourishing. The richness of religious expression and the traditions of older people, grounded in their cultural heritage, can be likened to a tapestry of life, interwoven with many colours and threads, to be honoured and loved.

Note
1. As the USA Census does not ask the question of religion, these figures cannot be accurately compared with other countries where this question is asked; it only provides numbers of people who are church adherents.

CHAPTER 2

The Interrelationship of Spirituality, Culture and Community in International Perspective

James Haire

Introduction

This chapter deals with the interrelationship of spirituality, culture and community from an international perspective. It begins by looking historically at types of cultures and types of spirituality in relation to community, with special emphasis on the development of Judaism, Christianity and Islam. Specifically it looks at the dynamics of cyclic cultures and word cultures, and the interaction between the two, particularly as they relate to community and spirituality. It uses as an example the search for the creation of communities of peace between faith-groupings around the world, by looking at the milieu of violence in which the faith-groups began, and then at the dynamics of their search for transformation to peaceful co-existence. From this, the paper seeks to draw out pragmatic conclusions in relation to spirituality, community and cultures.

Initially I seek to examine the interrelationship of spirituality, culture and community in international perspective by engaging in historical analysis. However, I do so not simply from a theoretical framework, but also from practical experience. I have had the privilege of lecturing in Indonesia for over 35 years. During this time I have been involved in Christian–Muslim dialogue, both in Australia and in South-East Asia, particularly in Indonesia, over many years. Indeed, I have had the privilege of lecturing at the Sekolah Tinggi Agama Islam Negeri (STAIN – the State Islamic University) in Malang, in East Java. I have also had the joy of engaging in public dialogue with K.H. Abdurrahman Wahid (Gus Dur), former president of the Republic of Indonesia. However, more than that, at the request of the Indonesian authorities I was engaged in the peace process for the Molucca Islands (Kepulauan Maluku) in Indonesia between 2001 and 2005, when I took part in persuading the Christian population to engage in the Muslim–Christian peace talks, which mercifully have been largely very successful.

Nevertheless, I speak as a Christian theologian. Who are we Christians? In theological terms, it is not precise to speak of our faith as 'Christianity', as if it were some sort of ideology competing with other ideologies in the marketplace of ideas. Rather, we are the ones who bear the mark of Christ upon ourselves, symbolically on our foreheads as it were (Williams 2006). In Rowan Williams' words, '(w)e carry the name of Christ' (Williams 2006, p.6). As he goes on to say, '(w)e are the people who are known for their loyalty to, their affiliation with, the historical person who was given the title of 'anointed monarch' by his followers – Jesus, the Jew of Nazareth' (Williams 2006, p.6). Our identity is not, first and foremost, as those who promote a particular ideology. Rather, it is as those who bear witness to God's action upon and within our personal and communal lives, including our personal and communal spirituality.

Moreover, it is not our task as Christians primarily to invoke God for our particular view of the world, but rather, in humility, to sit and listen as that divine voice comes to us. Therefore, we need to take up our task theologically. For Christians, the inexplicable will of God to be for, and with, humanity implies that Christian spirituality cannot be understood in terms of the structures and events of the world. Equally, God's inexplicable will to be God with, and for, humanity implies that we should always understand our spirituality as Christians in theological terms. These simple, yet profound, facts derive from the mystery of the triune God not to be God apart from, or separate from, humanity, but rather to make God's very life intersect with the unity of the Son of God with us. The theological basis of our spirituality as Christians and as the church is in the wonder of God's condescension, in the intentionality of God's solidarity with those who turn away from God, that is, with those who find their self-identity solely within themselves, and find their self-justification and sole solace in themselves alone, without any reference to God. The church is called to exist solely through the solidarity of Jesus Christ with those who are alienated from God, by Christ going to the extremes of alienation for humanity, so that humanity might through him come close to God. At the heart of our faith is expressed the fact that God does not wish to be alone in celebrating the wonder of his inexpressible love for humanity. God in Christ calls into existence an earthly body of his Son, who is its heavenly head, in order that humanity may responsively rejoice with God in the harmony and peace which God has established for creation. This is the theological basis of Christian spirituality. If the being of the church is predicated upon the grace of Jesus Christ as defining God's action in the world for the reconciliation of creation, including humanity, then its spirituality is that which it receives from him, who is its life. Thus the styles of Christian spirituality will each be shaped by the ways in which each spirituality confesses this truth to be its very life.

Origins

Let us, then, look at some of the interrelated and intercultural dynamics of the origins and growth of the three Abrahamic faiths, Judaism, Christianity and Islam.

All were born in worlds of violence. Christianity began as a despised minority of a despised minority (Judaism) within the Roman Empire. Islam also knew struggle and violence, as indeed did Judaism. However, within three centuries of being this despised minority of a despised minority, Christianity had become the official religion of the Roman Empire. This Constantinian settlement had a profound impact on the church. Its immediate source documents (the New Testament) had been produced for a tiny community suffering persecution and violence. Now that Christianity was in a powerful position, how was it still possible to hear God's voice so clearly through them? In fact, the church found its symbiosis with state power so congenial that it found, for its future, life outside this situation difficult to contemplate.

For Islam, too, the establishment of caliphates and sultanates and other forms of Islamic states provided great comfort after years of struggle. Equally, for Judaism, the establishment of the State of Israel in 1948 provided a symbiosis with state power unimagined in previous Jewish history. Christianity and Islam, along with Judaism, have known persecution, violence and oppression, but also congenial symbioses with state power.

Religion in intercultural history

Let us now look through one particular lens at the processes of the spread and development of one of these three Abrahamic faiths, that is, global Christianity. Let us see how the category of peace, and the ideal of communities of peace, developed on the one hand, or were restricted on the other, as Christianity expanded.

Christianity was born within an immediate Jewish cultural environment, surrounded by an Aramaic and Hebrew vocabulary, and Semitic expectations. However, this integrated Judaism, in its strict and official vesture, rejected Jesus of Nazareth and later turned against Paul as he championed freedom from the Law through Jesus Christ. As the New Testament and second- and third-century CE writings demonstrate, Christianity penetrated much more easily into Hellenistic culture, including Hellenistic Judaism, than into the culture of Judaism itself. From Hellenism, Christianity developed into the wider Greco-Roman culture, and subsequently moved into Northern, Western and Eastern Europe, in addition to its movements into Asia.

Cyclic culture

Why was it that Christianity found movement into Hellenism much easier than its movement into Judaism? It was because Hellenism was more of a culture in the original sense of that word (that is, related to agricultural growth) than was Judaism. Thus, Hellenism was much more related to primarily agricultural societies, whose deepest concern was with being in harmony with nature. The Christ Event spoke of birth, growth, development, maturity, death, resurrection, and new life. This was a cycle. It fitted the cyclic world of agricultural life. It was a cyclic culture. That world spoke of planting, development, maturity, harvest (or death), new life, renewed fertility of the soil and new growth. The Jesus story fitted the pattern of agricultural life. It had also been similar to the Old Testament dramas of the prophets and psalms, where they had spoken of destruction and rebirth.

However, in first- and second-century CE Judaism, a different world had emerged. There was no longer the drama of the Old Testament prophets and psalms. Now first- and second-century CE Judaism tended to stress the precise following of particular, divinely inspired words, which had been uttered up until the time of Ezra and the 'Men of the Great Synagogue', and thereafter had ceased. We see this in the first words of the Pirqê Abôth (Danby 1933, pp.446–461).

So the Gospel lived and flourished in a cyclic and agricultural mode as it was interwoven into agricultural societies. In this way, on the whole, the Gospel moved north and west, in addition to its movement east. However, it did not enter the world of Judaism to any large degree. As it moved west and north, and also east to some extent, the transfiguration of agricultural society meant that the Gospel was totally interwoven into the fabric of the culture. It also began to mould and to direct the cyclic impulses of the culture. Wholeness, harmony, rhythm and ritual (in water, and around a thanksgiving meal) were the means by which the Gospel was expressed.

Baptism was the water ritual; Holy Communion was the thanksgiving ritual. Both were central means of expressing the faith. Many parts of Central, Northern and Western Europe were evangelised in this way. The movement was slow and halting. Yet the interweaving continued. Celtic Christianity developed in this way – deeply cyclic, and deeply agricultural. There were limited movements also into Western Asia, to India and to areas further east, where Christianity developed in this way in the first millennium. There was, of course, from time to time, resistance to the Gospel, but on the whole the development of Christianity was communal. Christianity thrived in this cyclic world, and expressed itself communally. There were internal communities of peace, and frequently relations of peace with surrounding faiths.

Word culture

However, another world existed in which Christianity had not been able to develop so well. This was the world of a trading and word culture. It was the world of first- and second-century CE Judaism into which Christianity had not been able to develop in these centuries. However, with the rise of travel and trade, Christianity began to develop into a trading- and word culture, that is, into a culture in which wholeness, community, harmony and ritual received less attention, and more attention was given to common standards to guide diverse peoples as they sought to live together. The development of trading and word cultures occurred largely in the period from the fourteenth century CE, often referred to as the Modern Period, taking in as it did the European expansion in trade and commerce, the Renaissance and the Reformation, and industrial modernisation.

This was a world quite different from that of the agricultural world. Journeying individuals and communities needed clear-cut ordinances in warding off their dangers and temptations, far from the cyclic life of the soil which they had left behind. That cyclic world had been so clearly transfigured by the Christ Event, and celebrated in ritual as a means of expression and teaching. The trade and word culture was different. Guidelines were needed to bind communities together. Doctrine, ethics, church polity and management were all important. The emphasis was to be on the Book (the Bible), the Guides to the Book (confessions and catechisms), and the Interpreter of the Book (the preacher).

Parallel cultural emphases occurred in other trade and word religions, specifically Islam and Judaism. In Christianity, in this word and trade form, there was emphasis on the Bible, the confessions and catechism, and the preacher. In Islam, there was a parallel emphasis on the Koran (Qūrān), the

Sharī'ah, and the faqīh. In Judaism there was a parallel emphasis on the Torah, the Mishnah and Talmud, and the rabbi.

Within Western trade and word culture Christianity, of course, comes the European Enlightenment. Here we see radical changes, but they develop within Western Christianity in its trade and word form. Revelation, especially communal revelation, now has to prove its claim. The European Enlightenment does not deny the Christian faith, or indeed any religion, its place. That place is fundamentally in the private sphere. The Enlightenment relativises the Christian faith's exclusive claims, and thus places it firmly in the area of the individual's personal rights. Christianity, in this view, is thus no longer fundamentally communal. It is one logical development of Christianity in a word culture.

The interaction of cyclic and word cultures

So now Christianity succeeded in operating in two cultural modes, the cyclic and agricultural mode on the one hand, and the word and trade mode on the other. However, the critical issue arose during the period of international Christian evangelisation, from the late eighteenth century CE onwards. Could Christianity, which largely existed in a word and trade cultural mode in the mission-active nations, translate itself again into the cyclic and agricultural cultural modes of the receptor cultures? If the mission-active cultures had been those that were still in the original cyclic and agricultural mode, moving into new cyclic and agricultural receptor cultures, then the spread of the Gospel would have been relatively simple. However, mainly they were not. They were trade and word cultures. In the process of evangelisation a variety of reactions occurred. In some situations, it was extremely difficult, as, for example, in Japan, in parts of India, and in parts of China. However, in other situations the spread of the Gospel was highly successful, as, for example, in the Outer Islands of Indonesia, in North-east Asia, in much of the Pacific and in parts of Central, East and West Africa.

Indigenous Asian Christian spiritualities

This is particularly seen in a number of significant Indigenous Asian theologies and spiritualities (Wickeri 2000; Widyatmadja 2005; Yewangoe 1987, pp.289–323). Let us look, for example, at the Korean Minjung theology and its use of the concept of *han* (Bevans 2004, pp.77–78), at the writings of Kosuke Koyama (Bevans 2004, pp.95–99), and at the work of Choan-Seng (C.S.) Song (see, for example, Song 1975; Song 1979; see, too, Koshy 2004, p.219). In these, the concept of community and the related concept of spirituality relate both to the Christian community and to the wider community in each Asian society with which the Christian, minority community interacts.

Let us look at Korean Minjung theology. The Korean concept of the *minjung* is that of the people who have been put aside and robbed of their subjectivity in history, either by outsiders or by internal oppressors. The word is created from two Chinese characters, '*min*' and '*jung*', which can together be translated as 'the mass of the people' (Moon 1983, p.48). Its emphasis is on the people's loss of subjectivity. It thus has some similarity to the New Testament concept of 'ὄχλος (*ochlos*)', often translated as 'the crowd'. The Korean concept of *han*, so close to the heart of Minjung theology, refers to the sense of unresolved resentment against injustice and suffering, a sense of helplessness in the face of overwhelming odds, especially overwhelming violence, and a feeling of being totally abandoned. Again, we think of our Lord's cry, 'Why have you forsaken me?' (Mark 15:34; New Revised Standard Version). *Han* also points to a feeling of acute bodily pain, a feeling of helpless suffering, and an urge to right a wrong (Mol 1985, pp.20–21; Suh David Kwang-sun 1981, p.27). An example is given in the account of Miss Kim Kyong-sook. Miss Kim was an executive committee member of a Korean trade union. On 11 August 1979 she was shot dead during a demonstration organised by two hundred women workers demanding that the Government party (the New Democratic Party) work out a fair solution to their labour dispute. According to the letter which she left for her mother and younger brother (in case she should die during this labour dispute), she recounted that sometimes she was not paid for her work in the factory over the previous eight-year period. She had no opportunity to attend church because of her work on Sunday. Her testament was for a deepening of personal and community spirituality (church attendance and Bible study) and stronger support for the trade union movement (Suh Nam Dong 1981, p.54). For the Minjung theologian David Kwang-sun Suh this concern for communal spirituality is always central (see Koshy 2004, p.306).

Equally for Koyama it relates to the communal nature of Christian faith and spirituality in Thailand (see Bevans 2004, pp.96–99, 169–170), and for Choan-Seng Song it relates to spirituality and community in both Taiwan and China (see, especially, Song 1979; see, too, Po Ho Huang 2005). In parallel with Koyama's use of popular communal expressions in Thailand, Song uses the concept of the Mask Dance as a means of expressing communal theology in the public space. The dance helps the community overcome the toil of the day, including the effects of structural violence. However, for Song, its importance is much greater. Song sees the dance in its social, spiritual, political and theological contexts (Song 1986, pp.218–219). Through the dance, the plight of the poor and the achieving of justice without violence are portrayed in terms of spirituality. It inspires human resourcefulness in a merciless society. It exhibits the nearness of God to humanity, in God's favour as well as God's disfavour. So the communal Mask Dance, in the public space, is a political manifesto as well as a spiritual exercise for a community in trouble. According to Song, the dance comes from what is called the 'experience of critical transcendence' (Song 1986, p.219).

The outworking of the interaction of cyclic and word cultures

In the development of Christianity in the cyclic and agricultural mode, great emphasis was placed on the baptising of communities and cultures into the faith. Once whole Christian communities had been established, then there tended to be harmony and peace both within those communities and in relation to the surrounding societies. However, although trade and word culture communities encouraged peace within their community, they did not necessarily encourage community with those outside the faith-group. Often colonial Protestant communities were internally cohesive, but aggressive towards the world around them, including toward Indigenous religions. So in the West Indies and in the Southern States of the United States, the local population was enslaved, or slaves imported, and the slaves simply acquiesced to the colonists' religion. There was little attempt to translate the Gospel into the cultural terms of the Indigenous community. This occurred too in Australia.

In China, Japan and India, parts of the population were antagonised by Christianity. With the spread of Islam, such dynamics occurred too. However, here the dynamics are the opposite of those experienced by Christianity. For Islam they have been largely how a faith carried on a word and trading culture could be transferred to a cyclic and agricultural culture (on this issue in general, see further Boyd 1974; Haire 1981; Kitagawa 1992). This is very interesting in relation to the growth of the Ṣūfi movement within Islam. Ṣūfism, in the tradition of the ways of thinking originally associated with Ibn al-'Arabi of Murcia, for example, entered the territory of current Indonesia during the fourteenth and fifteenth centuries (Cady 1964, p.153). There was not a tendency in that situation towards asceticism, but rather an emphasis upon mysticism and the paths (ṭarīḳas) to achieving mystical and ecstatic union with Allah. This outlook also emphasised the manifold presence of Allah in nature and in human experience. There were thus both panentheistic and mystical tendencies in this movement, as seen in rural

Eastern Indonesia (Haire 1981, p.241). On the other hand, there was the development of conservative Wahhābism and other tendencies towards Islamic Puritanism in the Eastern Indonesian islands during this period (Haire 1981, p.243).

The interactions between these two movements in Islam and similar mystical and puritan movements in Christianity are striking. For, as Macquarie puts it,

> (a) thoroughly Calvinistic Christian, believing in the absolute sovereignty of God and believing that this is expressed in a meticulously regulated providence and predestination, stands closer in many respects to a Muslim, who has fatalistically submitted to the power of God, than he stands to many of his (sic) fellow Christians. (Macquarie 1977, p.163)

Specific implications of the interrelationship of spirituality, culture and community: violence, peace and cultures

Now we come again to the issue of violence and communities of peace. In our current world it is, of course, essential that we seek communities of peace. That we should do so is important, for four reasons. First, as Christianity and Islam represent by far the largest religious communities in the world, they have a responsibility for the existence of violence and peace in our contemporary world. Both Christianity and Islam have as their followers both the richest and the poorest on the planet. Moreover, the relationship of both Christianity and Islam to Judaism is central to this. Second, despite its strong peace traditions, Christianity has been involved in violence at many times of its history. This is also so for Islam. Third, we differ from other world religions in being truly inter-ethnic and international. For example, in Australia the countries of origin or birth of Australian Muslims is wider in number than in almost any other country in the world. Moreover, those countries of origin are more evenly spread in Australia in terms of the numbers of those originating from each one of them. Fourth, Christianity and Islam, in their 1400 years of common history, have both had ebb and flow in their influences. Throughout their common history there have been alternate advances and retreats for both faiths. Moreover, when Christianity or Islam has advanced in one place, it has often retreated in others. Where either of them has retreated in one area, often that one has advanced in another area. In this the dynamics of their history have often been similar (see, for example, Gillman and Klimkeit 2002; Moffett 1992).

Moreover, the contemporary reality of our world is one of deep violence. The irony of the ending of the Cold War is that it has coincided with the unleashing of uncontrollable violence. There is a pattern, in the words of Samuel Kobia, the General Secretary of the World Council of Churches, which 'legitimizes a culture of violence by invoking God arbitrarily to suit a particular agenda for aggression. As a result, insecurity, fear and anxiety characterize the lives of many people' (Kobia 2005; also see Burton 1990, pp.1–2, 13–24). This culture of violence manifests itself in many different ways.

There is the structural violence of domineering or negligent governments in relation to their populations. Corruption and the abuse of power often manifest themselves in violence. There are often structural forms of traditional violence. These result in gender discrimination, forced labour migration, discrimination against young people and those with disabilities, and discrimination based on race, caste and class. Surrounding human life itself is the violence against the environment.

Against this rather gloomy picture, positive signs must also be noted. There is a yearning among young people for true manifestations of peace and of peaceful communities. In the aftermath of the 2005 tsunami there were remarkable efforts to create communities of peace in various places. Again, the speed of reconciliation after ethnic and communal violence has often been very rapid. Despite violence, there is evidence of a vast amount of resilience among populations who have been deeply wounded.

I have myself been witness to a very significant process of reconciliation between Christians and Muslims. As noted above, between 2001 and 2005 I took part in the reconciliation process between Christians and Muslims in the Molucca Islands in Indonesia, where I had worked and carried out research from the 1970s to the 1990s. Both Muslims and Christians were involved in violence. However, since 2002 both the Muslim and the Christian populations have been slowly but surely working their futures out together, in a quite remarkable display of creating communities of peace. Towards the end of the peace process a remarkable communal act of reconciliation occurred. A rebuilt central mosque and a rebuilt Christian church were both dedicated. Both had been previously destroyed in the violence. At the beginning of the dedication of the mosque, Christians on their knees brought the *tifa* (the equipment used in Indonesia to call Muslims to worship), which they had had made at their own expense, to the Muslim community, as their gift for the new mosque. At the beginning of the dedication of the church, Muslims on their knees brought a large bell, which they had had made at their own expense in the Netherlands, as their gift for the new church. Both promised never to engage in violence again with their neighbours.

Violence and transformed communities

I wish now to look at the violent worlds in which the two religions, particularly Christianity, began, and then go on to look at the transformed communities of peace in the development of both religions, through examining the milieu of violence from which they developed, the transformed communities of peace then created, and the dynamics which created those transformed communities. In this I pay particular attention to Christianity, but also look at similar factors in Islam.

As a Christian I need now to look at this phenomenon of violence and peace from the perspective of the birth of Christianity. As noted above, Christianity was born in a milieu of political and social violence. The evidence which we have, both from the New Testament and from non-Christian sources of the first century CE, points to the constant struggle of Christianity to survive in such a climate. Clearly that climate of violence also influenced the language and concept-construction of many parts of the New Testament. Nevertheless, it is also very striking how early Christianity sought to transcend that violent world.

On the basis of our theological identity in Christ, Christians must take the New Testament writings, in this case with regard to spirituality and community, most seriously. A microcosm of the New Testament understanding of building communities of peace for all can be seen in the ethical sections of Paul's writings, especially in those ethical sections in his Letter to the Romans. It is arguable that no document in Christian history has played a more influential part than Paul's Letter to the Romans. One simply has to reflect on the pivotal impact of Romans on Augustine and the development of Western Christianity, on Luther and then on Calvin and Cranmer and the political, social and religious consequences of the Reformation, on Wesley and the emergence of the Evangelical Revival, on Karl Barth and his dominance of twentieth-century theology, and on the Second Vatican Council and the renewal of the Roman Catholic church. A primary impetus for Augustine, Luther, Calvin, Cranmer, Wesley, Barth and the Members of Vatican II came from Paul's writings, particularly from Romans. This letter is thus central to Christian self-identity and self-understanding. It forms a useful basis for the exploration of the understanding of Christian spirituality and community, based on identification with God in Christ, as it challenges the prevailing Greco-Roman culture of status based on potentially violent concepts through the ethical sections of Romans, particularly in Chapter 12.

The milieu of violence

In order to understand this ideal concept of community, we need to understand that it both reacts against, and transforms, Greco-Roman cultures of the first century CE. We need, first, of course to look at the results of socio-scientific research on first-century CE social organisation, on social interaction, and on religious organisations. We see parallels with this in the emergence of Islam.

As noted above, Christianity grew out of a situation of oppression, a despised minority of a despised minority. The rise of Islam in the seventh century of Christianity was not so oppressive, but involved an enormous struggle from a tiny minority. We look at the struggle of Christianity to create communities of peace in this world of violence. We look, initially, at the world into which it was born.

First, in the world of early Christianity, social groupings were based on kinship, ethnic issues, power and politics. Kinship was the central factor of social organisation. The kinship group was the focus of individual loyalty, and had decisive influence over individual identity and self-awareness. The security of each individual was grounded in the community, sharing as they did common interests, values and activities. Hence, the most basic unit of social awareness was not the individual. Individual consciousness was subordinate to social consciousness (Malina 1981, pp.55–66, 60–64; Meeks 1983, pp.90–91; also see Theissen 1992, pp.272–278). This dyadic consciousness, too, was the background for Islam.

Second, religion, like other social factors, was enmeshed in kinship and politics. Membership of a religious community was not necessarily based on religious relationships, but on bonds of kinship that gave structure to religious associations. Membership in religious groups was either involuntary or voluntary. Involuntary members belonged to a religion because, for example, they were born into a particular family. Voluntary membership in early Christianity stood in contrast to family-based religion. In the first century CE the religion of voluntary members resulted in a newly created kinship group (Theissen 1982, pp.27–40; also see Esler 1994, pp.6–12). Although it appeared similar to any other kinship group, it was in fact a created or fictive kinship grouping. In early Christianity, language of the natural kinship group, for example 'household (of faith)', was used for a created kinship group. Indeed, the struggle of the Christian community as a totality, for example in Rome, can be seen in relationship to these two types. It struggled as to which of these two types it in fact belonged to. Again, a similar background existed with the rise of Islam.

Third, there is considerable evidence in the first century CE within Greco-Roman culture of intense expressions of emotion, through outbursts of anger, aggression, pugnacity and indeed violence. Moreover, these appear to have been socially acceptable (Pearson 1973, p.193; Wedderburn 1988, pp.81–83; also see Loader 2002, p.177). Again, there is some evidence of this with the rise of Islam.

Fourth, in such an atmosphere, concern for honour and shame was significant. This was because honour determined social standing and was essential for social cooperation. Honour was the outward approval given to a group or an individual by others whose honour was not in question. The honour of an individual normally was dependent upon the outward approval given to one's group. On the other hand, people became shamed when they transgressed group standards or when they sought a social status to which public approval was not given. Honour was ascribed, for example, by birth into an honourable family, or by it being given or bestowed from honourable persons of power. It was acquired by outdoing others in social interchange. A person's sense of self-worth was therefore established by public reputation related to that person's associations, rather than by a judgement of conscience (Malina 1981, pp.27–40). This is not foreign to the experience of the early development and theological struggles of Islam.

Transformed communities of peace

Over against these four factors of community life in the Greco-Roman cultures of the first century CE, Paul summons Christians to a new form of religious organisation, a fictive kinship religious community and spirituality based on identity in Christ, in which membership is voluntary. He also summons them to new social roles. These social roles are based on the twin concepts of peace or harmony, and mercy, in a complex of cultures where expressions of violence seem not only to have been common, but also accepted, as has been noted.

To understand the significance of peace or harmony, and the related concept of mercy, in Paul's writings, it is helpful first to look more widely in the New Testament at the Greek words commonly translated as 'peace' and 'mercy'.

There are strong spiritual and communal elements in the New Testament uses of peace and of mercy. There are also strong elements of God's desire for a world which ultimately is to be under God's rule. These factors we see as we look at the two concepts more closely.

The Greek word 'εἰρήνη (eirēnē)' means harmony and peace. The verb 'εἰρηνεύω (eirēneuō)' signifies to be at peace or to live at peace or to keep the peace. *Eirēnē* is also closely associated with the Hebrew term for peace and harmony, 'םולש' (*shālôm*).

In the New Testament, *eirēnē* refers to two distinct states of peace. First, it means the final salvation and harmony of the whole community, and thus of the whole of each individual person. Zechariah proclaims this expected state of salvation and harmony of the whole community in Luke 1:76–79. The angels' song in Luke 2:14 refers to this salvation and harmony which has come to the earth. This concept is again referred to in Hebrews 13:20–21. It is this idea of peace which Paul himself uses in II Corinthians 5:16–19. There he speaks about Christian believers, being justified by grace in faith, having peace with God through Christ. These believers, Paul says, will be granted salvation. So the concept has a future orientation, referring to the final end of history. Moreover, spirituality has this future orientation too.

Second, on the basis of its future orientation, *eirēnē* refers to a condition here and now of peace and harmony, guaranteed by what will occur at the end of time. This divinely willed state in the here and now includes Christians' well-being, and their harmony with God, with one another and with all human beings. This idea appears in Hebrews 12:14. Paul uses it in Ephesians 4:1–3. So, again, the concept has also a present orientation. This present orientation refers in the first instance to the state of the whole community, and then to the individual as part of it. Moreover, Christian spirituality is to be based on this.

The first-century CE Greek terms for mercy are 'οἰκτιρμός (*oiktirmos*)' and 'ἔλεος (*eleos*)'. Both refer to mercy and compassion, while *oiktirmos* additionally means 'pity'. The verbs 'ἐλεέω (*eleeō*)' and 'ἐλεάω (*eleaō*)' mean 'to show kindness' or 'to be merciful'. Human mercy, therefore, denotes the divinely intended attitude of Christians towards others. It signifies sympathy and loving-kindness, which are to be exhibited in relationships, particularly through acts of help to the needy. This we see in Matthew 9:13, in relation to Jesus' attitude to eating with outsiders, and in Luke 10:37, in relation to Jesus defining the neighbour who may be an outsider. The neighbour was indeed none other than the despised outsider who showed mercy to the person who fell among thieves on the road from Jerusalem to Jericho. On this spirituality depends.

Thus, in the definitions of both of these terms as they were used in the New Testament, we see sustained communal elements, and also sustained pointers to the ideal of a society which is ultimately to be under God's rule. An example of this is in Romans. In Romans 12:1 Paul describes Christian life against the background of these terms, using metaphors from the sacrificial cult. This cult spoke of the offering of the central parts of a community's life to the power of God. For Christians, this is now to suggest that Christians are to give themselves permanently to the rule of God, as this way has been opened for them through God's self-sacrifice in Christ. The sacrificial cult continues to point to the rule of God throughout the community. It also points to an individual's relationship with God within the community's relationship with God. This is based on Paul's theological argument in Romans 5:1 and 9–10, where he describes how peace (*eirēnē*) and reconciliation ('καταλλαγή; *katallagē*') have been given by God to God's community in Christ. On these concepts spirituality is to be built.

The dynamics of transformed communities

So, if we now return to Paul, and specifically to Romans, we can observe how he deals with the four factors of community life in Greco-Roman culture outlined above.

Over against these four factors, Paul summons Christians to new social roles. They are based on mercy, peaceable conduct and reconciliation in a culture where expressions of violence seem to have been normative. The call for transformation now means new expressions of group identity. No longer based on kinship or ethnicity, group identity nevertheless seeks to retain the intense cohesion of former groups. Paul's community members bind themselves together as one body in Christ. This metaphor is poignantly suitable in a society where self-awareness arises from group association rather than from individual worth. The ideals of honourable and shameless conduct are altered in that they are not primarily derived from society outside. Rather, enhanced honour for the community derives from its incorporation into its risen Lord. Patterns of social cooperation are modified as a result. A new communal identity as one body in Christ is thus reinforced. Moreover, spirituality is to be built on these perspectives. Within Islam, we see parallel dynamics, particularly in relation to the formation and ongoing life of the community (*umma*).

The social groupings thus see their identity as coming from beyond themselves. Their self-understanding, their spirituality and their life together are defined by the kindness or mercy of God and by the truthful harmony (or peace) which God gives. The other factors in the transformation include cohesiveness within the group, based on an understanding of God's action from outside. For that reason, attitudes of peaceful harmony are central to the community's identity. Moreover, no other identity marker (ethnicity, gender, class or status) may be accepted as absolute. Honour derives from the faith-life of the community, originating from beyond. The original groupings are transformed by the new ideal of a central awareness of their relationship with God. Again, we can notice parallels with the development of the Islamic *umma*.

However, for Christianity, there is another factor of immense significance. Throughout the ethical sections of Romans, attitudes to those outside the newly created Christian social groupings are to be the same as to those within them. There is to be no distinction. All are to be treated in the same way. Again, we should note the parallels with Islam, particularly in relation to the other 'Peoples of the Book', Christians and Jews – for example in Muslim ordinances in relation to Muslim marriage to a Christian or Jew.

We thus see the radical way in which Paul took hold of Greco-Roman categories of group identity, and then applied to them new metaphors, including that of the body of Christ, so as to create in them a totally new identity. Present-day Western individualism makes it difficult for us to see the significance of the dynamism of Paul's total transformation of a received aggressive culture. Moreover, throughout world history Christianity has had both success and failure in presenting and living out this newly transformed identity in Christ.

In Christian terms, we need the Gospel in both cyclic and word cultures. Where the church has been primarily related to an agricultural or cyclic culture, it needs the struggle with the divine graceful criticism of that transfiguration. It needs to hear the voice in word form, so as to be constantly reformed. Equally, a church which is primarily related to the Gospel in a word- or trade culture needs always the struggle with the divine fact of incarnation, that God has placed God's church in the world. However, we need to be aware that the existence of the church in word and trade cultures has a tendency to work against building communities of peace.

This is frequently so, too, across religious divides, and especially where there is a meeting between two word or trading culture religions. There are four poignant examples of this. First, it is seen in the struggle between, particularly, the strident word culture form of Judaism and the word culture form of Islam in the Middle East. Second, it was observed in the tension of the past between Muslims and Christians in urban areas of Indonesia. Third, it is seen in the attack of word culture Christianity against word and trading culture Judaism in Germany in the 1930s. Fourth, it is observed in the antagonism between specific traditions of Islam and certain traditions of Christianity in the United States. In his 2007 Cyril Foster Lecture in the University of Oxford, the former British Foreign Secretary Jack Straw argued that the Cold War had eroded traditional political identities and encouraged people to retreat back to identities defined in terms of cultural, ethnic, national, gender or religious affiliations, and that the challenge has been to recapture civic political culture by finding ways of allowing space for these affiliations within a framework of shared values (Straw 2007). He was thus seeking to find ways of avoiding the violence between followers of religion in word or trade forms.

Spirituality, culture and community

Therefore, a number of things are incumbent upon us.

First, we need to be aware that creating communities of peace from the Pauline tradition means creating attitudes of peace and harmony towards those outside which are the same as attitudes to those within the faith-community (see, for example, from a Muslim perspective, Muhamad Ali 2003; Oasim Mathar 2003; Tarmiji Taher 1997). Here Christianity has significant parallels with Islam. Christians need to be reminded of the teachings of the New Testament, epitomised in Paul as we have seen, where Paul's ethics for internal Christian life are exactly the same as his ethics for those outside. You treat the outsider in exactly the same way as you treat your Christian sister or brother.

Second, we need to be aware that Christianity needs both its cyclic or agricultural culture forms on the one hand, and its word and trade culture forms on the other. However, we need to be aware that its word and trade culture forms have a tendency to go against the New Testament, and specifically Pauline, teaching, in that they can tend to foster an aggressive attitude to those outside the community, while fostering cohesiveness within the faith-group. Again, there is resonance with such tendencies in Islam.

Third, we need to stress the importance of cyclic and agricultural culture forms within the expressions of Christianity, and to see how word and trade culture expressions of Christianity can, in our time, be translated into cyclic forms (Haire 1981, pp.320–326).

Fourth, theology, therefore, is not simply a matter of engaging in word culture exercises (in, for example, spirituality, doctrine, ethics and polity). It is as much an expression of faith through liturgy, drama, dance, music and communal living.

Fifth, this way of communal harmony is necessary in the ways in which the churches live their lives. Consensus decision-making, mutual celebration, the interest in others' rituals and festivities are important in being Christian. Here, too, there are parallels in Islam.

Sixth, truth can be communicated without aggression (see, for example, in the history of Asian Islam and Asian Christianity, Leimena 1941, pp.626–642; Leimena 1968, pp.57–64; Simatupang 1967; Simatupang 1973; Van Klinken 2003. Regarding Leimena, Soekarno, a nationalist of joint Muslim and Hindu background, had been one of his colleagues, and Leimena refused to join in activity to betray or discredit him). Therefore, the ecumenical movement internationally, in and of itself, as it brings the churches together, is central to the creation of peaceful communities (see, for example, Thomas and Abrecht 1967). Again, the style of interfaith dialogue is pivotal in creating societies of peace.

Seventh, the communal nature of expressing theology calls both Christians and Muslims in particular to advance, at all opportunities, the eight goals of the Millennial Declaration (MDG) of the United Nations – that is, to:

- eradicate poverty and hunger

- achieve universal primary education

- promote gender equality and empower women

- reduce child mortality

- improve maternal health

- combat HIV/AIDS, malaria and other diseases

- ensure environmental sustainability

- develop a global partnership for development.

(United Nations 2009)

These are indeed expressions of communities of peace.

We in our time live in a deeply ambivalent age, an age of high technology and of medieval conflict, and an age until recently as strangely confident of the saving powers of the marketplace as a previous age was strangely confident of the saving powers of collectivism. Yet both these ages have reflected inbuilt cultures of violence. One of the great leaders of the Christian ecumenical movement, Archbishop William Temple, served as Archbishop of Canterbury for only two years, from 1942 to 1944. One of his lasting images to the ecumenical movement was that of the Christian with bifocal lenses. In his writing he says that we should look through the top part of our glasses to see the world as God intends it to be, united and in harmony. With the bottom of our lenses we see the world as it actually is, divided. Although we look at life day-by-day with the bottom part of our spectacles, we should also always live as if the top part were reality, as if there was true harmony in the world. So it is with spirituality, culture and community. With the top part of our spectacles, as it were, we see a world community of peace and harmony. With the lower part of our spectacles, we observe the world as it is. Although we daily look at reality through the lower part, we must live as if the upper part is reality too.

CHAPTER 3

The Cultural Diversity of Older Australians

Ingrid Seebus and Ann Peut

Introduction

Australia is a culturally diverse country with a growing number of Aboriginal and Torres Strait Islander Australians, and a high proportion of overseas-born Australians. Australia's cultural composition shares commonalities with a number of other English-speaking countries such as the United States, Canada and New Zealand. In 2006 Australia's Aboriginal and Torres Strait Islanders made up 2.5 per cent of the total population, making it proportionally larger than the Indigenous populations of the United States (1.5%). Canada's Indigenous population made up almost 4 per cent of the population while New Zealand Maori made up 15 per cent of the total population (AIHW 2009). Like Australia, the United States, Canada and New Zealand are all countries of high immigration. Of these four countries, in 2006 Australia had the highest proportion of overseas-born people (24%), followed by New Zealand (21%) and Canada (20%), while the United States had 13 per cent (OECD 2009).

The proportion of people aged 65 and older is increasing in all Organisation for Economic Cooperation and Development (OECD) countries, a trend which is expected to continue (OECD 2009). Consequently, countries with culturally diverse populations can expect to have increasingly larger populations of culturally diverse older people. This has implications for many facets of public policy, including developing and maintaining social cohesion and social connectedness, and ensuring adequate and appropriate provision of services. The aim of this chapter is to explore some of these implications in the Australian context. The chapter examines the nature and extent of the cultural diversity of older Australia, and looks at aspects of social participation by different cultural groups. It illustrates the potential implications of cultural diversity for a key area of service provision to older people, namely formal aged care. As the number of older people increases, the needs of culturally diverse groups within the aged care system must be understood in order to plan for future care needs. While the focus of the chapter is on the Australian context, many of the issues raised will be of relevance to other countries with culturally diverse populations.

Older Australians

In Australia it is conventional to define 'older people' as those aged 65 and over, as this is the age at which people become eligible for the aged pension. However, definitions of 'older people' can vary depending on the context and the issue under discussion. For example, the age from which usage rates in aged care services become noticeably higher is 75. Consequently, some of the discussion in this chapter will define 'older people' as 75 and over. On occasion, this age group will be compared to the 55–74 age group, who are treated here as a future 'older' cohort. Indigenous Australians have a lower life expectancy and poorer health status compared to the non-Indigenous population, which results in their need for services at younger ages. 'Older Indigenous people' in this chapter are generally defined as those aged 50 and over. The chapter uses published data sources: the definition of 'older people' in this chapter is also constrained by the age ranges used by published data.

Older people make up a considerable and growing proportion of the total Australian population. In 2006, 1.3[1] million people were aged 75 and over accounting for 6 per cent of the total population (ABS 2007a). A further 3.7 million people were aged between 55 and 74, accounting for 18 per cent of the population (ABS 2007a). The number of Australians aged 75 and over will increase to an estimated 3.4 million by 2036, over a tenth (13%) of the total population (AIHW 2007b). The rate of growth in the older population is highest among the very old. The number of people aged 85 and over doubled in the 15 years to 2006, when it reached almost 322,000 (AIHW 2007a). In 2036, Australians in this age group are estimated to reach over 1 million (AIHW 2007b).

The age structure of the population varies across the states and territories. In 2006, South Australia had the highest proportion of people aged 75 and over (7.6%), followed by Tasmania (6.9%), NSW (6.5%) and Victoria (6.4%). The Northern Territory had the lowest proportion (1.4%) (ABS 2007a). Older Australians aged 75 and over were slightly less likely than those aged under 74 to live in *Major cities* (67% compared to 69%) or *Remote* areas[2]

(1% compared to 2%), and slightly more likely to live in *Inner and outer regional* areas (31% compared to 29%) (ABS 2008c).

Indigenous Australians

Available data shows that the age distribution of Aboriginal and Torres Strait Islander people in 2006 differed greatly from that of the non-Indigenous population. Overall, Indigenous Australians have a much younger age structure, with numbers decreasing considerably after the age of 45 (AIHW 2007b). In 2006, Aboriginal and Torres Strait Islander people aged 50 and over accounted for only 11 per cent of Australia's total Indigenous population. In contrast, the same age group made up almost a third (31%) of the non-Indigenous Australian population (AIHW 2007b). However, despite the smaller representation of older people in the Indigenous population, in 2006 there were around 55,000 Indigenous Australians aged 50 and over, including 14,000 who were aged 65 and over (AIHW 2007a).

Estimating the size and age composition of the Aboriginal and Torres Strait Islander population is difficult for several reasons. These include differences in how Indigenous status is recorded on births and deaths records across jurisdictions, and high rates of incomplete records, although efforts are being made to improve the quality and completeness of data collections (ABS and AIHW 2008). Because of uncertainty about the estimates of the total Aboriginal and Torres Strait Islander population, indirect methods have been used to calculate life expectancies. The most recently published data, which used the indirect Bhat (2002) method for the period 1996–2001, estimated that life expectancy at birth was 59 years for Indigenous males and 65 years for Indigenous females, compared with 77 years for all Australian males and 82 years for all Australian females for the period 1998–2000; a difference of approximately 17 years for both males and females (ABS and AIHW 2008). At the age of 65, however, the life expectancy 'gap' between the Indigenous and non-Indigenous Australians was less than at birth, namely six years for men and eight for women (AIHW 2007b).

These life expectancies should only be used as an indicative measure of the level of mortality of the Indigenous population (ABS and AIHW 2008). Recent work by Barnes *et al.* (2008) suggests that direct methods of estimation are more robust than indirect methods, and should be used for estimating Indigenous life expectancy. The Australian Bureau of Statistics (ABS) is investigating alternative approaches to calculating life expectancy estimates (ABS 2008a).

The distribution of the older (i.e. 50 and over) Aboriginal and Torres Strait Islander population is similar to that of the Indigenous population as a whole. In 2006, NSW and Queensland had the largest numbers of older Indigenous people (20,343 and 17,037 respectively), while the Northern Territory had the highest proportion of older Indigenous people (17%) (ABS 2008b). Older Aboriginal and Torres Strait Islander people, like the Indigenous population generally, were more likely than the non-Indigenous population to live in a *Remote* area. About a third (30%) of older Aboriginal and Torres Strait Islander people lived in a *Major city,* with 44 per cent living in *Inner and outer regional* areas, and 26 per cent in *Remote* or *Very remote* areas. In contrast, almost two-thirds (66%) of non-Indigenous Australians aged 50 and over live in *Major cities*, while almost a third (32%) live in *Inner and outer regional* areas, and only 2 per cent live in *Remote* or *Very remote* areas (ABS 2008c).

Language and religion

The heterogeneity of Aboriginal and Torres Strait Islander people is reflected in their linguistic diversity. In 2006, older Aboriginal and Torres Strait Islander people, defined here as aged 45 and over, and those aged 25–44 years, were slightly more likely to speak an Indigenous language at home (13% and 14% respectively) compared with younger people under 0–14 years (10%) and those aged 15–24 (12%) (ABS 2008d).

Older Aboriginal and Torres Strait Islander people living in *Remote* or *Very remote* areas were more likely to speak an Indigenous language (87%) than those living in *Inner* and *Outer regional* (9%) or *Major cities* (4%). Just over half (51%) of all Aboriginal and Torres Strait Islanders who spoke an Indigenous language lived in the Northern Territory, and almost two-thirds (60%) of the Territory's older Indigenous population spoke an Indigenous language (ABS 2008d). The most commonly spoken Aboriginal and Torres Strait Islander languages across the total Indigenous population were Torres Strait Creole, Kriol, Arrernte, Djambarrpuyngu and Pitjantjatjara (ABS 2008d). Of those aged 45 and over who spoke an Indigenous language, 81 per cent also spoke English 'well' or 'very well' (ABS 2008d). English-language proficiency reported in the 2006 Census is based on self-assessment, and so there may be some variation in English-language skills among those who report the same level of proficiency (ABS 2008d).

Although the 2006 Census includes a question about religious affiliation, it is an optional one (ABS 2008d). In 2006, 13 per cent of Aboriginal and Torres Strait Islander peoples did not respond to this question, compared with 7 per cent of the non-Indigenous population (ABS 2008d). Among Aboriginal and Torres Strait Islander peoples who did respond, 24 per cent had no religious affiliation. This compares with 21 per cent of non-

Indigenous Australians (ABS 2008d). (Disaggregation by age has not been published.)

Less than 1 per cent of Indigenous respondents had an affiliation with an Australian Aboriginal traditional religion. Those living in *Very Remote* areas were more likely (6%) than those in all other areas (less than 1%) to have such an affiliation. Almost three-quarters (73%) of the Indigenous population who responded to the question on religious affiliation were Christians, of whom about one-third were Anglican and one-third were Catholic (ABS 2008d).

Social participation

The National Strategy for an Ageing Australia includes as one of its goals the development and encouragement of public, private and community infrastructure to support older Australians and their participation in society. A culturally diverse population poses issues about how different cultural groups participate in the broader community and the extent to which they are at risk of social isolation. These questions can be partly addressed for Aboriginal and Torres Strait Islander people by some of the results of the 2002 ABS National Aboriginal and Torres Strait Islander Social Survey (NATSISS).

Two measures of social participation included in the 2002 NATSISS were being 'involved in social activities in the last 3 months' and 'attended cultural event(s) in the last 12 months'. A lower proportion of older Indigenous people (defined in NATSISS as aged 55 and over) were involved in social activities in the last three months (81%) compared with the younger age groups 15–24 (94%) and 25–35 (92%). However, there was no difference in attendance of cultural events in the preceding 12 months between older Indigenous people (68%) and the total Indigenous population aged 15 and over (68%) (ABS 2004).

Overseas-born Australians

Australia has long had a high proportion of overseas-born people. In 2006, Australia recorded the second highest proportion of overseas-born people among its total population of any OECD country (24%), behind Luxembourg (35%) and alongside Switzerland (24%) (OECD 2009). The OECD average of 12 per cent was just over half the proportion in Australia, with many countries having close to half Australia's proportion, or less.

The cultural profile of different age cohorts varies, reflecting different immigration policies and programmes over time. In 2006, over a quarter

(27%) of Australians aged 75 and over were born overseas (344,000) (ABS 2007b[3]). Of this group, 43 per cent came from the main English-speaking countries of New Zealand, the United Kingdom, Ireland, USA, Canada and South Africa. More than half of overseas-born Australians (57%) came from countries where a language other than English (LOTE) was the main language spoken. The proportion of people aged 55–74 who were born overseas was higher, reaching almost a third (31%), with the proportion born in LOTE countries remaining the same (57%) (ABS 2007b). This means that, overall, the proportion of people with a LOTE background was higher in the age group 55–74 than in the 75 and over age group.

The profile of the overseas-born aged 75 and over reflects the immigration policies of the post-World War II years (AIHW 2007b). While China was the largest LOTE country across the total population in 2006, European birthplaces dominated in the older age groups. The 2006 Census identifies the 50 most common countries of birth for overseas-born Australians. However, 71 per cent of the older LOTE population aged 75 and over came from just 10 countries, with Italy, Germany and Greece the three most common birth countries. These three countries also dominated the 55–74 age cohort, although the order was slightly different, with Greece overtaking Germany as the second largest country of birth (see Table 3.1).

The size of the overseas-born population with a LOTE background aged 75 and over varied across the states and territories. The largest populations were in NSW and Victoria, accounting for about a third of the LOTE population each (NSW: 68,800; Victoria: 67,500). Queensland, South Australia and Western Australia accounted for a further 28 per cent of the LOTE population between them. The Northern Territory had the lowest number (388). The spread was similar for the 55–74 age group, where NSW and Victoria again had the largest numbers of people with a LOTE background (234,200 and 219,000 respectively).

The proportion of the older overseas-born population with a LOTE background also varied across states and territories. The cultural diversity of the older population was greatest in Victoria (21%) followed by ACT (19%), while Tasmania had the lowest proportion (6%). The pattern changes in the 55–74 age group. While Victoria retained the highest proportion (25%), it was followed by NSW (20%). Tasmania again had the lowest proportion, with 5.7 per cent.

In terms of the composition of the older overseas-born population with a LOTE background, people born in Italy were the largest LOTE groups in all states except for Tasmania. The Netherlands was the most common birthplace here, with Italy the fourth largest group. There was more diversity between states in terms of their second and third largest LOTE group. In the two largest states, NSW and Victoria, those born in China and Greece formed the second largest groups respectively. The Dutch-born were the second largest group in both Queensland and Western Australia, while German-born older people were the second largest group in four of the states and territories (South Australia, Tasmania, ACT and Northern Territory).

Table 3.1 Top 10 LOTE countries of birth,* 2006

	Aged 55–74			Aged 75 and over			Total population		
		Number	% of LOTE pop		Number	% of LOTE pop		Number	% of LOTE pop
1	Italy	106,399	16.9	Italy	46,943	24.0	China**	206,589	8.9
2	Greece	64,140	10.1	Germany	16,217	8.3	Italy	199,122	8.6
3	Germany	51,751	8.2	Greece	15,960	8.2	Viet Nam	159,849	6.9
4	Netherlands	40,835	6.5	Netherlands	14,100	7.2	India	147,106	6.3
5	China**	30,535	4.8	Poland	13,547	6.9	Philippines	120,540	5.2
6	Malta	25,181	4.0	China**	11,076	5.7	Greece	109,989	4.7
7	Croatia	23,786	3.8	India	6486	3.3	Germany	106,524	4.6
8	India	22,457	3.6	Malta	5228	2.7	Malaysia	92,334	4.0
9	Viet Nam	20,999	3.3	Hungary	5000	2.6	Netherlands	78,924	3.4
10	Lebanon	17,614	2.8	Viet Nam	4890	2.5	Lebanon	74,850	3.2

Notes: *Figures exclude 'born elsewhere' and 'not stated'.
**(excl. SARS and Taiwan province).

Source: Derived from ABS (2007b) Census of population and Housing Australia, 2006. Cat. no. 2068.0. Census table: Country of birth of person, by age by sex.

Language and religion

English-language proficiency is an important factor in terms of need for ethno-specific services, as poor English-language proficiency may increase hesitancy to access formal services (AIHW: Benham *et al.* 2000; AIHW 2004a). In 2006, those born in a LOTE country and aged 55–64 had the highest level of confidence in their English-language skills, with just over three quarters (76%) of this age group reporting that they spoke English 'well' or 'very well' (ABS 2007b). Those aged 85 and over reported the weakest level of confidence, with just over half (51%) reporting that they spoke English 'well' or 'very well'. However, as this is cross-sectional data, it cannot be concluded that English-language proficiency necessarily decreases with age. There may be a cohort effect, which is in part related to different waves of immigration and settlement processes, and the fact that English-language proficiency varies among different birthplace groups. Factors affecting English-language proficiency at an individual level include age at migration and the length of residency in Australia (AIHW 2004a).

Australia's religious profile has changed as a result of British settlement, and ongoing immigration (ABS 2008e). European migration in the post-World War II years increased the size of the Orthodox and Catholic churches, and established the Reformed churches (ABS 2008e). In more recent years, migration from Southeast Asia and the Middle East has increased the total number of people with a Buddhist or Islamic affiliation, and diversified the cultural profile of existing Christian denominations (ABS 2008e).

Published data from the 2006 Census does not provide a breakdown of religious affiliation by country of birth, and so the discussion here looks at the religious affiliation of the total older Australian population aged 75 and over, and the future cohort of older Australians (aged 55–74).

Christianity remains the dominant religion in both the age groups 75 and over, and 55–74; however, the proportion was higher in the 75 and over group (80% compared with 75%). Conversely, the proportion of those aged 75 and over who indicated that they had no religion was lower (7%) than for the 55–74 age group (12%).

Judaism and Buddhism were the second largest reported religions in the age group 75 and over, with almost 1 per cent each. However, a smaller proportion (0.5%) of the 55–74 age group had a Jewish affiliation. Conversely, a higher proportion (1.4%) of the younger age group had a Buddhist affiliation. Islam and Hinduism were also more predominant in the younger age group. This suggests that the religious profile of older Australians will change with the next generation, influenced in part by changes in the ethnic and cultural characteristics of the cohort.

Social participation

A wide range of measures of social participation were collected through the 2006 ABS General Social Survey (GSS). The measures of social participation collected by this survey differ to those collected by the 2002 ABS National Aboriginal and Torres Strait Islander Social Survey discussed earlier and cannot be compared.

The GSS survey results indicate that family was a prime source of social contact for older people (AIHW 2007a). Australian-born people aged 75 and over, and those from a main English-speaking country, had similarly high levels of contact with family members living outside their household

(79% and 78% respectively) (ABS 2007c). However, a lower proportion of older people with a LOTE background had this kind of contact (72%) (ABS 2007c). Possible factors accounting for this difference include the fact that older people aged 75 and over with a LOTE background are more likely to be living with other family (20% compared with 10% for the Australian-born) and less likely to be living alone (24% compared with 35%) (AIHW: Benham *et al.* 2000). As such, contact with family members by those with a LOTE background may be more often satisfied within the home context.

In relation to the measures 'Actively participated in social groups (last 12 months)' and 'Participated in a community event in last 6 months', Australian-born people were less likely than those born in a main English-speaking country to have been active in a social group (54% compared with 62%). Similarly, Australian-born people were slightly less likely than those born in a main English-speaking country to have participated in a community event (43% compared with 46%). Older people from a LOTE background had the lowest rates of active participation among the three other groups on both measures (47% and 36% respectively) (ABS 2007c).

'Feeling able to have a say within the community on important issues' would seem to be an area in which Australians generally lack confidence. Just over half (54%) of the total population aged 18 and over felt able to have a say. Older Australian-born people had a similar proportion to the population as a whole (53%), while the proportion drops five percentage points for older people born in a main English-speaking country. However, older people from a LOTE background were far less likely to feel able to have a say within the community on important issues (34%) (ABS 2007c).

Aged care programmes
A culturally diverse older Australia has implications for the provision of aged care services. A range of care service programmes for older people is funded by the Australian, state and territory, and local governments. Permanent residential aged care provides accommodation and care services to people who are no longer able to support themselves or be supported by others in their own home. At 30 June 2007, 146,959 people aged 65 and over were permanent residents of Australian Government-funded residential aged care homes (AIHW 2008b).

Community Aged Care Packages (CACP) and Extended Aged Care at Home (EACH) packages provide care in community settings for people who are eligible for, and might otherwise need low-level and high-level residential care respectively. At 30 June 2007, 32,983 people aged 65 and over received a CACP, while 2793 received care through an EACH package (AIHW 2008a).

The Home and Community Care (HACC) Programme aims to promote and enhance the independence of frail aged people, and younger people with disabilities, and their carers, by providing a range of essential community care services (DoHA 2008). The HACC Programme, which is a joint Australian government, state and territory initiative, is the largest aged care programme, with a total of 612,428 clients aged 65 and over receiving assistance during 2006–2007.

Indigenous Australians

The number of Aboriginal and Torres Strait Islander people receiving formal aged care is generally under-reported in all programmes. These underestimates are partly due to the exclusion of some aged care places from routinely reported data, but also to under-reporting of Indigenous status. Some reasons for this include whether or not individuals choose to self-identify as being of Aboriginal or Torres Strait Islander descent, and whether service providers collect information on Indigenous status (AIHW 2007c).

During 2006–2007 at least 858[4] permanent aged care residents (all ages) identified as an Aboriginal or Torres Strait Islander, while 1293 Indigenous Australians (all ages) received a CACP or EACH package. Over a quarter (28%) of Indigenous Australians in residential aged care and about a third (32%) of Indigenous CACP/EACH care recipients preferred to use an Indigenous language. At present only limited data have been collected on the actual Indigenous languages spoken. Of those which have been identified, the four most commonly spoken by both residents of residential aged care and CACP/EACH recipients alike were Arrernte (Aranda), Warlpiri, Alyawarr and Pitjantjatjara.

The Aboriginal and Torres Strait Islander population has a younger age profile and higher rates of disability than the non-Indigenous population. In 2006, 13 per cent of those aged 55–64 needed assistance with core activities of daily living (i.e. self-care mobility and communication) compared with 5 per cent of the non-Indigenous population (ABS and AIHW 2008). As a result, Aboriginal and Torres Strait Islander people tend to access aged care programmes at younger ages than their non-Indigenous counterparts (AIHW 2008b).

At 30 June 2007, Aboriginal and Torres Strait Islander people aged 50 and over made up 0.5 per cent (795)[5] of permanent residents in residential aged care, compared with 3 per cent (1240) of CACP/EACH recipients on the same date. Indigenous Australians aged 50 and over also made up 2 per cent (13,113) of HACC recipients (2006–2007).[6] As Aboriginal and Torres Strait Islander people make up less than 1 per cent of the total population aged 50 and over, this group appears to be slightly under-represented in residential aged care and over-represented in both CACP/EACH and HACC programmes.

A comparison of age-specific usage rates for residential aged care and aged care packages indicates that Aboriginal and Torres Strait Islander people had higher usage rates than their non-Indigenous counterparts in both types of formal aged care, and across all age groups (see Table 3.2). However, in residential aged care, the difference in usage rates between Indigenous and non-Indigenous groups was lower in the older age groups. While the Indigenous rate in the age group 65–69 was over twice that of the non-Indigenous population, in the oldest age group reported here (75 and over) the difference was negligible (102 per 1000 for the Indigenous population compared with 105 per 1000 for the non-Indigenous).

Table 3.2 Formal care programme usage rates, by Indigenous status as at 30 June 2007 (per 1000 population)

	50–54	55–59	60–64	65–69	70–74	75+
Residential aged care						
Indigenous	2.0	5.3	9.3	15.5	24.5	104.7
Non-Indigenous	0.6	1.3	2.6	5.9	12.8	102.1
CACP/EACH						
Indigenous	4.7	10.7	19.8	36.8	53.3	90.7
Non-Indigenous	0.1	0.3	0.8	2.4	4.9	22.9

Note: Recipients with unknown status have been pro rated.

Source: AIHW analysis of the Commonwealth Department of Health and Ageing's Aged and Community Care Management Information System (ACCMIS) database as at July 2008.

In contrast to residential aged care usage rates, the usage rates of CACP/EACH programmes among Indigenous Australians remained much higher than non-Indigenous rates across all age groups. For example, in the oldest age group reported here (75 and over) the difference between the two groups was still over three times (91 per 1000) that of the non-Indigenous population (23 per 1000). It should be borne in mind that differences in age structure between the two groups and the relatively low percentage of Aboriginal and Torres Strait Islander people aged 75 and over affects comparisons of usage rates (AIHW 2007a).

The use of HACC by Aboriginal and Torres Strait Islander people bears some similarities to usage patterns for CACP/EACH. For the age group 50 and over, the usage rate for Indigenous Australians (270 per 1000) is two-and-a-half times that for non-Indigenous (108 per 1000).[7]

Overseas-born Australians

The cultural diversity of older Australians discussed earlier is reflected in the cultural profile of aged care residents and CACP/EACH clients. A total of 22,050 (15%) aged care residents aged 65 and over were born in LOTE countries, while 7466 CACP recipients (23%) and 702 EACH recipients (25%) aged 65 and over were born in LOTE countries. Over 150 LOTE countries and over 70 languages (including Indigenous) were represented among aged care residents. Like the older population generally, there was, however, considerable variation in the size of each birth country represented. Among the total aged care residents, the 10 largest LOTE countries of birth accounted for almost two-thirds (64%) of the overseas-born population with a LOTE background, while the top five countries accounted for almost half (47%). Conversely, at the other end of the scale, there were over 50 countries from which there were only small numbers of people, with each country accounting for only one, two or three people. In 2007, the top six birth countries among aged care residents were: Italy, Germany, the Netherlands, Poland, Greece and China (excluding SAR (Special Administrative Region of the People's Republic of China) and Taiwan). The top six preferred languages among aged care residents who preferred to speak a language other than English were: Italian, Greek, Polish, German, Dutch and Cantonese.

The relationship between the top ten countries of birth and the top ten preferred languages is not a direct one. This is because different immigrant groups in Australia have different first-language maintenance patterns, with some immigrant groups maintaining their first language at higher rates than others.

The diversity of aged care residents' cultural backgrounds has implications for service provision in terms of a need to provide culturally sensitive services and bilingual support. The challenge in meeting the needs of older immigrants is perhaps greatest for numerically smaller or widely dispersed cultural groups (AIHW 2007a).

The overseas-born population had different patterns of use compared to the Australian-born population. Those from the main English-speaking countries were the most consistent in their representation across the four aged care programmes, making up 12 per cent of both the residential aged care and CACP/EACH populations and 11 per cent of the HACC population. These figures suggest that this group was slightly under-represented across all programmes, as they made up 14 per cent of the total population aged 65 and over. The overseas-born population with a LOTE background was more varied in its representation across the different types of formal aged care. Older people with a LOTE background made up 20 per cent of the total population aged 65 and over, and so were under-represented in residential aged care, where they made up 15 per cent. However, they were over-represented in CACP/EACH programmes where they made up 23 per cent. They were 'normally' represented in HACC making up 19 per cent of the population.

Age-specific usage rates for those born in one of the main English-speaking countries showed considerable variation across the programmes with no clear pattern. Usage rates of residential aged care by people born overseas in a main English-speaking country were lower than those for the Australian-born population. CACP/EACH usage rates for this group were also lower than those for the Australian-born in the age groups 65–74 and 75–84, but higher in the oldest age group (85 and over). HACC usage rates for this group were consistently lower than both the Australian-born and those from a LOTE background.

Age-specific usage rates for overseas-born people from a LOTE background in residential aged care were also lower than for the Australian-born across all age groups reported here. They were also lower than those for people born in a main English-speaking country in the two older age groups (75–84, and 85 and over) but higher than the rate for people born in a main English-speaking country in the youngest age group (65–74). Usage rates of community packages by overseas-born people from a LOTE background were lower than those for the Australian-born in the younger age group (65–74), but higher than for the Australian-born in the older age groups (75–84, and 85 and over). The difference was most marked in the oldest age group (85 and over) where the usage rate by overseas-born people with a LOTE background was 60 per 1000 compared with 45 per 1000 for the Australian-born population.

Perhaps surprisingly, usage rates for HACC did not follow the same pattern as those for CACP/EACH. Overseas-born people with a LOTE background had lower usage rates than the Australian-born population across all age groups. This prevents a simple conclusion being drawn that overseas-born people with a LOTE background have a preference for community-based services over residential aged care. It is very likely that a variety of factors are at play.

First, the data presented here is highly aggregated, thereby obscuring variation in usage patterns between different cultural groups, some of whom may well have a preference for home-based care. Space constraints prevent a finer level of analysis being provided here. Second, service delivery structures vary between programmes and may influence accessibility and take-up of service options. For example, entry into CACP and EACH packages is through a single entry and assessment point managed by Aged Care Assessment Teams (ACAT). However, HACC has multiple entry points. Some immigrants from LOTE backgrounds may find it easier to enter and navigate the service system when a single entry process is available.

Table 3.3 Formal care programme usage rates, by birthplace, 2006–2007 (per 1000 population)

	65–74	75–84	85+
Residential aged care*			
Australian-born	10.4	55.8	251.6
Overseas-born, main English-speaking country	6.6	46.9	234.4
Overseas-born, LOTE country	7.1	46.5	192.5
CACP/EACH*			
Australian-born	4.0	14.9	41.0
Overseas-born, main English-speaking country	2.6	13.9	44.1
Overseas-born, LOTE country	3.8	20.5	53.2
HACC**			
Australian-born	114.0	309.0	526.0
Overseas-born, main English-speaking country	75.0	254.0	441.0
Overseas-born, LOTE country	95.0	286.0	480.0

Notes: *Residential aged care and CACP/EACH data as at 30 June 2007.
**HACC data for the year 2006–2007.

Source: Residential aged care data and CACP/EACH data: AIHW analysis of the Department of Health and Ageing's (DoHA) Aged and Community Care Management Information System (ACCMIS) database as at July 2008; HACC data: DoHA analysis of HACC data, provided August 2008.

Other potential factors include the availability of services in particular areas, including culturally appropriate services (see also the following section: 'Aged care programmes and cultural specialisation'), English-language proficiency among the overseas-born people with a LOTE background, and the availability of informal carers at home.

Higher usage of CACP and EACH may also suggest that overseas-born people with a LOTE background and their carers are not accessing services until their needs are severe, resulting in referrals from medical practitioners to an ACAT assessment. In support of this claim, overseas-born people with a LOTE background have a higher level of dependency upon entering residential aged care than other new admissions (Gibson 2007).

Aged care programmes and cultural specialisation

One service response to the cultural diversity of the aged care population is through the provision of ethno-specific services. In 2007, 17 per cent of residential aged care homes and 47 per cent of community care outlets catered for specific ethic groups (Martin and King 2008). A key issue in being able to provide culturally appropriate aged care services is the availability of staff with bicultural and bilingual skills. Figures provided by Martin and King (2008) indicate that overseas-born people with a LOTE background were more highly represented as direct care workers in residential aged care facilities (20%) and as community care workers (15%) than they were in the Australian population as a whole (9%). However, this does not necessarily mean that there is a complete match between the cultural and language background of care recipients and care workers.

In residential aged care, the most commonly catered for groups were those with an Italian, Aboriginal, Chinese, Greek, Dutch or Polish background (Martin and King 2008). In those facilities where more than a third of personal carers spoke a LOTE, the most common cultural groups among carers (in order of size) were Philippino, Asian (unspecified), Chinese, African, Italian, Greek, Fijian, Aboriginal and Torres Strait Islander, and Dutch (Martin and King 2008).

Another way to examine the match between aged-care workers and aged care residents is to look at how many workers used their LOTE in their work. According to Martin and King (2008), while almost a third (29%) of personal carers and a quarter of nurses (25%) and allied health workers (24%) spoke a LOTE, only about half of personal carers (47%) and nurses (52%) used their language in their work. Allied health workers were more likely to use their LOTE in their work (63%) (Martin and King 2008).

In community care programmes, the cultural groups most commonly catered for included those with an Aboriginal and Torres Strait Islander, Italian, Chinese, Greek, Dutch or Polish background (Martin and King 2008). The most common cultural background of community care workers in outlets employing community care workers with a LOTE background were: Italian, Chinese, Aboriginal, Spanish, Asian, Greek, Dutch and Philippino (Martin and King 2008).

About a quarter of community care workers (24%) and allied health workers (22%) spoke a LOTE. Two thirds (66%) of community care workers and seven in ten (71%) allied health workers used their LOTE in their job. A much smaller proportion of nurses in community care spoke a LOTE (11%) but most of these used it in their work (83%).

Martin and King (2008) concluded that neither Aboriginal and Torres Strait Islander nor overseas-born people from any LOTE country were represented in the aged care workforce in proportion to the specialisation of services for older clients from their communities. In particular, Aboriginal and Torres Strait Islander workers were 'very rare' (Martin and King 2008, p.150). While those with a LOTE background were better represented, many did not share the same cultural background as aged care residents, or clients of community care providers (Martin and King 2008). While service providers may seek to employ those with appropriate language and cultural skills, such workers with relevant qualifications can be difficult to find. Some aged-care workers with a LOTE background are employed for reasons other than their specific language and cultural knowledge. In some cases, this is more to do with limited employment options available for low-skilled workers (Martin and King 2008).

Conclusion

Over the course of the twentieth century Australia has, like several other countries, become very culturally and linguistically diverse. This is also true of older cohorts. The pattern of diversity among the older population will change with future generations. While Aboriginal and Torres Strait Islander people currently form a small proportion of the older population, this is likely to change in future cohorts. Further, there is considerable diversity within the older Aboriginal and Torres Strait Islander population in terms of languages spoken and cultural heritage.

A high proportion of overseas-born people in the 55–74 age group provides some evidence that the proportion of overseas-born people with a LOTE background among future cohorts of older people will be higher than it currently is. The cultural composition of Australia's older overseas-born population varies between age groups, reflecting the history of immigration and settlement in Australia over the past 80 years or so. The cultural makeup of future cohorts as they enter old age will continue to reflect historical migration patterns.

A culturally diverse older society has implications for social cohesion and connectedness, as well as for service planning and delivery, with formal aged care services being one example. This chapter has illustrated how in the Australian context older Aboriginal and Torres Strait Islander and overseas-born populations are represented among users of formal aged care services in different ways, possibly reflecting different cultural preferences and practices in relation to the care of older people, and differences in knowledge about and access to these services. The challenge for all governments with culturally diverse populations and their respective aged care industries will be to ensure that the needs of culturally diverse older people can be responded to in a timely and effective manner. This same challenge is also relevant to other service sectors, such as health and housing.

Notes

1. All numbers and percentages cited in the text have been rounded.
2. The ABS Australian Standard Geographical Classification (ASGC) Remoteness Areas classification has five remoteness categories for areas, depending on their distance from a range of five types of population centre. Areas are classified as *Major cities*, as *Inner regional* or *Outer regional* (*Regional* when taken together) or *Remote* and *Very remote* (*Remote* when taken together) (AIHW 2004b).
3. Numbers exclude the categories 'born elsewhere' and 'not stated'.
4. Numbers exclude 'status unknown'.
5. The numbers and proportions cited here exclude persons for whom Indigenous status is unknown.
6. The proportion of HACC funded agencies that submitted HACC MDS for 2006–2007 was 83 per cent. This means that actual client numbers will be much higher than those reported here.
7. Rates based on AIHW analysis of HACC data tables supplied by the Commonwealth Department of Health and Ageing.

CHAPTER 4

The Ageing Spirit

Rachael Kohn

Hundreds of people, young and old, from different religious backgrounds and spiritual sensibilities have shared their thoughts with me on 'The Spirit of Things'.[1] Although ageing has not been the usual topic of discussion, their individual stories often reveal the secret to living a good life well into old age. And that's no small feat, given how tempting it is to be very gloomy about the current state of the world, with its contradictory tendencies to overwhelming decadence and shocking neglect. At a personal level things are no less apocalyptic, since living longer has only increased the possible ways we will meet our inevitable deaths, while it has cultivated an unrealistic belief that we should be able to live without the normal visible signs of ageing and without pain right to the end. In the midst of this dark satire of life and death, however, a persistent bunch of optimists tell us that by good deeds and a positive outlook, not to mention love and prayer, we can increase our happiness in old age, and as a bonus the world can become a better place (Kohn 2007).

Whether or not the theories are right, every single individual meets the onset of old age in a way that is meaningful for them, and occasionally instructive for the rest of us as well. The people who I remember here did strike me as being comfortably, sometimes powerfully, *in* their old age. They were still of *use*, even if some of their mental faculties were diminished. In fact, I'll begin with Emily, an Aboriginal woman who had dementia. She was nonetheless a lovely artist. Her life had been difficult, as she was a 'half-caste', a 'creamy' as they used to call them, and had essentially been taken from her mother and placed in a convent school where she was educated and later lived as a laundry hand and kitchen helper. She painted beautiful pictures of hills and dales, filled with flowers, trees and streams. These were magical scenes of such serene beauty and happiness, that inevitably prompted her to describe them as if they were snapshots of her early life. Made up or true, the half imagined stories of her youth repeated a theme of visiting her mother who picked her bouquets of flowers. The paintings were a visual reminder of her past, which of course is an abiding aspect of dementia, where the present often fades as the past moves in with increasing clarity. When she spoke to me about each painting, and the stories contained in it, she beamed, and it was clear that painting was an aide mémoire for the things she wanted to remember about her life.

Her happiest moments, however, were when she burst into song. All the words and melodies were intact, whenever she sang the hymns she learned in the convent as a child. I shall never forget the sweet girl's voice that emitted from her when she sang.

The details that Emily told me about her life were far from accurate in a journalistic sense and I soon stopped trying to order them into a coherent time line. I found that the best way to be in this situation was to accept that it was the experience of her storytelling and painting that was most real and satisfying to her. A woman and art gallery owner, who understood this, provided her with the ways and means to paint, and her paintings were exhibited and sold, with most of the proceeds going toward her care. Emily basked in the attention, being quite a pretty woman who dressed beautifully even in her senescence, and she must have felt that she was fulfilling some wonderful destiny to share her story with others.

I met another Aboriginal woman in Alice Springs whose life could not have been more different. She was full-blood, an elder and not in the least pretty. She was in fact formidable, even scary-looking to me all those years ago when I had not met many Aboriginal people. To my surprise, she wanted to meet me and was anxious to take me under her wing and tell me what was going on in her community. There was death and drugs and unhappiness all around, yet she seemed proud to be in an authoritative position. The others deferred to her, but for this woman there was no relief, no comfort and very little rest, except when she was in church. Even there, she was all too aware of who was present and who wasn't, and the reasons why, which she was determined to tell me even in the midst of the service. She was shouldering an impossible burden.

I often think of her, and wonder if she's still alive. Surely, many of the young men she pointed out in the congregation would not be. What she wanted most of all was support from people like the nuns who worked alongside her women folk in the outback. And although she initiated contact with me, I did feel that without real help to give her, I was just a temporary diversion, perhaps a glimmer of hope. I think she sensed my feelings of inadequacy, and considerately took me under her wing for what turned out to be one of the steepest learning curves of my life, as I observed the physical deprivation and spiritual decay of her people. I did learn that day, however, that the Aboriginal matriarchs were ready and able to give direction to a younger generation that had lost their way.

Back in Sydney, some years ago, I received regular letters from Tom. He wrote in a neat, small hand, always full of intellectual and spiritual engagement with the subject matter of 'The Spirit of Things' that week. I was impressed by his desire to engage with so many different subjects, and all with a consistent optimism, as if each week the programme posed a challenge to him: what wise insight into life could it provide this time? You see, he always found the positive angle in whatever topic was up for grabs that week. I detected that Tom was an elderly gentleman – the penmanship gave him away, as much as the courteous style in which he expressed himself. But what stood out for me, was that he never betrayed a hint of the old nostalgia that envelops so many people past a certain age. One day I wrote, asking if I could visit him. It was in 2003, because he was keen to get a copy of my first book, *The New Believers. Re-imagining God* (Kohn 2003), which I duly brought to him.

So, there I was in an aged care facility up on the Colloroy Plateau in Sydney's northern beaches, visiting Tom in his room. It was neat, as I expected, and yet not without books and letters, and magazines. Tom was a letter writer extraordinaire, and I was only one of dozens of people who heard from him regularly, including the letters editor of the *Sydney Morning Herald*. What I wanted to learn was what made him tick, because it was clear he had a keen interest in world events as well as the quality of spiritual life. His own story, as it turned out, was interwoven with twentieth-century history: World War I, World War II, the Temperance Movement, the Oxford Movement or Moral Re-armament, now called Initiatives for Change. Tom's life was full of purpose and direction.

He had seen how drink had destroyed so many lives in his native Glasgow. He knew that taking care of others was not the only religious duty; you also had to care for your own body. That was a religious duty too, and it had social consequences as well. Tom's teetotalism wasn't born of a naïve fundamentalism – he was too intellectually keen to fall for that. It was born of an understanding that life is a gift, which you can either treat shabbily and consign to the dustbin before its time, or treat with care and determination, with a sense of a higher purpose, and an understanding that it will repay you.

Above all the things that ensured Tom had a long life, however, I would bet that it was his innate gift (or was it learned?) for cultivating friendship. With good humour, a positive interest in others and a love of music, the twinkle in Tom's eye was as discernible at 91 as I'm sure it was at 19. Tom died at 92, and at his funeral his friends and family played an excerpt from my interview with him, which I was very touched to learn about. There were hundreds of people who came to say goodbye to Tom, which is testament enough, isn't it, that Tom's dedication and good humour touched a lot of people. A life well lived, which really didn't change its character, even into his nursing home years. And prayer had a lot to do with it. This is how Tom Gillespie explained it to me:

> I think it's this question of the Lord's Prayer, which I say every night and every morning, 'Our Father which art in heaven, hallowed be thy name; thy kingdom come, thy will be done on earth as it is in heaven.' That is really it for me... Well, the point is, I do believe that God can speak through one's mind in an intelligent way, and that to me is the important thing. As well as me praying to God and speaking to him, *I listen and see what comes into my mind, because after all, God made mind; who made your mind?* There must be a creator, therefore I listen and try and get the thoughts. *And I listen to people too, because I learnt a lot from other people.* The chap at my table at lunchtime and at breakfast time, he's got a great experience of all kinds of things, and I like to listen to him and he tells me all about his work in radar and the army, and his knowledge of Australia, and many things. Very interesting. *So I like to listen to people.* (Gillespie 2003)

There is so much profundity in these words. It is as if Tom's belief in God laid the groundwork for his interest in other people and the respect he paid them with his curiosity and attention. Valuing friendship is surely the best antidote to measuring the quality of your life by the things you have.

Not long ago, I spoke to an older gentleman, who I think was in his 60s. His skin was smooth and the colour of café au lait. His chocolate dark eyes were clear and shining. He looked healthy. But like all devout followers of the Jain religion, he follows a strict dietary code, which doesn't include meat or other animal products, nor green vegetables on certain days of the month, and never root vegetables, like potatoes and carrots. He looked in fine fettle. But here's the thing: he was a diamond merchant, a traditional occupation among Jains, and I imagine would be doing well financially. He and his wife and adult children lived in a small modern apartment in Sydney's central business district, which afforded a spectacular view of the harbour, but had little space for furniture. I was conscious of how efficient and elegant his wife was in that tiny space, preparing refreshments for us without being intrusive. He said to me, 'We Jains believe that it's best to live without too much, but just enough.' That is, their lives were not preoccupied with chasing lots of material things – larger homes, larger cars, larger sofas, gigantic TVs, and other accoutrements of the so-called 'good life'. And yet Jains are the most economically successful segment of the

Indian population. They constitute one per cent of the population in India and pay approximately 30 per cent of its taxes. They love education and regard hard work and discipline as virtually mandatory. Yet the fruit of their success is not materialistic. Rather, it is having the time to return home early enough to eat dinner before sundown – a Jain rule – and having time to do one's devotions at the home shrine. Relaxing with the family and getting to sleep early was all part of the rhythm of Jain life.

Jains don't believe in the kind of salvation which Westerners hanker for, and they don't even have the concept of a creator God. Instead the universe is believed to go on for eternity, in cycles, some up, some down, and each eon or era is led by a type of messianic figure. It may sound depressing, as if they are caught in an endless wheel of time, but like all religions, Jainism offers its followers a means of attaining a higher path, leading to the lightening of the soul, freeing it from the emotional burdens that bring it down and prevent a good death and rebirth. It is not a passive world view, but on the contrary it invites you to participate in the care of your soul and those around you.

When I met the Jains, I never expected their practices to bear any similarity to the Jewish tradition, but wasn't I surprised to learn that the festival I was there to investigate involved an eight-day period of deep soul-searching, of fasting, and then of forgiving of others, and asking forgiveness from those whom they have hurt, culminating in a joyous celebration of thanksgiving to the Lord Mahavira, whose exemplary life and teachings are the inspiration for the Jains. Anyone familiar with the Jewish high holidays will immediately see how similar it is to the period between Rosh Hashana and Yom Kippur on the Jewish calendar. I could only smile inwardly and say to myself, here is an instance of profound similarity in the way human beings strive to lead an exemplary ethical life that is focused not only on making one's life right with God, but on making it right with others. To assist in the redemption of the world is important, and Jains, like Jews, believe that in doing good deeds for the world, not just for their own community, which after all is small, they are fulfilling a sacred mission. For them, God is the good you do.[2]

In early 2007 I went to visit the Sikhs, who have a large *gurdwara*, or house of worship, in Western Sydney.[3] Its seven golden onion domes can be seen from the highway, and I often wondered what it was like inside. I soon got my chance to see when I recorded the daily service, which is followed by the *langar*, the communal meal. Although the *langar* is served every day, it is a very large affair on the weekends. The *gurdwara* is built large enough to accommodate all the Sikhs who come together, first to read the *Guru Granth Sahib*, the sacred text of poetry and praise, and then to partake in the *langar*, which is always taken seated on the ground or floor. Business and professional leaders of the community alongside labourers and housewives prepare the meal and serve it, and all sit and eat together.

The leaders of the community, who were a mixture of older and younger men, and one woman, were all eager to talk to me about the philosophy and values of Sikhism which underlie the *langar* – the most practical expression of religious duty one could imagine: preparing food, serving it to one and all without discrimination, and eating together. In this way, the Sikh tradition guarantees that no one in their community goes hungry due to indifference or neglect. Sikhs are also committed to doing charity for others outside their own community. For example, they were active in raising money for the 2008 earthquake in Burma. It was soon evident to me that a culture of serving and providing for one's own also breeds a more general ethic of helping others beyond one's community. Indeed, no one would turn you away from a *langar* because you were not Sikh, although women and men would be required to cover their heads during the service.

The chanting of the Sikh sacred text, the *Guru Granth Sahib*, which constitutes the service, is accompanied by all attendees proceeding to the front of the hall and dropping a donation into the box, or leaving food for the next day's *langar*. It is not mandatory, but as most people do it, everyone is encouraged by example to take responsibility for the maintenance of the community. Indeed, this simple and central ritual, which involves everyone, struck me as the embodiment of a basic humanitarian principle whereby the most basic need of a community is met: sustenance.

As most religions demonstrate, however, the material necessities of survival are useless without a purpose for living. I would venture to guess that for the Sikh community it has much to do with keeping the wisdom of the *Guru Granth Sahib* alive, which means ensuring that the Sikh community survives, and which in turn is aided by instilling in its members the key obligation to serve others. Thus, a cycle of mutual support is embedded in their consciousness: serve others and they will serve you. Being a member of a faith community in this active way is not only uncomplicated and practical, it is founded on the most profound value of communal sharing. Once this is witnessed as a child and practised from youth on, imagine how it informs one's attitude to others, and to life in general. *You are never alone.* Suicide must be a rarity in the Sikh community, where from childhood on you know that others care for you, and, more important, you care for them.

Last year I had a most unusual encounter with a Chinese professor from Shantung. He was a specialist in Jewish studies. Jewish studies, you might ask in disbelief! Why not? First, there was a large Jewish community in Shanghai – refugees from the Russian revolution and then later from Nazi

Germany. Second, many of the great Asian scholars of the twentieth century were Jewish. So why not the other way around? My Chinese scholar of Judaism was not merely interested as an academic, but, with the characteristic practicality of the Chinese, he wanted to learn how it was that Jews survived the most horrible act of annihilation in the modern world, yet still held on to their identity and their traditions. Furthermore, he wanted to know how these traditions co-existed with a robust engagement with modern norms and values. He was, therefore, very interested in the practical expressions of Jewish thought – its ethics.

He had embarked on a major study of Jewish philosophy and rabbinic thought and was busy translating it into Chinese. Beyond his interest in classic Jewish texts, however, the thing that had most impressed him was his one year of living with a Jewish professor in Washington. He could scarcely comprehend the way in which Jewish people give large amounts of their money and time to others. Whether they have a lot of money or not, all Jews do it. Indeed, most do not have a lot of money, despite the rumour to the contrary, which he himself had to dispel. The voluntary involvement of Jews was something he admired because, from a Confucian point of view, *you are on your own* – you pull *yourself* up by your bootstraps, and if you fall down it's your own fault and your own fate. No one is going to pull you out of it. This, he told me, was the Confucian ethic. The curious thing about the Jews he met was that they did not want to see others fall, nor expose them to the public shame of failure. It is a rabbinic principle which has produced a deeply ingrained Jewish attitude that it is kinder to give someone a job and preserve their self-esteem than to hand them charity and watch them stoop to take it. Similarly, it is better to build up facilities and institutions for everyone, than to single out the needy and provide assistance just for them. In this way, no divisions are set up within the community between the haves and the have-nots – and that is most evident, for example, in the Montefiore Homes for the Aged, for which everyone is eligible, and which are supported by a larger communal funding body to which everyone contributes.

Speaking of Jewish wisdom, I recently had the delight of interviewing someone I'd first learned about 35 years ago. He was quite a cult figure then, amongst Jewish students who were interested in living their faith in ways that were more 'spiritual' than their parents – or so they thought. Zalman Shachter was the new wave of Judaism in the 1970s. So, 35 years later, after an eventful life, and accumulating a new wife and an additional name (Zalman Shachter Shalomi), he came to Sydney and talked about getting old. In fact, he wrote a book called *From Ageing to Sage-ing* in which he tells people who don't like getting old that they should shift from ageing to sage-ing.

> The first step is to face our mortality. When I look ahead, I see the end. I'm going to die. Most people have an aversion to looking in the direction of dying. [But] the future inexorably comes, and if I'm not facing it, I'm backing into it...
>
> Once they've looked directly at their mortality they can ask a realistic question: How long have I got? And most of the time it's not so bad. If I've lived to today, the likelihood is that I'm going to live some more, and maybe a lot longer. Once people realize that they can begin *to plan*. (Schachter Shalomi 2006)

Zalman Schachter also pointed out that the problem with growing older is that we haven't really got a positive way of describing or appreciating that period beyond the sixties. He calls it 'the harvest'.

> The first thing is one needs to take real responsibility for the harvest time in [your life]. [When] you come [to] the age of 63, you get into that period for which we don't have models in society, and this is why it is so important to be able to create a cadre of elders who will tell people what [is] possible.
>
> ...One is only old by the calendar, but one becomes an elder when one knows how to use those years, and that means life review, life repair, relationships repair, and a way of thinking about, how do I want to harvest what I learned in life. And there are good memories and there are some other memories that are not so happy, but they contain in themselves some gold too, if one looks into them.
>
> So in order to be able to do this work, one has to learn how to use contemplation, because one needs to be able to reflect, contemplate and... time travel, to go over the past and do harvest from there. (Schachter Shalomi 2006)

Some years ago I visited a former Anglican priest. He was actually the chaplain of Cranbrook Boys School in Sydney when my husband was a student there. The Reverend Peter Newell had been through the ups and downs of the Anglican church in New South Wales and Adelaide, and eventually left the priesthood in order to practise his faith with more creative flair and less institutional pressure. When I visited him in Adelaide he was suffering from very serious cancer, and I didn't think the pale-skinned, delicately featured fellow who came to meet me in Glen Elg had much time to live. At that time, neither did he. But, he persevered, and after getting a good deal worse, he also recovered substantially. I think his remission was certainly helped by his ministry – if I can use that word – through a beautiful 'magazine' which he issues about every two months. *La Campanella*, which means 'little bell', is a collection of religious, literary and personal reflections, which Peter Newell injects with his love of poetry and art and his deep spiritual knowledge and sensitivity. His beautiful insights never cease to amaze me. Each time I receive *La Campanella*, I know that it is a gift of love which surely keeps him alive and thriving.

I say thriving, because Peter Newell actively reveals through his reading and writing that the Word, the Christian term that encapsulates salvation as Jesus communicated it, can also take to a canvas, a poem, a waltz, a threnody and even the insights of history. The Word was there for Peter when he first saw Van Gogh's *Sunflowers* in London's National Gallery. And in the nineteenth-century Scottish author, poet and minister, George MacDonald, who famously said 'If you are in a prison, the first step to freedom is to sweep the floor.' What far-sighted wisdom is born of practical necessity! Take charge, put your place in order, care enough to keep your little habitat clean. It is in the doing that God finds ethical expression: God is in your hands. And it is also in the command to be still and seek the inner places within you, and know that even in the midst of your sorrow, perhaps especially there, God's presence can be felt.

Peter wrote, with the extraordinary understanding of someone who knows from experience both sides of the equation, 'Visiting a sick friend is difficult. We must give away altogether the half thought that we are doing the other a favour. We need to unearth the love that is in us, to give our friend a sense of his or her worth' (Newell 2008). He is also a sensitive poet:

Addressing You
I touch your hand, hold your eye,
This is our bodies' poetry
And such word that we can say
Come borrowed from another day
So read the face, trust our heart
And reckon this a healing art.

(Newell 2008)

The spiritual dimension of the healing arts has been with us since the beginning of time – we find it in ancient sources, as abundantly in the East (such as in Taoism's search for the elixir of immortality) as we do in the West (such as in Jesus healing the sick and even raising the dead). Today spiritual healing has resurged into a huge movement, with a particular tendency to see spiritual practice as having salutary biological and physical effects which are scientifically verifiable. I've written about this trend of thinking in my book, *Curious Obsessions in the History of Science and Spirituality* (Kohn 2007), which examines, among other things, the historical and the contemporary relationship between the mystical and the medical. And although the combination has at times given rise to beneficial scientific discoveries as well as increased spiritual maturity and understanding, it has also resulted in pseudoscience, where outlandish claims are made that sell both science and spirituality short. Yet, there is a powerful urge to merge these two realms of knowledge, and at the very least one must proceed with caution, especially as one grows older and is more vulnerable to the signs of mortality and the desire to hang on to life at any cost.

Rather than list the desperate measures to which some people have fallen victim to at the hands of charlatans selling snake oil and bogus healing waters, let me end with a gentle nod toward the nineteenth century, which in America saw the rise of new religious movements that were imbued with a concern for health and longevity. Their legacy today is not entirely a good one. The Jehovah's Witnesses, for example, refuse some of the fundamentals of modern medicine, such as blood transfusions, without which most operations would be impossible to perform successfully. The Seventh Day Adventists, on the other hand, promote their profound interest in health and well-being through the establishment of medical schools and hospitals offering outstanding care, as well as a vegetarian and caffeine-free diet. Not only is their strong emphasis on cereals, beginning when J. Harvey Kellogg famously invented a new kind of breakfast food, good news for the older person who needs to keep his digestive system in good working order, but their belief, following Paul's teaching in Corinthians, that the body is the temple of the God and the dwelling of the Holy Spirit, diminishes the likelihood of substance abuse and obesity.[4] Adventists have conducted important studies which also show that an active religious life and a steady pattern of altruism increase longevity and lower the incidence of depression.

This discovery is not specific to Seventh Day Adventists but is a generally valid observation that has had a long history of supportive research. It is this area of knowledge that is giving us another insight into why religion is so persistent, despite its current legion of naysayers. Put simply, 'it works'. It is now regularly shown that the religious life not only extends one's longevity, it also increases the emotional reserves that people have to cope with illness and death. Researchers like Dr Harold Koenig, Professor of Psychiatry and Behaviour Sciences and founder of the Centre for the Study of Spirituality, Theology and Health at Duke University Medical Centre, and Dr Stephen Post, Director of the Institute for Research on Unlimited Love at Case Western Reserve University, have been increasing our appreciation of the positive role that the spiritual life plays as we get older and face the inevitable challenges of encroaching physical debilitation and death.

Most religions experience increased involvement on the part of the grey-haired members of their community, not only because older people have more time and perhaps more wisdom to impart, but clearly because it does them more good than staying away. Religion is not simply a refuge for the generation that is closer to mortality, but also for many it is an opportunity to 'give back' in the form of helping others, and this has profound psychological and physiological effects. As Stephen Post related on 'The Spirit of Things':

> It turns out that in general, older adults who are involved in volunteering and again – the caveat always is not to be overwhelmed – but they do have reduced mortality rates. We have four or five really wonderful studies that look at older adults, aged 60 and older, for periods of three years, and five years and seven years, and these all are done by researchers at premier universities, and it really turns out to be the case, that 'tis better to give than to receive, and science says it's so, that the giving is more beneficial than the receiving of support.[5]

Thanks to a large reservoir of research on ageing we now appreciate that religion reorients people's perspective and revises their priorities, so that they can actually face their mortality with less fear and more understanding. We would do well to respect this basic truth and learn to embrace it.

Notes

1.   The Spirit of Things is heard on ABC Radio National, Sundays at 6:05pm, Tuesdays at 1:05pm and Wednesday mornings at 2:05am. It can be downloaded or heard online at www.abc.net.au/rn/spiritofthings.
2.   With a nod to Michael Benedikt, author of *God is the Good We Do*. (New York: Bottino Books, 2007).
3.   Gurdwara Sahib Parklea, New South Wales, Australia.
4.   Seventh Day Adventist, Dr. Gerald Winslow, who teaches Ethics and Religious Studies at Loma Linda University, California, explained the theology underlying the Adventist focus on health on 'The Spirit of Things' 21 October 2007, www.abc.net.au/rn/spiritofthings.
5.   Stephen Post on 'The Spirit of Things' 29 April 2007. See www.abc.net.au/rn/spiritofthings.

CHAPTER 5

Friends and Neighbours: Pastoral Care and Ageing in Christian Perspective

Elizabeth MacKinlay

Introduction

This chapter offers a broad perspective of the pastoral role of Christians in spiritual care, while briefly outlining types of religious care that may be needed by different denominations within Christianity. At the same time the core beliefs of Christianity and differences between denominations are acknowledged. Concepts of belonging, of separation and of friendship are explored in the context of providing pastoral care to, by and with older people in a multifaith and multicultural society. The model of being a neighbour, exemplified by the *Good Samaritan,* is used to examine concepts of Christian pastoral care. This model delivers care to any in need, regardless of religion and ethnic grouping. The needs of older Christians for spiritual growth and care are examined within this context. Sensitivity of the care providers to spiritual and religious needs of others is essential and based on effective listening and assessment skills.

Pastoral and spiritual care in a pluralistic society

Attitudes towards people of other cultures and faiths may be coloured, at least to some extent, by our own feelings of belonging, or of separation from others. Jean Vanier raises questions of the importance of belonging together, in a pluralistic society. He says that belonging begins 'with human contact, with friendship, and as we listen to each other's stories' (Vanier 1998, p.62). He notes that we are all touched when a person from another culture treats us kindly, 'even though we are not a member of their group, or when they reveal their inner pain, weakness, and difficulties'.

Jean Vanier says:

> Perhaps it is then that we feel more deeply this bonding in a common humanity. Friendships grow between people of different backgrounds and cultures because they meet as persons, not because they share a common heritage. Such friendships grow because we all belong to the largest group of all, the human race. (Vanier 1998, p.62)

Vanier also writes of the tensions of balance between belonging to a group, such as a religious group, and the broader category of being Christian. It is possible that a particular religious group may become the primary focus, with the result that all other possible friendships outside this one group become excluded. He writes:

> When religion closes people up in their own particular group, it puts belonging to the group, and its success and growth, above love and vulnerability towards others; it no longer nourishes and opens the heart. When this happens, religion becomes an ideology, that is to say, a series of ideas that we impose on ourselves, as well as on others; it closes us up behind walls. When religion helps us to open our hearts in love and compassion to those who are not of our faith so as to help them to find the source of freedom within their own hearts and to grow in compassion and love for others, then this religion is a source of life. (Ranier 1998, p.63)

In this chapter I will focus on pastoral care in a Christian context, with emphasis on love and its practical outpouring in friendship and in being neighbours. I want to begin by asking: what are Christian beliefs about the nature of being human that underlie the care that is provided in pastoral care?

Different expressions of Christianity

We often take for granted that most people will know what Christianity is about, and what beliefs and doctrines guide its followers. While 64 per cent of Australians still acknowledged a Christian denomination on the 2006 Census data (ABS 2006), we cannot make the assumption that those who care for others, often young people caring for elderly people, will know about the Christian practices of those they care for. If we look more broadly at our multifaith society, it then becomes apparent that community understandings of Christianity simply cannot be assumed or taken for granted. Therefore, in the context of this book on ageing and spirituality across faiths and cultures, it is wise to endeavour to set out what the major beliefs and practices of Christians are, but even this is not so simple. In other chapters, the religious beliefs and practices of faiths with larger numbers of older people will be set out.

There are different expressions of Christianity in the various denominations. One example of this is a life-skills coordinator, brought up in a Catholic tradition, who found it hard to understand the way a group of older Latvian residents expressed their faith. These residents were Lutherans, for whom English was a second language, and their formative years had been lived in the midst of World War II. Thus their practice of their faith was different from what the life-skills coordinator could expect, based on *her* faith experience; they came from a different culture and they were from a different and older cohort of people. It is hard for workers caring for the aged to provide religiously and culturally sensitive care when they do not have experience or understanding of the beliefs and cultural heritage of those they care for.

We might think that all Christians are the same, that is, have the same faith, see their faith in the same way and hold similar world views (except perhaps for some very fundamentalist groups). In fact this is not the case; although the central tenets of the Christian faith hold across most denominations, some views are held by some more strongly than others. For instance, central tenets of Christianity are recognising Jesus as Son of God, believing in the incarnation of God's Son, and the life, crucifixion and resurrection of Jesus. Yet even these central tenets may be understood at least slightly differently by different groups of Christians.

Further, ways of worship are often different across denominations; ritual is more important for some than for others, likewise the use of symbols and the importance given to scripture, and there is a variety of interpretations of scripture. For some denominations the Eucharist or Holy Communion is central, while for others the preaching of the Word of God forms the central component of the practice of their faith. Even within Anglicanism there is a range of liturgies, from the Anglo-Catholic to the Evangelical.

Often older people come from a long tradition of particular ways of being Christian and are familiar with a particular type of worship, and the hymns, words of the service, types of prayers, wearing of vestments or not by clergy will all be important for them in making the attendance at a service of worship meaningful or not. In addition, different Christians will view their faith and religious practices differently, and so variations exist even within families and in the same community of faith.

I clearly remember a woman with dementia in a particular congregation, who said the great thanksgiving prayer along with the priest. This was a special time of connecting for this woman, who was finding it difficult to talk with others and connect in normal conversation, but she was able to participate fully in the words of the Eucharist. This was a time of sacredness in worship, a time when she could become immersed in worship, despite her dementia.

The way faith is lived may have bearing on ideas of life and death and quality of life. Sanctity of life is valued by Christians. However, Christians recognise that life in this world is temporary and that earthly life does naturally come to an end, recognising that saving life in this world at any cost is not the whole story. Yet often people feel confused about issues of eternal life – for example, one elderly woman told a nurse that she couldn't believe in eternal life, but she was afraid to talk with her minister about that. The fears around death and dying are as old as humanity itself. The Christian response to dying and death is not to cling to life, but to live each day fully in the knowledge of being made right with God through the saving work of Jesus. In the face of this there is no need for fear. The work that has been done in recent years in palliative residential aged care is valuable in developing strategies for providing appropriate spiritual and pastoral care (MacKinlay 2006). While issues around death and dying are important ethical issues, of concern to all of us, they are not, however, the topic of this chapter.

What kind of pastoral care is needed?

Given that there are so many differences between groups and communities, even within Christianity, questions are raised about what spiritual care is appropriate. How do care providers know what kind of pastoral care is going to be effective in any given situation? Does this mean that pastoral care can have no guidelines for practice? While there are many differences, there are also certain principles that can operate as guidelines for all pastoral care. A foundation for pastoral care can be laid. However, individual differences in faith development and expression of faith do mean that individual needs must also be assessed and addressed. I distinguish between the role of the pastoral carer and the role of the chaplain in care of the aged – the chaplain providing both pastoral care and religious care. Also important are the roles of the health professionals in aged care; I suggest that these roles become more important in care of frail elderly people and those with dementia.

What kind of broad framework can be used in Christian spiritual and pastoral care, and in pastoral care offered by Christians to others?

Friendship: A model for pastoral care

Relationship is crucial to the well-being of humans. Friendship is one way of looking at a model of the relationship between the one cared for and the carer in the pastoral care relationship.

Elisabeth Moltmann-Wendel (2003) has explored biblical images of relationship and found that, as well as the image of family that is often used for the Christian model of relationship, a model of friendship was also used by Jesus, especially in John's Gospel. Jesus describes the special closeness of relationship that is to exist between him and those who follow him. 'I do not call you servants any longer...but I have called you friends, because I have made known to you everything that I have heard from my Father' (John 15:15). Jesus speaks of the depth of commitment of friends to each other, saying 'No one has greater love than this, to lay down one's life for one's friends' (John 15:13). Jesus did ultimately lay down his life for his friends, on the Cross.

Jesus instituted the sharing of a meal between friends, the Eucharist or the Lord's Supper, before his death. He asked his disciples to remember him each time they did this. It is significant that this breaking of bread between friends is a central practice of many Christians throughout the world. This meal epitomises the type of community that was to arise (McFague 1987, p.172). This simple event is also the oldest Christian ritual of friendship. Further, McFague notes that as we extend hospitality to strangers, we must keep in mind that the church 'can in no way be a community of like-minded friends but must have at its very heart the inclusion of the others, the different' (1987, p.174).

Friendship is seen as relationship of equality, rather than an hierarchical relationship. In our overcrowded planet, the

> old ideal of friendship with strangers presses forward again: Friendship with strangers and those who are different as individuals and as nations and cultures. After centuries of hierarchical and polarizing models, such friendship models are needed for the survival of humankind. (Moltmann and Moltmann-Wendel 2003, p.38)

According to McFague (Moltmann and Moltmann-Wendel 2003, p.39), 'in Hebrew thinking the counter-concept for friend is not enemy but stranger. The stranger is therefore the potential friend'. Moltmann-Wendel maintains that Jesus' model for friends is the 'different ones', the outsiders, the strangers that he wants to make into his friends, both male and female (p.39). Moltmann-Wendel says that currently, friendship 'offers itself as a long-forgotten possibility of making God real in the world' (p.40).

Further, friendship is a special relationship between God and humans, and according to Hauerwas (Hauerwas and Yordy 2003, pp.176–177) involves three aspects, of first, enabling and assisting each friend in developing and practice of Christian virtues, second, building up the Christian community as the Body of Christ, and third, making possible 'under God's gracious favour through the Holy Spirit, friendship with God' (p.177).

The nature of Christian pastoral care

Christian care is based upon the Jewish experience that came before Jesus, and then on the example of Jesus himself. As previously stated, Jesus said, 'I do not call you servants, but I call you friends' (John 15:15). Relationship of love is at the very basis of being human, and so I want to develop two aspects of the understanding of love, of friendship and of neighbours, found in John's Gospel and in Luke's Gospel. I see these as underpinning the whole nature of Christian pastoral care.

- In John's Gospel Jesus spells out his relationship with his disciples as that of friendship, based on love. 'Love one another, as I have loved you. No one has greater love than this, to lay down one's life for one's friends' (John 15:12–13).

- Jesus said, 'I do not call you servants, but I call you friends' (John 15:15). Friendship is not a hierarchical relationship but one of equality.

- Friendship is seen as openness, based on love; it is 'other' centred.

The general model for pastoral care, of course, is Jesus, both his actions during his ministry and in his teaching. In John's Gospel Jesus spells out his relationship with his disciples as that of friendship based on love. In this context a rich understanding of friendship is offered. What it means to be a friend of Jesus is to be close to him, to be in a trusting relationship that is open; that deep and important secrets will be shared; a relationship that involves learning and growing with the teacher.

Friendship is seen as openness, based on love; it is 'other' centred. It is the love that is so great that one would give up one's life for a friend. It is sacrificial love. There is a sense of being in journey with another. This is the kind of friendship that is on offer for those who would provide and receive pastoral care. And yet, there is something more; where the relationship of friendship does not exist, where the players are strangers to each other, we find that it is still possible to reach out to others, without need for the intimacy of deep friendship and commitment to enter into a pastoral relationship. Friendship, then, is the relationship that Jesus calls his followers to. What can be offered to those who are not his followers? What can be the vehicle of love moving out of an exclusive relationship of friends to become love among strangers?

Another context is offered, also based on love: that of neighbour. In a sense, the relationship understood by 'neighbour' gives another entrance into the pastoral relationship. A neighbour does not need to be a friend. But a neighbour is understood as someone with whom you stand in relationship. There is a potential duty of care. There is a sense of at least a shared environment, if not shared values and goals. But the concept of neighbour, in the context of pastoral care, needs to be further spelt out. In Luke's Gospel, the question of 'who is my neighbour' is directed to Jesus. The context is: 'What do I need to do to inherit eternal life?' or 'What is most important in life?' The answer given by Jesus in Luke 10:27 is, 'You shall love the Lord your God with all your heart and with all your soul, and with all your strength, and with all your mind; and your neighbour as yourself.' Love is at the centre of this commandment.

The question then becomes, who is my neighbour? Who do we have to love as ourselves? Not more than, nor less than, but as ourselves?

The neighbour and pastoral care

I suggest that it is the neighbour that we serve in pastoral care. Jesus' teaching on relationship with neighbours is exemplified in the story of the Good Samaritan.

In this parable Jesus takes love and care right outside of formal religious duties to place it centrally in love and care of the stranger: he places care in the context of loving and caring for another human being who is in need.

The parable famously arises from the question: 'Who is my neighbour?' In the parable the question has another layer: if I can know who my neighbour is, if I can define who are those I need to regard as neighbours, then I can see who is a non-neighbour. Then my duty of care can be easily seen. My duty of care is to my neighbour, not to anyone else who might not be regarded as my neighbour.

So, first, the definition of 'neighbour' is needed, or so it would seem at first glance. The story of the Good Samaritan is well known across Christian circles and beyond. We 'know' what is meant when we say 'he or she's a Good Samaritan', without even knowing the story from scripture well. The 'man who fell among thieves' may have been Jewish, but we don't know. In fact this point was apparently of no interest to the Samaritan. The man was left stripped, beaten and robbed; left 'half dead' on a lonely and remote part of the road; it might have been some time before help would arrive. A priest and a Levite passed the victim by – on the other side of the road. According to the laws established by their faith, and their perception of the situation, it did not warrant care to be given to this stranger by another – at least this can be inferred from the actions of those who passed by.

The point in the parable is that there is no 'non-neighbour'. There are no boundaries that can be set to say that someone is *not* my neighbour. We cannot define our neighbours, we can only 'be' a neighbour. Thus there is no obligation, but a challenge to care and take responsibility. In the parable the Samaritan stops, and, 'moved to pity', he helps. It is not some duty that drives him to help, but an inward attitude that draws him into relationship, that leads him to being a neighbour.

Not only does he do this, but he acts generously towards the victim. He renders first aid and sets the man on his own animal and brings him to an inn. Then he also provides money to the innkeeper and offers still further support, if needed, when he returns by the same road. He goes beyond all community expectations.

The final question from Jesus goes back to the questioner: 'Who do you think was a neighbour? Which of the three?' The answer is obvious; no one can argue. It was the one who stopped to help, the one who showed mercy. Jesus responds, 'Go and do likewise.'

It is interesting that over the centuries, this requirement to care has not changed. So often people seek for new ways of doing things; for those who are Christians, new ways of being church; but there is also the need very carefully to examine and remain faithful to our roots. Things like love and care do not change, but the danger may be that we cease to love and care in the face of staffing shortages and tensions in families and communities. We may even 'burn out' in the course of 'duty'. However, it seems there is an underlying attitude assumed. At the base of pastoral care lies the desire to reach out to others in love. The desire to reach out must not be based on duty alone, but on love. Fulfilling duty may flow from love, but duty must not be based solely on obligation. If it is, the duty becomes an emptiness.

A model for pastoral care based on love: Friends and neighbours

A model is established. How can it be used? The concepts of friends and neighbours can be examined in terms of ways of providing care, or responding in pastoral ways to others. There is nothing in this model of care that includes specific religious symbols or rituals. This is straight loving and generous care. It is holistic care, it is spiritual care – care of the human spirit, but in a very practical way, by caring for the body.

So it can be seen that pastoral care also has cultural and spiritual tones; it is holistic care. We can all be Good Samaritans, whatever our job designation or whoever we might be, but how we do this depends on our own cultural and faith perspective. We know from our own enculturation that certain acts and symbols give comfort to those from our own cultural and faith background. However, if we are meeting with others from faiths and cultures that we are not familiar with, we will lack the knowledge of the specifics of care; but we will still know that we should act as Good Samaritans, in loving kindness towards others.

The basis for pastoral care is not so much a specific faith or religion, but an attitude to life, and so to other people. This attitude is exemplified in the life and work of Jesus. First, Jesus did not exclusively minister to, or associate with, those of his own faith or culture. Is it necessary to learn how to love and provide this kind of spiritual care? Perhaps some need to. Love lies at the basis of relationship with a loving God, and was clearly modelled by Jesus. Yet even people of his time did not necessarily show love, nor do all people demonstrate love in their lives these days. This can only too readily be seen in burdened carers and staff and in those who are in need.

Paul wrote on love in his first letter to the Corinthians (1:13) and said that anything that we do, if it is not based in love, will be useless. But even love cannot achieve its potential, if it is offered in a situation of ignorance.

This book is about ageing and faith and culture. So far I have focused mainly on issues of faith and culture and the relationship with pastoral care. Now I want to shift the focus to ageing. If we fail to understand the nature of older and frail people, if we fail to listen to their stories and to see them in the context of the totality of their life meaning, faith and culture, all our love will not be able to provide appropriate care. If our love for others is real, we will want to learn about how we can give the best and most appropriate care, and we will seek to find how this can be done.

A Scriptural base for attitudes towards older people

Through the Bible, both Old Testament and New Testament, the position of elder is recognised as a special place in the community of believers. This place emphasises the wisdom, and therefore the leadership roles, of elders, and also the respect due to elders in their latter years. In the New Testament, the place of widows having a particular role is included. In I Timothy 5, a widow over 60 years of age who has been faithful and well known for good deeds may be put on the list of widows. In Acts 6:1 and James 1:27

the need to care for widows by the community of faith is highlighted. Care of the elderly is advocated. Simeon and Anna, in Luke's Gospel (2:25–38), have a special place in history at the presentation of Jesus in the Temple, acknowledging him to be the redeemer of Israel.

Pastoral care and older Christians

Pastoral care is not the same throughout the life cycle. Older people have particular needs for spiritual growth and care related to their life stage. The potential for spiritual growth never comes to an end. Spirituality of ageing is set in context alongside the ageing body and mental, social, emotional and spiritual factors of ageing. In the Christian perspective, the Scriptures provide a clear picture of the need to respect and care for older people. Against these values are the values of Western societies that value youth against ageing, and it remains a continuing tension to keep the Christian values of ageing alive against the societal values that seek to devalue older people and their worth.

Earlier, I spoke of friendship as a model for pastoral care. How is this played out in later life? Hauerwas and Yordy write: 'Christian friendship as described here is much tougher than a diversion *from* the preoccupation of ageing; rather, it is a redirection *to* the gift of ageing in a Christian community' (Hauerwas and Yordy 1993, p.177). The later years of life can be a time of growth, of transformation and even growing in the virtues.

Connecting points in the journey

Story is an essential ingredient of the process that links with identity for each of us. Who we are as people is coloured by our culture, our faith and our whole lived experience. For Christians, but not only Christians, the sharing of journey is of immense value. Too often in current Western societies, ageing is marked by loneliness and isolation for those living alone without access to friends and the support of a caring community.

I now suggest a model of pastoral care for older people. This model engages with knowing and loving, responding generously and facilitating the discovery of meaning and hope in the current situation.

- *Knowing and loving* is a way of reaching out to the one in need of care with a desire to be in open and trusting relationship, in friendship with that person. To know someone, in a pastoral setting, is to be vulnerable and willing to enter the interaction with the other person. Inherent in this is willingness to journey with the other. The initial stranger becomes friend through this process. It is in friendship that the other is served. Further, it is love that enables the interaction to flourish. Knowing and loving presumes attitudes and characteristics in the carer of respect, truthfulness, integrity. It is only in this way that the spiritual or pastoral carer may be authentic as provider of care.

- *Responding generously* becomes possible, through the initial act of entering into the relationship of knowing and loving.

- *Facilitating the discovery of meaning and hope in current circumstances* can then be commenced. It must be remembered that the spiritual or pastoral carer can only journey *with* the person; they cannot find the meaning and hope *for* that person (Frankl 1984). A means of facilitating this process is from within a model of spiritual tasks of ageing, in this context.

Response to life meaning

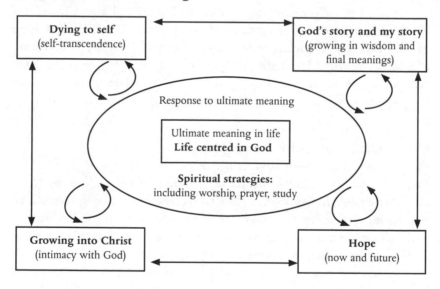

Figure 5.1 Spiritual tasks and process of ageing – a Christian perspective

In relation to meaning, it is essential to address the issues of the individual person, their needs to connect with ritual, with symbol and with liturgy. Spiritual assessment is a means to understanding the person's need for prayer, study and other spiritual strategies, such as meditation. Spiritual assessment is an important component of spiritual and pastoral care, to understand the particular needs for care of, for example, Catholics, whose need for the Eucharist is central, and for Anglo-Catholics, who likewise share a deep and central need for regular Eucharist. Other Protestant Christians, for whom the Bible is so central, for prayer and intercessions, will have a different emphasis on needs. For Pentecostals, who seek a very informal and often spontaneous way of worship, there are further variations for meeting their needs for worship and responding to ultimate meaning.

Meditation is also a means of responding to life and ageing. The practice of mysticism seems to fit with ageing itself, with a growing movement, from mid-life onwards, towards the interior life and deepening personal relationship with God. There are many differences, set around centuries of tradition.

Assessing of spiritual needs

A model such as the one I have briefly outlined assists in establishing the needs for pastoral and spiritual care. Always, pastoral carers must be aware of their own spirituality before attempting to assess and provide for the spiritual needs of others. It is essential that the older person is given opportunity to express his or her needs for spiritual and pastoral care. Spiritual assessment forms can be valuable in this process (MacKinlay 2006).

Differences between spiritual and pastoral care and chaplaincy roles

Spiritual care is a relatively new concept of care, and the term is often used in the context of care provided by a range of disciplines, including nurses, social workers, medical practitioners, life-skills coordinators and other providers of care for the aged. Spiritual care is provided in the context of the particular discipline of the carer. Pastoral care is an evolving discipline closely associated with chaplaincy, but usually the pastoral carer works in caring and journeying with people in their faith journeys. It is a supportive role that fits very much with the friendship and neighbour models described in this chapter. Pastoral carers can provide spiritual and emotional care to people in secular settings in a broad caring role. On the other hand, chaplains are usually ordained or more highly trained individuals, who work more closely with the religious needs of people, as well as their pastoral needs.

Conclusion

Who can deliver pastoral care to Christians? Anyone can provide the broad basis of pastoral care, as long as they are self-aware and have a high level of respect and love for others. Likewise, Christians can deliver effective pastoral or spiritual care to people of other faiths, or none. What must be recognised is the need to listen to the expressed needs of the person being cared for, and to endeavour to come alongside them in their journey. Pastoral care must be delivered with a sense of humility and honesty.

Referral to chaplains, other clergy or the religious providers of one's choice is important, where specific religious needs are to be addressed. Specific religious care, such as the administration of the sacraments, confession and pronouncement of forgiveness, is the domain of the particular religion and denomination. It is important to recognise the cultural differences among Christians, as well as denominational differences. Not all Christians are the same, just as members of other faith traditions are not all the same.

CHAPTER 6

From Ageing to Sage-ing: Judaism and Ageing

Jeffrey Cohen

With the ancient is wisdom; And in length of days understanding.

Job 12:12

Introduction

Being a 'child of the sixties', whenever I begin thinking about ageing I think first of the Beatles' song 'Eleanor Rigby'[1] which speaks of her 'dying alone in her bed', as well as 'And all the lonely people, where do they all come from?' That song is combined in my head with another Beatles' song by Paul McCartney, 'When I'm Sixty-Four'.[2]

These songs, written when Paul McCartney was in his teens and early twenties, reflect a view of the time about ageing. Admittedly it was an idea of that generation where ageing was so foreign to all of us. Someone once suggested to me that 'aged' was 15 years older than one is. To be 64 was to be ancient, perhaps even older than one's grandparents!

Overview

Nearly all words in Hebrew are based on three Hebrew letters. Based on the same three-letter root Z–K–N we can note the following is a play on words:

za-kein, aged

za-kan, beard

The term *za-kein* is applied first to Abraham and then to other Biblical characters, including Isaac, Jacob, Joshua, Eli, Samuel and David.

While it would be nice to claim uniqueness for Judaism, this is similar in Chinese and other Asian societies, where traditionally, at least for males, that wisdom was represented by a beard, however wispy. That beard was usually grey and long, and believed to be indicative of both age and wisdom. (As an aside, it is interesting that Japan actually holds an 'Honour the Aged Day' which owes its origins to deference to the elderly rather than the greeting card industry!)

We all know about the ageing demographic and we hear economists and futurists predict the complex fiscal issues as those born after World War II leave active employment, and how this will be funded. Ageing is a normal part of life – it is one of life's stages. Judaism has a lot to say about ageing.

The twentieth-century Jewish philosopher Abraham Joshua Heschel has suggested in his book *The Insecurity of Freedom* (1987) that 'One ought to enter old age the way one enters the senior year at a university, in exciting anticipation of consumption' (quoted in Schachter Shalomi 1995, p.21). What an exciting concept. It refocuses the way we approach ageing!

Heschel takes the Levitical principle of the seven-year cycle, primarily applied to agriculture and still by observant Jews today to produce from the Holy Land.[3] Heschel applies the seven-year cycle to the cycle of life and then relates it to the months of the year:

January – childhood

February – puberty and transition to adolescence

March – approaching adulthood

April – cleaning up the emotional and intellectual debris previously acquired from family, education, etc.

May – settled in work and family

June – finished establishing social identity and place in the world, for at this point the morning of life is over and the evening is approaching

July, August, September – periods when mind, body and soul are unified

October, November, December – a time for harvesting. An opportunity for reflecting on achievements and feeling pride in contribution to family and society. At the same time one is also finding/recognising one's place in the cosmos

Texts relating to old age

Judaism has always been a text-based religion, drawing initially from the Torah, then from the remainder of the Hebrew Bible and finally turning to rabbinic texts.

In the Bible we only find one definite statement on the limit of life: 'The days of our years are threescore years and ten; and if by reason of strength they be fourscore years, yet is their strength labour and sorrow' (Psalms 90:10). In the Talmud[4] we find a similar statement: 'If one dies at eighty, he has reached old age.'

Deuteronomy 32:7 states: 'Ask your father, and he will declare to you, your elders, and they will tell you.'

The Book of Leviticus commands us to honour elders (regardless of whether scholars or 'simple folk'): 'Rise up before the hoary head and honour the face of the old man.' Although the Torah says that 'one must rise in the presence of the elderly', there is no clear definition of when that should happen. It is left to the later commentary on this text, which is known as the *Chaye Adam* (69:3), to answer the question of when should this be done, with the following definition of when it is appropriate: 'but [one] should wait until the elder is within four cubits [two metres] so that they know the honour is due to them.'

The Bible (Hebrew Scriptures 1917)[5] does not necessarily paint a rosy image of ageing for it also recognises the physical ills attendant upon old age. The author of Ecclesiastes, in his celebrated dirge (Ecclesiastes 12:1–7), indicates the failing powers of age:

1. Remember then thy Creator in the days of thy youth, before the evil days come, and the years draw nigh, when thou shalt say: 'I have no pleasure in them';

2. Before the sun, and the light, and the moon, and the stars, are darkened, and the clouds return after the rain;

3. In the day when the keepers of the house shall tremble, and the strong men shall bow themselves, and the grinders cease because they are few, and those that look out shall be darkened in the windows,

4. And the doors shall be shut in the street, when the sound of the grinding is low; and one shall start up at the voice of a bird, and all the daughters of music shall be brought low;

5. Also when they shall be afraid of that which is high, and terrors shall be in the way; and the almond-tree shall blossom, and the grasshopper shall drag itself along, and the caperberry shall fail; because man goeth to his long home, and the mourners go about the streets;

6. Before the silver cord is snapped asunder, and the golden bowl is shattered, and the pitcher is broken at the fountain, and the wheel falleth shattered, into the pit;

7. And the dust returneth to the earth as it was, and the spirit returneth unto G-d who gave it.

And the Psalmist (Psalms 71:9–18) makes pathetic reference to the infirmity of his declining years:

9. Cast me not off in the time of old age; when my strength faileth, forsake me not.

10. For mine enemies speak concerning me, and they that watch for my soul take counsel together,

11. Saying: 'G-d hath forsaken him; pursue and take him; for there is none to deliver.'

12. O G-d, be not far from me; O my G-d, make haste to help me.

13. Let them be ashamed and consumed that are adversaries to my soul; let them be covered with reproach and confusion that seek my hurt.

14. But as for me, I will hope continually, and will praise Thee yet more and more.

15. My mouth shall tell of Thy righteousness and of Thy salvation all the day; for I know not the numbers thereof.

16. I will come with Thy mighty acts, O L-rd G-d; I will make mention of Thy righteousness, even of Thine only.

17. O G-d, Thou hast taught me from my youth; and until now do I declare Thy wondrous works.

18. And even unto old age and hoary hairs, O G-d, forsake me not; until I have declared Thy strength unto the next generation, Thy might to every one that is to come.

The first rabbinic text drawn upon is taken from the Talmud (*Baba Batra* 10b): when asked who will be honoured in the world to come, Solomon answered, 'Those that show honour to the aged.'

It is as if the rabbis of 2000 years ago were anticipating today's reality, for the Talmud (Kiddushin 32a) tells us that it is incumbent upon us to 'respect even the old person who has lost his learning'. Another text (Seder d'bei Eliyahu) goes so far as to admonish a child (of whatever age) with 'Even if one's father's spittle is running down his beard [e.g. with Alzheimer's disease] his children should obey him.'

The Midrash on Exodus goes so far as to argue that it is the merits of the aged that enables the Jewish community to prosper, for 'it is always the aged who uphold Israel. When does Israel stand upright? When they have their aged with them. For he who takes counsel with the old never falters' (Exodus Rabbah 3:8).

When Moses' father-in-law pointed out to Moses the burdens of leadership, Moses was commanded to appoint a Council of Elders. There were actually 70 appointed Elders, which later became the basis for one of the Sanhedrins (there were a number which had different numbers according to the types of cases they tried. The larger the Sanhedrin the more important the case, similar to the role of the Supreme Court in a number of countries today. Capital cases could only be tried by a Sanhedrin of 120 and even then the Talmud states that a Sanhedrin who condemns a person to death once in 70 years shall be known as a 'killer Sanhedrin') (Mishna Makkot 1:10).

There is a rather strange story recounted each year during the Passover meal known as the Seder. There the following passage is found:

> Rabbi Elazar ben Azaryah said: Behold, I am like a man of seventy, and I never understood why we talk about the Exodus from Egypt at night...[6]

The commentaries point out that Elazar was only 18 and had assumed the role of Head of the Sanhedrin. According to the lore, overnight his beard grew long and all his hair went grey. This was to add to his authority as head of the Sanhedrin! For it is often said that grey hair is the 'crown of glory'.

The story of Rabbi Elazar seems to point to a value consistent throughout biblical and rabbinic texts, that the experience of years is the best guide for deciding vexed and complex questions. After the death of Solomon (1 Kings, 12:13–14), his son Rehoboam looks to the counsel of young men rather than accepting the counsel of the elders, and ultimately this brings about the division of the kingdom.

Within the apocrypha the importance of turning to those who are wise is found in the Book of Ecclesiasticus[7] (25:4–6) as follows:

4. O how comely a thing is judgment for gray hairs, and for ancient men to know counsel!

5. O how comely is the wisdom of old men, and understanding and counsel to men of honour.

6. Much experience is the crown of old men, and the fear of God is their glory.

From this passage we learn about the insight that comes with years!

Failing to respect the elderly has its consequences

When one thinks of the Ten Commandments (Exodus 20:12) as usually taught and displayed, it is only in terms of 'Honour your father and mother' – overlooking the fact that this clause is part of a complete sentence which continues 'so that your days may be long on the soil which G-d, your G-d, has given you'. This makes it clear that if one honours one's parents, then one is assured length of days. The collorary is that if one does not honour one's parents, then one will experience a shortened life.

In the Talmud[8] there is an interesting prediction that a sign of the troubled days preceding the coming of the Messiah is a lack of respect and courtesy shown by the young toward their elders!

Does age automatically lead to wisdom? There are statements in the Bible and the Talmud to the effect that mere length of years provides no claim to reverence. Job (32:6–9) advises thus:

6. And Elihu the son of Barachel the Buzite answered and said: I am young, and ye are very old; wherefore I held back, and durst not declare you mine opinion.

7. I said: 'Days should speak, and multitude of years should teach wisdom.'

8. But it is a spirit in man, and the breath of the Almighty, that giveth them understanding.

9. It is not the great that are wise, nor the aged that discern judgment.

The Psalmist exclaims, 'I understand more than mine elders, because I have kept Thy precepts' (Psalms 119:100).

The writer of the Book of Ecclesiastes[9] declares, 'Better is a poor and wise child than an old and foolish king' (Ecclesiastes 4:8–9).

More emphatic is the author of the Book of Wisdom of Solomon, which states: 'Honourable old age is not that which standeth in length of time, nor is its measure given by number of years: but understanding is gray hairs unto men, and an unspotted life is ripe old age.'

The Midrash[10] highlights the underlying tension: 'There is an old age without the glory of long life; and there is long life without the ornament of age: perfect is that old age which hath both.'

Ferrucci, Mahallati and Simonsick (2006, p.260) expand the Midrash as follows:

The Book of Jubilees (23:11) reinforces the lack of equivalence between aging and frailty by stating that the 'calamitous days' of old age only occur as the effect of premature aging (opposed to normal aging), which is the consequence of sin: 'Abraham was perfect in all his deeds...all the days of his life... [on the contrary] the generations which shall arise from this time until the day of the Great Judgment shall grow old quickly...' Note that this interpretation is consistent with the notion of frailty as a condition of 'accelerated aging.' However, many passages that presuppose the revered notion of the aged take vigorous issues with the assumption. (Psalms 119:100; Job 12:12, 32:9; Ecclesiastes 4:13)

The magic 120

Moses had three stages of his life, and according to the Midrash each was of 40 years' duration.[11] It was only in the last 40 years that he assumed the role of leader. This has led to the traditional greeting, often given at a funeral, that each of the survivors should 'live to 120'.

Also there is a tradition that when a traditional Jew is asked his age, the response will be 'xx nach ein hundred and svanzik [xx till 120], i.e. 'xx after 120 [xx before 120]'.

Physical changes as we age

The Bible recognises that in ageing there are physical changes to the body including grey hair, loss of eyesight, loss of hearing, loss of potency – which includes both inability to enjoy sex and the inability to conceive – loss of strength and loss of taste.

- *Grey hair* – there are a number of texts, including:

  'As for me, I have grown old and grey.' (1 Samuel 12:2)

  '...and even into old age and hoary hair, O G-d, forsake me not.' (Psalm 71:18)

It is not always seen as a negative, for Abraham (Genesis 15:15 and 25:8) and David (1 Chronicles 25:28) show that each died not only blessed in old age, but contented with their lives.

- *Loss of eyesight* – this was seen as normal, for with ageing comes the dimming of eyesight, if not total blindness. Isaac's 'eyes were too dim to see' (Genesis 27:1) and Jacob: 'now Israel's eyes were dim with age; he could not see' (Genesis 48:10) and Eli, the High Priest and mentor to Samuel: 'and his eyes had begun to fail and he could barely see' (1 Samuel 3:2). The one exception was Moses, about whom the Bible tells us 'His eyes were undimmed' (Deuteronomy 34:7).

• *Loss of hearing* – the Bible offers few examples, for Barzillai responds to David's invitation to Jerusalem with 'Can I still listen to the singing of men and women?' (2 Samuel 19:35). Ecclesiastes warns us that not only is old age dark, but it can also be silent, devoid of the beauty of music and song 'and all the daughters of music will be brought low' (Ecclesiastes 12:4).

• *Loss of potency* – this refers not only to the ability to conceive, but also to the ability to enjoy sex. David is offered the maiden, Abishag, when he is in his old age and is cold but 'he knew her not' (1 Kings 1:4). Sarah, when she is informed that she will have a child within the year, responds with 'Now that I am withered, am I to have enjoyment with my husband so old?' (Genesis 18:12). While she is questioning her ability to have a child, she is also questioning whether sexual enjoyment is still possible for either Abraham or herself.

• *Inability to conceive* – this is not when a woman in the normal course of her life was unable to conceive, such as Rebecca, Rachel or Hannah. This is the case of the woman who had passed menopause. The first is Sarah (above) but also the Shunamite woman whose husband was old (2 Kings 4:14), for she is rewarded with a child. Naomi tells her daughters-in-law, Ruth and Opah, that not only is she left without her sons, but she has no hope of bearing any more. This is contrasted at the end of the Book of Ruth where Naomi suckles her grandchild.

• *Loss of strength* – Proverbs sets the scene, when it reminds us that strength is in the hands of the youth: 'The glory of the youth is their strength; the majesty of old men is their grey hair' (Proverbs 20:29). In Jerusalem in the time of the prophet Zechariah, the old men sat in the square 'each with staff in his hand because of their great age' (Zechariah 8:4). The onset of old age is described by the author of Ecclesiastes thus: 'in the day when the watchmen of the house tremble, and the strong men are bent' (Ecclesiastes 12:30). Part of being old is the inability to feel warm. David is described as constantly cold, 'and although they covered him with bedclothes, he never felt warm' (1 Kings 1:1).

- *Loss of taste* – the only direct statement about this is from Barzillai (2 Samuel 19:36) who says to David, 'Can your servant taste what he eats and drinks?'

The twenty-first century

It has often been argued that today, 60 is the new 40! Is this praise or criticism, or just commentary? It does recognise that more people are living longer. It also identifies that many will not be able to retire at 65. Not only are we living longer but we have under-invested in the future – and there are times when this is compounded by the economic environment. In the middle part of the twentieth century it was considered that the average man would die within two years of retirement, work having been a large component of his life. In the twenty-first century, it is likely to become the norm to live for decades after what is currently the age of retirement.

Harold Koenig (2007), in his presentation at the Health and Spirituality conference in Adelaide in 2007, reported that the US Congress' Office of Budget notes that at the current rate of increase in government health care expenditure, such expenditure would consume the total US Government budget before 2030. Politically, it will be hard to control the continual expansion of health care costs.

Stages of ageing – a rabbinic view

With the focus on studying, the rabbis in the Talmud (*Avot* [Ethics of the Fathers] 5:24) articulated what they saw as the stages in a person's life:

> At five years old a person should study the Torah, at ten years for the Mishnah, at thirteen for the commandments, at fifteen for the Talmud, at eighteen for the bride chamber, at twenty for one's life pursuit, at thirty for authority, at forty for discernment, at fifty for counsel, at sixty to be an elder, at seventy for gray hairs, at eighty for special strength (Psalm 90:10), at ninety for decrepitude, and at a hundred a man is as one who has already died and has ceased from the affairs of this world.

Within this model, there is a focus for about a quarter of one's life on study; the reality is that one is expected to study at all stages of one's life.

The rabbis also recognised that it is not just one's age that is important but also what one does. Here are two statements (*Avot* [Ethics of the Fathers] 4:26, 27) which seem at first to be opposed to each other.

> Rabbi Meir used to say: 'Do not look at the flask but at what is in it; there may be a new flask that is full of old wine and an old flask that does not

even have new wine in it.' On the other hand, Rabbi Yosi bar Judah of Kefar ha-Bavli said: 'He who learns from the young, what is he like? He is like one who eats unripe grapes and drinks wine fresh from his wine press. But he who learns from the aged, what is he like? He is like one who eats ripe grapes and drinks old wine.'

Yet in both texts, old wine is synonymous with ageing and wisdom.

How does society see 'successful ageing'?

The very concept of 'successful ageing' is based on the Victorian ideal of healthy, self-reliant old age, free from dependency and physical debility. Underlying this concept is a series of lifestyle changes, with the implication that they are approved by society and do not call upon society's resources, especially financial ones.

Harry R. Moody, who has served as Director of Academic Affairs for the American Association for Retired People (AARP) for many years, has observed that in modern gerontology, successful ageing basically boils down to achievement and activity, which are the hallmarks of Western culture (Moody 2005). To put it another way, society focuses on whether you are active and busy. It does not allow for the person who enjoys just sitting around, perhaps reading or just watching people go past.

Such a model rejects the contemplative traditions, for this will never be seen as 'productive retirement'. Contemplation and reflection are seen as the antithesis of activity and how can you measure their achievement? This flies in the face of evidence from groups such as religious contemplatives and those active in religious leadership who seem to live long and satisfying lives (Kirkwood 2003). In the Jewish world, it is not uncommon to find the head of an orthodox rabbinical institution in his eighties, and even nineties. It also stands in the way of medical evidence that shows that those who practise meditation and contemplation have lower stress levels.[12]

Julia Neuberger, a liberal rabbi who is also a member of the House of Lords in the United Kingdom, recently published what can only be seen as a manifesto for ageing, entitled *Not Dead Yet* (2008). The book is built around ten points (lest I suggest ten [new] Commandments for the twenty-first century). The chapters, under the rubric 'Our Call to Arms', are:

1. Don't make assumptions about my age.

2. Don't waste my skills and experience.

3. Don't take away my pride.

4. Don't trap me at home.

5. Don't make me brain dead, let me grow.

6. Don't force me into a care home.

7. Don't treat those who look after me as rubbish.

8. Don't treat me like I'm not worth repairing.

9. Don't treat my death as meaningless.

10. Don't assume I'm not enjoying life.

Brian Groombridge, in his review in the *New Statesman*, noted:

> She opens and closes the book and ends each of the ten chapters with ten-point manifestos to counter age discrimination. These deal with work, pensions, public safety and facilities, learning opportunities, housing, care assistants, community beds and hospitals, the right to die well and much else, and then, summing it all up, 'grey rage'. (Groombridge 2008)

The book is quite descriptive in the realities of ageing although it is less proscriptive about how to move forward and to turn 'lemons into lemonade'!

Some would suggest that Julia's book is not 'Jewish'. She does not quote continually from biblical and rabbinic sources. (One of the ongoing tensions in the Jewish world is over what does it mean to be 'Jewish'.) It as if she wants the book accepted in spite of her being a rabbi. Being 'Jewish' in today's world is a mixture of both cultural and religious values. (It is clearly reflective of Jewish values and concepts.)

What has happened in our post-industrial society? We have warehoused the elderly in segregated ghettos. This becomes obvious especially when one thinks about retirement villages and nursing homes, where the residents experience both isolation and disempowerment. As Neuberger points out, in the UK only one in 20 seniors wishes to be 'in care', yet one in five dies in a nursing home. Some years ago, Jewish Care in the UK developed a plan which would be a village-type arrangement in London: the mixture of residents would be one-third elderly, one-third people with physical and/ or mental handicaps, and the last third would be college-age students – the underlying idea being that the people would interact. For reasons about which I do not know, it did not proceed.

Reality is that the modern post-industrial society tends to treat people as 'cogs in a machine'. When they are no longer contributing, then they are surplus to requirements.

The care model

In many Jewish communities around the world, the local community established care facilities for those who can no longer care for themselves. In most cases, one of the values they practised was the provision of kosher food and religious/liturgical services. This was usually important to the first generation of migrants to the community. It was funded out of community resources on an 'ability to pay' model, with the deficit seen as part of the wider community's responsibility.

Since 2000 there have been two significant changes. One has been the shift to offering kosher meals as an option. The second has been rebuilding and expansion to include an 'up-market' option for those who can 'afford it'. This has not always worked, with at least one facility going to court to stop a foreclosure.[13]

In Sydney, Australia the local Jewish funding agency has encouraged the various agencies of the community to offer a seamless system of aged care delivery from home care through hostel to nursing home. Although it reflects three independent agencies, they cooperate, and two operate from within the same campus in Randwick.

The medical model

There are many involved in modern medicine who sincerely believe that we are chemical machines and that when there is a chemical imbalance, then, with 'minor' adjustments, all can be fixed. The extension of this is the application of surgery, for the expunging of the 'bad humours' will lead to 'perfect' health. This approach has been extended to modern gerontology. The philosophy here is that ageing is a problem of social engineering which can be solved by technological means (Kirkwood 2000)!

We can see from the above that the medical/gerontological model is antithetical to what Judaism holds as important values.

The Sage-ing

Sage-ing is the last step. It is the passing on of the learned wisdom from previous generations. As Rabbi Abraham Twerski has opined,[14] the human being is the only point in the animal kingdom which can pass on knowledge from one generation to another. Today this is done in many ways. It can be through the recording of oral history, or it can be through the creation of an ethical will. The most important part is for the next generation to recognise that previous generations do have stories and values that are worth hearing and perhaps using as a guide.

The ethical will

In the medieval period within the Jewish communities of Europe there emerged a document known as an ethical will. This is a document where one speaks not of passing on physical belongings, but, instead, of passing on lessons, stories and dreams.[15] Recently, interest in this form of will has emerged beyond the Jewish community[16] and a number of guides to writing such documents can be found on the Amazon website. The earliest known ethical will is attributed to Eleazar, the son of Isaac of Worms, and was written about 1050 CE. Riemer and Nathaniel (1991) have focused more on those written at the end of the nineteenth century and during the twentieth century.

Conclusion

Judaism from the time of the Bible till today has honoured its ageing members. Like the characters of the Hebrew Bible, Judaism has not idealised ageing but has presented it 'warts and all'. In recent times, and in reflecting the world in which it functions, Judaism has adopted most of the values of the world around it. This has led to the institutionalisation of some of the most weak and vulnerable, but most live in the community, usually still in their own homes, and experience healthy ageing. Judaism does not operate in a vacuum. There is much material from within Jewish tradition that supports the care of those ageing, as well as turning to them as sages to be heard!

Acknowledgements

This paper was inspired by the writings of Zalman Schachter Shalomi in his co-authored book *Age-ing to Sage-ing*. The first draft of this article was presented at the 'Ageing and Spirituality: A Diversity of Faiths and Cultures' conference sponsored by the Centre for Ageing and Pastoral Studies in August 2008.

Notes

1. 'Eleanor Rigby' by the Beatles on the album *Revolver* (Capitol #SW2576).
2. Released in 1967 on the Beatles' album *Sergeant Pepper's Lonely Hearts Club Band* (Capitol #MAS 2653).
3. 2008 was such a year when the land was to lie fallow. Observant Jews do not purchase any produce from Israel which was grown in that year.
4. Moed Katan 28a, Baba Batra 75a.
5. I have used the *Hebrew Scriptures*, the Jewish Publication Society (Philadelphia) 1917 edition, for all biblical translations.

6. The original text is found in Berachot 28*a*.
7. In Rabbinic literature Ecclesiasticus is known as *The Wisdom of Ben Sira,* and was included in the Septuagint.
8. Soṭah, 49*b*.
9. *Wisdom of Solomon* 4:8–9. [King James Version Apocrypha.]
10. Genesis Rabbah [also known as the Midrash to the Book of Genesis] 69.
11. Genesis Rabbah 69: 'Amongst a number of great men who all reached the same age are Moses, Hillel, Rabbi Johanan b. Zakkai, and Rabbi Akiba. Moses' years were divided into three equal portions, viz., forty years in Pharaoh's palace, forty years in Midian, and forty years as leader of the Israelites in the wilderness.'
12. See www.mayoclinic.com/health/meditation/HQ01070 and http://nccam.nih.gov/health/meditation/overview.htm, accessed 15 February 2009.
13. www.stltoday.com/stltoday/news/stories.nsf/story/8e04e43b023093658625746b0 0101f8a?opendocument.
14. The author heard Rabbi Twerski propound his theory at a series of launches of several of Twerski's books. The theory goes along the lines that a horse which wins a race does not pass onto its progeny the secrets of winning a particular race, say the Melbourne Cup, by telling the progeny where on the course it can speed up, slow down, or the quirks of the particular track.
15. Jack Reimer and Nathaniel Stampfer (eds), in *Ethical Wills, A Modern Jewish Treasury* (2003) (New York: Schocken), built on the earlier work of Israel Abrahams: *Hebrew Ethical Wills*, first published in 1926.
16. Kate Murphy: 'The virtues and values of an ethical will.' *Business Week.* 8 April, 2002. See also Friedman, S.T. and Weinstein, A.G. (2005) 'Reintroducing the ethical will: expanding the lawyer's toolbox.' *GP | Solo Law Trends and News 2,* 1.

CHAPTER 7

Dorothy, Oodgeroo and Blackfella Ageing: The Role of Spirituality When You're Short on Culture and Can't Find Your Red Shoes

Dennis McDermott

When first invited to comment on spirituality in relation to Aboriginal ageing, I declined. There was the question of diversity: against commonalities in Aboriginal spirituality across Australia, the unique notions and practices of two hundred or more pre-colonisation language groups needed to be ranged. The part of Eastern Australia that I'm from – an arc that stretches from New England and the northwest of New South Wales down to Sydney – has endured many assaults. The impact on the structures that preserved and passed down traditional knowledge and practices has been profound, and yet uneven. Traditional culture persists, even in those places – Sydney and the Hunter Valley – where colonisation hit my mob early and hard. Yet there is no doubt that Indigenous knowledge in such places has been fragmented. Some Kooris have been left with no connection. For others, there's been a profound disturbance, a scattering, beyond even the usual Aboriginal strategy of farming out to family stewardship various bits of the cultural repertoire. Then there was the question of me: one of the things that worried me was that I'm not party to any of my own mob's unique nation or clan knowledge. I'm also not an initiated man. My invitation, though, was renewed with a question: *What about your poetry? There are important things that you touch on in some of those poems.* I started thinking of a way that I could do justice to the themes of this book, as a Koori man, without exceeding my right or authority to talk about matters spiritual. I came to two conclusions.

The first was that I deal with the spiritual every day. As one of a small number of Indigenous psychologists – there were 40 of us at last count and we've, just now, arrived at the point where we're founding the Australian Indigenous Psychologists' Association – as one of such a mob, my philosophical base is not confined to the Western understandings of mental health. Such approaches are variously referred to as the bio-medical model, or the biological-psychiatric model, or at worst – given the level of pharmaceutical company dubious practice involvement in *which* drugs get the nod for *which* psychological presentations (Breggin 2000, 2003/2004) – the psycho-pharmacological model. Rather, Aboriginal and Torres Strait Islander psychologists work from a holistic Indigenous model of social, spiritual and emotional well-being. And the spiritual is not a gloss, but an integral part of how well people are travelling.

My second conclusion was that there is a great need to speak to, and talk through, this fragmentation: to deal directly with major cultural dislocation. For many blackfellas, and this grouping includes me and members of my family, such processes aren't optional. They constitute our reality. I decided that I wanted to include the perspectives of those who have come from a stronger base in terms of cultural continuity, or cultural renaissance, but also pay solid attention to those who are trying to make their way from where some colonial tide has left them, to a point of reconnection with an Indigenous spirituality. This chapter, then, will draw on Aboriginal perspectives and psychological and public health research to explore what it means for Indigenous Australians to grow older well, and not so well; in culture, and out of culture; with traditional spirituality, and with little knowledge of such things – and less access. There are resonances here, I feel, for those who support or care for older people in general; probable points of leverage for those grappling with the contradictions of a surviving, ageing Aboriginal and Torres Strait Islander Australia; and potential implications for those making policy or delivering services.

Why Dorothy, then, and why Oodgeroo? In juxtaposing ageing, spirituality and Indigenous Australia, I want to draw particularly on the experiences of my mother, Dorothy, and the woman who could have been her twin – in looks, style and spirit – Oodgeroo of the Noonuccal, the poet and rights activist originally known as Kath Walker. From the mid-1960s to the early 1970s, Kath Walker was one of the best-selling poets in Australia.[1] Her poetry was unabashedly polemic. It broke no new ground in poetic structure, yet transformed what could be said about Aboriginal Australia – and said it in 'mesmerising' fashion (McDermott 2004a). In

1988, in the bicentennial year of British colonisation of Australia – two centuries characterised, for Aboriginal people, by a humiliation and brutality for which (the then) Kath saw no proper Crown acknowledgement – she gave the empire back its MBE, and changed her name. Like Oodgeroo, I believe that it's hard to really 'get' what happened in this country – and its contemporary consequences – with mere prose. So, I'm going to thread poetry through this chapter: poems of mine that deal with these issues through the lens of my family, especially my mother, and of Oodgeroo. I'll also draw on an ekphrasic poem, one that began life as an expression of my admiration of the painting of Rover Thomas, but ended up exploring cultural and spiritual renaissance in the Kimberley. Rover's work, and the renaissance it helped trigger, emerged within a locality where potent understandings and practices persist, despite a history of colonial trauma that incorporates massacre and widespread cultural suppression.

The first poem deals, amongst other things, with identity. A reader might also draw some links between parental behaviour that appears puzzling and awareness of a process that, in the era of the poem, had not yet been described as the 'stolen generations' – the suspicion of all official-looking cars that might pull up outside, the ever-present fear of forcible child removal. The poem is called 'Page Three Story'. It remembers a time in this country when, to survive as a black man or woman, you might have had little choice but to collude with your own cultural suppression. At that time, you might not have been free to speak your language, nor have the access to country – nor to those with the right knowledge – necessary to pass on your spiritual practices to your children. For many Aboriginal and Torres Strait people, their very identity had to be downplayed – at worst, denied. The poem is set in the late 1950s, an era with a whole circuit of Australian/ UK/American Idol progenitors, known as Eisteddfods.

As children, as part of my mother's drive to secure our social acceptance, my siblings and I had elocution and singing lessons: I started at four. First, my elder brother and sister, then I, did the circuit from our home town of Tamworth, through the Welsh-influenced mining towns of the Lower Hunter Valley, down to the big one, the City of Sydney Eisteddfod. Rupert Murdoch was also learning lessons: before he became an American citizen and global behemoth, he refined his US Fox Network aggression and his London *Sun* 'tack' on Australia's tabloids – including Sydney's (then) *Daily Mirror*. From the early 1960s on, in Australia (from 1970 on in the UK), the Page Three girl was a sexy pin-up, mostly bare-breasted, but acceptable enough – by the standards of the time – for a bloke to check out in the tram or train on the way home from a boring factory job. So, 'Page Three Story':

Page Three Story
Locks in the fifties
went rusty: apart from mixed-up children
no one ever took anything
away. Pure news. No Page Three girl
peeping from *The Mirror*. Instead
my sister's lubra-lips were captured,
a prize grin above the tag:
First Aborigine Wins City
of Sydney Eisteddfod.

The only person apparently not pleased
was my mother. Didn't they know
the Trinidad connection? Our honourable line
of West Indian descent? The line
we'd heard for years. The life-line that
bound us mix-ups to our parents. My mother called it
slur, called for apology, asked for
and got a printed retraction. Page Three.
That put them in their place.

(McDermott 2003a, p.17)

A poem, then, about denial, but one that also begs the question: what are the effects of such denial on identity – and of identity on well-being?

Here we need to bring in the stories and experiences of the 'stolen generations'. If you're an Indigenous Australian who's been forcibly removed from family, country and community, then the issue of healing – of satisfactorily dealing with multitudinous concerns arising from the original act of removal – is one of the most complex, yet important, facing Aboriginal Australia (Link-Up and Wilson 1997; Department of Victorian Communities 2003). There are clues from experience and research, but no clear, comprehensive approach to guide us. Our meagre understanding of how this complexity plays out confounds the work of those providing services to removed people and their families (McDermott *et al.* 2008). Yet, there is great necessity not to avoid this complexity, neither in working through the consequences of such experiences, nor in what genuinely helpful responses might look like. We need to factor in the unexpected, potent ways that individual circumstances can combine: the multiple losses engendered by one act of removal; the inhumanity and abuse of institutionalisation; the desolation of later indentured labour, or of racism when you were brought up to believe yourself white. Indeed, the especially hurtful consequence reported by a number of removed people is rejection by a community to which – through no fault of your own – you've become stranger (Bowden 2006). It's more than difficult and painful: it's layered trauma, under a worn-thin skin.

If grief goes sideways through family and community, then trauma, unchecked, goes down the generations (Danieli 1998). Brutality was visited upon many removed children on isolated farms or inside suburban foster homes; within institutions it descended both individually and collectively. Many such institutions, it needs to be remembered, went about their business for decades. In New South Wales, for example, between 1920 and the 1960s around 600 Aboriginal boys, and a few girls in the early days, were interned in Kinchela Boys' Home. These inmates were part of a recorded '5,625 Aboriginal children...taken away from their families in that state up to 1969' (AustLii 2007).

Although there were variations in legislation and practice from state to state, eddies of family and community grief found every corner of the continent. Removed people had not only their own grief and loss, but also de-humanising institutional experience, serf-like farm and domestic experience, and high rates of physical and sexual abuse to deal with. My clinical experience, working with the distress of removed people, echoes the accounts of both Holocaust survivors and veteran populations in the evidencing of effects of their trauma on subsequent relationships, including those with their children. It is hard to overestimate the potential for transgenerational trauma arising from generations of forcible removal. Nationally, estimates concur that, overall, at least one in ten Indigenous Australian children was forcibly removed, and thus profoundly affected. This baseline percentage, however, may be an under-representation, reflecting narrow definitions of the application of 'force'. Power could also be deployed through trickery – such as offers by officials to give the children a short 'holiday' – or by intimidation or misrepresentation of legislation. Allowance also needs to be made for earlier reportage of removal defining Aboriginality narrowly, in terms of 'full-blood' status (Jackson Pulver 2003). A case can, in fact, be made that total forcible removals were two to three times higher than earlier thought. Nationally, this would translate to a figure for the key period 1910–1970 of between 20,000 and 30,000 removals. In 2007 the NSW Link-Up organisation alone reported having around 7000 'stolen generations' clients (or the partner or child of a 'stolen generations' member) on their books, with six to ten new clients approaching them every week (Stubbs 2007).

Peter Read, the historian who coined the phrase 'stolen generations', estimates that – as with my mother in her earlier years – there are 100,000 Australians who either deny, or are denied, their Aboriginality (Read 1981).

Identity, culture, spirituality: all are complex businesses in a colonised land. Recently, an academic colleague sought my help, then, gently, refused my suggestion of a particular Aboriginal speaker for a planned seminar on psychology and Indigenous spirituality. The person I'd suggested, a Murri man from Central Queensland, was raised in a setting of ongoing cultural connection, but was also a Christian pastor. He ran an inner-city church that was strongly engaged with the Aboriginal population of the area. His complex spirituality pervaded everything that he did – he was deeply involved in 'stolen generations' issues, he took sporting and other role models to kids in the outback and he was a moving speaker, who yet hung on to his sense of humour. The man was no 'God-botherer'. The colleague asked me, instead, for someone who could provide a 'pure Aboriginal spirituality'. I pointed out that many of the blackfellas whom I knew to have a powerful grasp of traditional spiritual understandings also had connections to Western religion. I have yet to hear back from him.

After two hundred years of colonisation, such notions of a frozen authenticity are spurious. Echoing the Taoist maxim that 'the only constant *is* change', Aboriginal Australian spirituality manifests in multiple ways, in forms that are mutable rather than set for all time. The appearance of fresh dimensions is consonant with a 'Dreaming' that is not bound to erroneous Western notions of a (long past) 'Dreamtime'. Profound insights, revelations – even visions – may emerge at moments of desperate need, at community or cultural 'tipping points'. When the tag 'authentic' is awarded solely to static, perceived 'traditional', Indigenous cultural perspectives, it is time to question that commentator's grasp of history and contemporary reality – if not their motives. Such tagging is particularly demeaning to those Indigenous Australians whose connection to land, clan and culture have been ripped away through forcible removal or other workings of Australia's 'virtual' apartheid (McDermott 2004b).

A few years ago, at an Aboriginal men's health conference on the NSW Central Coast, the Aboriginal educator, Dr Bob Morgan, asked the rhetorical question: 'How do you get cured of spiritual sickness?' His comment can be read as shorthand for the multifaceted difficulty of recovery from not only initial dispossession and concomitant cultural suppression, but also the consequent loss, grief, violence, child removal, racism and official marginalisation of the last two hundred years. It helps us to comprehend a phenomenon whose enormity and pervasiveness is hard to grasp. Yet, it's more than a handy metaphor: it actually goes to the nub of the dilemma itself. A de-spirited person – or community – needs the means to *heal* their spirit before their circumstances can change (McDermott 2003b).

That Aboriginal and Torres Strait Islander peoples have survived the rolling effects of colonisation at all is, accurately, put down to resilience. But resilience is more than an individual matter. Beyond the personal capacities and adaptation to circumstances exhibited by individual people – such as the survivors of the Nazi concentration camps; people who, rightly, sparked decades of research into how they managed it – one arrives at an additional perspective: *cultural* resilience. The findings of North American work on cultural resilience augment, in a pan-Indigenous context, Australian research by Westerman in Western Australia and McKendrick in Victoria: if you connect, or reconnect, Indigenous people to country, culture and – where possible – language, you do remarkable things for their health, mental health and well-being (Heavy Runner and Marshall 2003; Raphael and Swan 1997; Westerman 2004). In some research, such measures were protective of suicidality (Raphael and Swan 1997). The research of Strand and Peacock in particular, along with some others, offers clues from a pan-Indigenous context to fruitful explorations of spirituality in relation to Indigenous Australian lives. These authors found that Indigenous adolescents who reported higher levels of connection to culture and greater affiliation with traditional spirituality came up better, not only on levels of well-being, but – also surprisingly – with respect to educational outcomes (Strand and Peacock 2002).

A connection between research with adolescents and ageing, and in particular between such research and growing old well, may not be immediately apparent. There is indicative value, though, in staying with this notion of a real and demonstrable linkage between personal and community malaise, 'spiritual sickness', and some significant cultural renaissance, one at least partly mediated by spirituality, through one more exemplar – one that may extend our understanding. There is much to draw from the work of the East Kimberley artist, Rover Thomas. Here was a man with tribal connections extending from the top of Western Australia into the Northern Territory, but who spent his last years before his death in Warmun, or Turkey Creek, not far south of the Ord River scheme. There, after a life as a stockman, he started painting. Although his works, some of which are must-see items on any tour of the Canberra's National Gallery, can sell for hundreds of thousands of dollars, his original motive was to spark cultural renaissance in his people. He wished to respond properly to visions he connected to a visitation by the spirit of a relative who'd recently died. An old woman, a classificatory mother to him, had been seriously injured in a car accident, then died – somewhere over a significant whirlpool, off the Kimberley coast – as the air ambulance was flying her to a tertiary-care hospital. Rover started with placards, painted under his instructions, to accompany a corroboree, he 'found' (i.e. was given by the vision). The ritual dances, known as the Krill Krill ceremony, described the journey back to Warmun of the old woman's spirit, accompanied by various others, culminating in a distant view of Cyclone Tracy wreaking havoc on Darwin in 1974. Gradually, the paintings became more Rover Thomas' own works: big slabs of black, brown, red, mustard and white that used, or echoed, the earthiness of ochre. Even when there was a long-simmering, brutal story to tell, the narrative emerged through a depiction of the spiritual and geographic topography of Rover's own country, deceptively simple in execution, yet charged; almost, but not, abstract. To the Western eye, they could look more abstract than they were ever intended to be by Rover Thomas. Amongst the paintings' range of life and site-specific denotations, rather than representations, they ended up telling of the infamous massacres that took place as late as the 1920s, as pastoralists rendered The Kimberley safe for cattle. Rover's spirituality, the full-blown visions of a senior man with important work to do – once he'd emerged from his stockman persona – are implicated in the cultural renaissance of his people – and are capable of working magic on the viewer. So, I wrote a poem about it all, called 'That Snake Wind'.

That Snake Wind
There's a breeze up. When I emerge with coffee,
paperweight refilled, I find the *Saturday Herald* has
quickly colonized the most part of the yard.

I've lost the *Good Weekend*, find it in the house.
My daughter's left it open at Darwin, how things are
28 years after these shots of harvest stubble,

sticks and air, once houses. It lies on a bookcase
full of Reich and Jung and words like synchronicity,
beside the back cover of a catalogue, a painting

of no stars, bounded by white dots. I see the shape
of a two-legged stool on dirt, an invoking: storm in,
storm out. On the front cover, a cow's rear turns

on second look into a thought balloon, black,
devoid of easy meaning. It's become half the canvas,
a killer's eye inside a rain of crooked spears, yellow

interspersing dirty red. On the Science Show,
Robin Williams' guest said that in this void
called the universe, there is something leaping around

called energy. I paused before this sunless,
monsoonal thought on a Canberra morning
sucked clean of tourists save me in the Rover Thomas

retrospective I was about to leave, when the didge player,
back from his cuppa, back on the platform started softly
behind me, as I stopped fighting, surrendered to Cyclone Tracy,

found my tears, the mud, lightning and a Rainbow
Serpent, Rover's black wind, at work destroying Darwin.
Once, I stopped in Melbourne, forgot to keep

in motion. Straightaway, this dry-gully, suburban gum
came through the window, bark shards in full 3-D.
Images no longer kept their distance – behaved

as images – were no longer flat, but thick and real
and frightening. Rover paints in reverse:
a massacre's just a skull up a tree.

The Kimberley night is black ochre
and three or four stars, almost incidental,
round the edge. He makes the sky fall in

on how things are held to be: ground takes shape,
becomes visible; what we thought figure
now looks ground. The grizzled stockman

has removed his disguise: Rover paints revelations
from that old woman, skin-system mother, the one
who died high above the Rainbow Serpent that is

that whirlpool on the Kimberley Coast, the one
whisked from the ambulance flying her, car crash victim,
uselessly to Perth. Rover got the message, saw

the whole corroboree, the Krill Krill
dances and the images – her spirit journey back –

then Tracy, renaissance Tracy, viewed from afar.

Then more: Bedford Downs Killings, Texas Downs,
Ruby Plains. Rover shows no blood, but when I stop
driving, become a passenger, I see. Now, vision seeps

through canvas. I see the earth turning, people
wound to the point of discharge, serpent winds
that dance, like Kali, the desperate's renewal.

(McDermott 2003a, p.53)

Notions of Indigenous Australian ageing have not always served the development of better practice. Indigenous Australians over the age of 50 with 'premature illnesses' have often been shunted into age-inappropriate services with people over 70, as though they were 'prematurely aged' (Cotter, Anderson and Smith 2007). Paradoxically, despite the reality of the near two-decade gap between Indigenous and non-Indigenous Australian life expectancy, the steady growth of an older cohort of Aboriginal and Torres Strait Islander people is also real (Broe and Jackson Pulver 2009). A national workshop was inaugurated in 2008 not only to address these issues, but also to reset the parameters of the discourse around Indigenous Australian ageing (Australian Association of Gerontology 2008). What was deemed missing was a whole-of-life approach to Indigenous ageing. This workshop reshaped the landscape within which Indigenous ageing policy and service delivery operated: although improved policies and services directed at older Aboriginal people were still considered vital, it emphasised the longitudinal health impacts – the state in which people actually arrived at old age – of early and mid-life experience, and, hence, how the needs of those periods could be better addressed. Its whole-of-life purview suggests that benefit would arise from this chapter considering questions of spirituality and Aboriginal ageing from a life-*course* perspective, as much as from life's *end*.

The approach taken by the organisers, drawing on the growing literature on dementia prevention, suggest useful tags to characterise what helps at each life stage of Indigenous ageing: early life – *grow your mind*; mid-life – *mind your mind;* and late life – *save your mind*. Thus, a key early life issue for Indigenous children, one powerfully relevant to later life, becomes the recognition, then addressing, of the impact of transgenerational trauma – and consequent violence, abuse and neglect – on the developing brain. In turn, this foregrounds the significance and urgency of developing culturally regardful, accurately evidenced interventions and programmes for traumatized children. One such approach, emerging from the extensive psychoneurobiological literature, is Bruce Perry's Neuro-developmental Adaptation Model (Perry 2001). Perry's model assists our understanding of, and response to, North American and Australian Indigenous contexts of widespread disruptions to parenting. Violence, abuse and neglect are rooted in colonisation's direct effects, but also follow in the wake of, for example, such second-order intergenerational effects as those engendered by Canada's Residential Schools Movement and Australia's 'stolen generations'. As well as effects that pass down the generations, there may be a further iteration sideways, as trauma-related reactivity has an impact on the extended family or community, through eruptions of what has been termed 'lateral violence' (Wilson 2004).[2]

A succinct, and sufficiently accurate, rendering of the work of Perry, together with his colleagues and peers, is that chronic, unpredictable and off-the-scale fear and trauma actually 're-wire' the developing brain – with enormous implications for adult and late-life functioning. Neurotransmitters and spirituality aren't often considered together, yet the most promising interventions with traumatised children re-invent, in a Western psychiatric context, the spiritual/ceremonial dance, drumming or other body-based – in fact, Perry would say brain-stem-based – healing practices of many Indigenous cultures (Perry and McDermott 2007).

Early life experiences are crucial, but understanding Indigenous mid-life contexts also suggests how we might better support or intervene to promote ageing well for Indigenous Australians. At an Aboriginal men's health conference in 1999, the Aboriginal educator Bob Morgan's push for a recognition of 'spiritual sickness' was designed to draw attention to the profound negative impact of the diminution of Indigenous men's roles and worth. Nineteenth- and twentieth-century colonial tactics of infantilising Indigenous men (Broome 2002) have receded in favour of demonising them: headlines can range from 2006's 'Raping children part of "men's business"' to 2009's 'Violence the way of traditional life' (Jarrett 2009; Kearney and Wilson 2006). Many Aboriginal or Torres Strait Islander men report an automatic suspicion that they're either child-abusers or wife-bashers: they see the regard in which they are held – or, rather, not held – in the gaze directed from the next supermarket queue. The assumption of Indigenous male mendacity is a widespread default position, with unknown dispiriting consequences. Anecdotally, many Aboriginal men in the Northern Territory, who've born the brunt of such assertions, are withdrawing from public life (Miller 2009).

If we're going to implement changes in the mid-life period that can boost the chance of blackfellas growing old well, we also will need to reverse the massive, destructive over-incarceration of Indigenous Australians.

Angela Davis has noted the Australian Indigenous parallel with the over-incarceration of 'people of colour' in the USA. Both, she holds, have been exacerbated by the interaction of racism and the political ascendancy of neo-liberalism over recent decades (Davis 2008). Krieg has detailed how systemic failure, unconcern and institutional racism can make post-release re-integration a phrase with little practical meaning. Amongst a range of concerns, 73 per cent of South Australian Aboriginal prisoners in her study 'expected to have insecure or no housing on release' (Krieg 2006). She notes Mick Dodson's apt, chilling summation that the '…whirl of the revolving door is never far away' (Dodson 1996) and goes on to capture succinctly the consequences of Indigenous over-incarceration:

> If we are serious about breaking the cycle of disadvantage and incarceration, we must honestly address the stigmatising and discriminatory practices occurring across all service sectors, from targeted policing and unachievable bail requirements, to the difficulties of access to health services for people with a history of correctional involvement. (Krieg 2006, p.535)

Whether we examine the contexts of Aboriginal ageing in mid-life or older age itself, an inescapably central issue is the adequacy of the current workforce to deal with the demonstrated needs of Indigenous clients. An obvious shortfall is in the insufficiencies in recruiting, funding places for, financially supporting and mentoring to graduation, Indigenous practitioners of all kinds. The less obvious inadequacy is the lack of models of non-Indigenous practitioner training that go beyond *de rigeur* cultural awareness to encompass, in some integrated, mutually reinforcing way, aspects of cultural competence, cultural safety and a tenet I've tagged 'cultural ease'. The last-mentioned builds on a developing familiarity with Aboriginal protocols and an incorporation, where possible, of Aboriginal cultural notions and 'ways' into practice – in essence, an Indigenising of praxis (McDermott and Gabb 2009). Much current training still under-prepares the non-Indigenous aged-care workforce to work effectively with Indigenous Australians – which brings me again, full circle, to my mother.

My mother, born Dorothy Lennis, between Sydney's Newtown and Redfern, become Dorothy McDermott and, finally, Dorothy Stace. She nursed her second husband, a TPI (Totally and Permanently Incapacitated) prisoner of war from World War II – a man irrevocably changed by the grind and terror of Changi – through the last few years of his life. Perhaps understandably, it got her down – we psychologists once referred to this as a reactive depression. Like many Aboriginal people before her, the totality of her life context was ignored, and, like many elderly people generally, she was inappropriately prescribed medication – in her context, anti-depressants.

I've described the family battle with the medicos elsewhere – and some of the lessons I believe can be gleaned (McDermott 2006). The point here is, rather, the lack of cultural competence – the *unsafe* cultural practice – of the medicos involved, both in this and other aspects of her treatment.

A participant in a professional development workshop I'd co-facilitated – a workshop on 'deep listening', and other ways to indigenise one's praxis in the service of more effective work across cultural divides (McDermott and Gabb 2009) – reminded me that I'd used the phrase 'right relationship' to better describe cultural ease and to foreground the humility, flexibility and self-reflexivity required for culturally competent and culturally safe practice. I reconsidered my throwaway line: here might be a way to characterise those aspects of Indigenous Australian spirituality that were, potentially, *common* to those raised in traditional culture, with knowledge of, and (hopefully, though not always) access to traditional country and the ceremonies related to it, and those denied those things by the processes and consequences of colonisation. I'd thought of my mother's spark, her connection to all aspects of life itself and her lifelong connection to music – our whole family sang and a number of us played musical instruments. Music therapists understand the link between singing and spirituality. Perhaps – especially as we grow old – in finding, and then giving voice, we can clear away some of the overburden on our selfhood. Simply in the title of her paper, given at the conference on which this book is based, Robertson-Gillam sums up the dual effects, in the last years of my mother's life, of that spark and those connections: 'The effectiveness of choir therapy to reduce depression and meet the spiritual needs of people with dementia' (Robertson-Gillam 2008). Dorothy had no brush with dementia, but when my mother was no longer able to look after herself, at around the age of 85, and was living in a Catholic-run nursing home just outside the NSW country town of Tamworth, she used to travel around with a choir to all the nursing homes in the area. She couldn't stand for long, so she sat to sing, for 'all the old people'. It's hard to describe how positive this was for her identity, purpose and sense of well-being. I'd also thought of my mother's nominally Anglican, but eclectic Christian faith. Finally, in relation to those potential commonalities, I'd particularly thought of Mum's commitment to, and love of, people and sociality. It was that workshop participant, though, who reminded me that what I'd articulated in one context had relevance in another: that 'right relationship' to everything around you – and notably engaging transparently and whole-heartedly with people – was in fact a hallmark of a spiritual life. Undeniably, it was part of an Indigenous spiritual life. The perceptive Aboriginal psychologist and academic, Tracy Westerman, has stressed that not only can a 'spiritual dimension' be recognised within people raised outside of traditional

Indigenous culture, but that – in relation to successful non-Aboriginal professional engagement with Aboriginal people – the Aboriginal client may need to recognise such a dimension within a *non-Aboriginal* service provider (Westerman 2004). Westerman's work resonates with that of Gabb and McDermott in their noting of a central need for 'transparency' on the part of health and welfare workers:

> ...lift[ing] the traditional clinical boundaries of self-disclosure a little, so that a level of rapport can be achieved between the Indigenous and non-Indigenous members of the dyad. (Gabb and McDermott 2008, p.8)

It also articulates a profound precursor to real engagement by aged-care workers with Indigenous clients and communities:

> ...a sense of the person's strength and goodness of spirit is often the basis upon which engagement will occur. It...importantly, matches the strong sense of spirituality that Indigenous people have within themselves and are able to see in others. (Westerman 2004, p.5)

Other Indigenous cultures reflect this sense that one of the strongest things a non-Indigenous professional or carer can bring to an encounter with an Indigenous person is their own wellness, a *good spirit* (Weaver 1999). It's as if one's spirit is almost visible – it shines through – or is, almost, tangible.

This sense of someone's spirit 'shining through' was something my mother shared in common with Oodgeroo of the Noonuccal. Oodgeroo, however, was a woman with substantial Aboriginal cultural resources on which she could call. When I was finishing my studies in psychology at the University of Queensland in the first half of the 1970s, I would travel from Brisbane, across Moreton Bay, to North Stradbroke Island. On 'Straddy', Kath Walker (as she was then) was setting up an Aboriginal cultural education centre, called Moongalpa, and invited people to come and help her in her enterprise. I learnt a lot from Oodgeroo, things that my mother never had a chance to learn. I would have liked to put the pair together, and let them loose to stroll and yarn on a beach. I've tried to capture all this in a poem. It's called 'Dorothy's Skin'.

Dorothy's Skin
At fourteen, my daughter knows why The Old Couple on the Beach,[3]
    not The Tiger,
leaps at her from her Christmas gift. She likes Dali. I don't, except for
    one image
that I flip pages for, until I realize they've left it out: Lifting the Skin of
    the Water

to See the Dog Sleeping in the Shade of the Sea. Down the road from
     Tamworth,
from Christmas at my mother's, Goonoo Goonoo paddocks wear bright,
     bad toupees.
Surreal colour wraps Wallabadah hills from ridge to highway, like an
     over-packaging
of something subtle. Look there! Kath Walker would stop you. She'd
     peel back the veil
of leaves so you'd see the slender swamp orchid growing up the
     paperbark. Kath, then,
in the Seventies, on my visits to Stradbroke Island – Noonuccal land –
     before she became,
or reclaimed, Oodgeroo. I still don't know whether she lifted a layer, or
     added another.
When I met Oodgeroo, I met my mother: not just Dossie's poise, eyes
     and Lindt-like
skin, but the funny-bugger with a steak knife, buried, a serrated intensity
     that
unsettled me – a boy of elocution lessons and an easier ride, a man of
     lighter brown
travelling, whose tab of overt intolerance came in at insults and one lost
     girlfriend.
I wasn't there when indignity did its daily round – rarely blunt, rather,
     a pointed
needling that cut near the core, left wounds that broke their stitches
     every morning.
I did know that the sharp steel about Oodgeroo was also about my
     mother. On campus –
UQ – a doctor's daughter from Ingham or Innisfail, some sugar town,
     told me Queensland
houses on their skyscraper stilts were the perfect metaphor for non-
     Indigenous Australia's
perch on the land. Then she described the GTO,[4] that Seventies model
     of sexual intimacy
popular where she came from: Gravy Train On – Wooh-Wooh!! – the
     only girl she knew
her age, in her town, that hadn't been gang-raped. I had no reason to
     disbelieve her.
I thought about targets: when you're a candidate for grief, keep moving.
     I knew some of

the men's stories: my sister's man, jumping from a moving car on a
lonely Tassie road

to miss a bashing; my sister's son, dodging a splintered pool cue in that
high-culture,

high-altitude, cold and broken town, Orange; but not the women's.
When we were kids

mum kept us in motion, in baths and out, to school and back: the devil
had a thing about

motors on the idle. Doss draped protective layers on us all: cardigans,
scholarships and

singing lessons, and more manners and mannerisms than the middle-
class we aped.

I like Queensland houses. I want and don't want to lift the skin of
settlement.

If Oodgeroo were alive, I'd take Doss to Straddy. Maybe they wouldn't
hit it off – just

fight like the sisters they seem. Yet they might walk alongside each
other, an old couple

on the beach. Oodgeroo could lift the skin of sea and land – when, and
when not,

to harvest oysters – show mum the swamp orchid, tell her of the
Grannies

that walk some nights, stories she's never heard. In the Link-Up office,[5]
counsellors talk

to me in supervision of taking clients, their stolen generation clients
home. Everyone

seems to know just where the fucking place is. Doss Lennis from old
Newtown, black

with steam-train soot, respect-full Dot, from the Ladies Auxiliary,
Tamworth RSL[6] –

mum's many layers peel so slowly. The West Indian cover is an old
friend. Eighty-four

years along – long wait – I hear the word 'Aboriginal' creep into a self-
descriptive

sentence. Dorothy's skin is so thick and yet so thin. Where can I find
those red shoes

you simply click to teleport you home?

(McDermott 2003a, p.60)

Notes

1. Oodgeroo/Kath Walker managed to combine an activism, deemed 'radical' at the time, with a poetry and prose that successfully invited reluctant, non-Aboriginal readers to engage with Aboriginal perspectives. She opened the eyes of non-Indigenous Australia to the Indigenous culture and experience of their nation, at the same time as she set out to discomfort and change that same nation politically. She drew inspiration, and recharged her energy, from her 'country', a long, sandy island near the mouth of the Brisbane River known as North Stradbroke Island, or 'Straddy'.

2. Policies resulting in widespread forcible removal of, so-designated, half-caste children from their Indigenous Australian parents (as well as subjective interpretations of parental 'neglect' provisions) brought major loss to a minimum 30,000 victims over the decades, grief to their extended families and communities and, often, physical and/or sexual abuse through placement in institutions or foster homes. Australia's 'stolen generations' and their descendants struggle with manifestations of a transgenerational trauma that parallels that evidenced by those affected by Canada's attempt to educate the 'native' out of the native Canadian, the Residential Schools movement. There are more than 85,000 Canadians still alive who passed through this system.

3. The titles 'The Old Couple on the Beach', 'The Tiger' and 'Lifting the Skin of the water to See the Dog Sleeping in the Shade of the Sea' refer to paintings by Salvador Dali.

4. The initials GTO, in Australia in the 1970s, were shorthand for a sports model spin-off of one of the leading brands of sedans. They were also, at times, shorthand for a situation where consensual sex with one partner was parlayed into pack rape – casually, and chillingly, given the euphenism of Gravy Train On – with either subtle, steam-whistle hand-pull signals or not-so-subtle noises.

5. Each state in Australia has a Link-Up organisation that works to trace the family and community of members of the 'stolen generations', then counsels and supports those forcibly removed through a challenging reunion process.

6. The Returned Services League (RSL) has a long history of providing a range of family support services to veterans of Australia's wars. It often includes a social gathering place (the RSL club) where a number of roles in the past – such as event catering – fell to the women of the 'Ladies' Auxiliary'.

CHAPTER 8

An Islamic Perspective on Ageing and Spirituality

Mohamad Abdalla and Ikebal Mohammed Adam Patel

Introduction

The word 'Islam' is derived from the root word *slm* meaning 'peace'. Lexically, 'Islam' means 'submission', which in a religious context means submission to one God, known in Arabic as Allah. A Muslim is a person who submits to God and is a follower of the religion of Islam. In the past, Western writers referred to Islam as 'Mohammedism', a misnomer that insinuates the worship of the prophet Muhammad as a deity, which is not accepted in Islam. As a religion, Islam is known in its Arabic term *Din*, meaning a complete way of life – a more comprehensive connotation than 'religion'.

Given that Islam is a way of life, its teachings encompass the legal, moral, ethical and spiritual dimensions of a human's life. It has powerful moral and ethical imperatives that govern the everyday behaviour and practice of its adherents, and an equally strong recognition that true success and happiness can only be found in the cleansing of one's heart and self. This latter process is commonly known as spirituality (or Islamic psychology), and this chapter will explore the meaning and significance of spirituality in Islam. In addition, Islam places great importance on old age and ageing, and next to the command of worshipping God, Islam demands from its adherents that one's parents, particularly when they reach old age, be treated with *ihsan*, or excellence. In fact, in Islam it is inconceivable to be spiritual without respecting, honouring and caring for the elderly.

Islam: A brief outline

Original sources dating back to the time of the Prophet Muhammad (570–632) relate that in 610 Muhammad, who was then 40 years old, received the first revelation from God through the angel Gabriel, who recited to him the word of God, today written down in the Qur'an, Islam's Holy Book. Muslims believe Muhammad was simply God's prophet and messenger and that he was not divine in any way. They also believe that all of God's prophets and messengers, including Jesus son of Mary, were human beings without any divine attributes.

Tawhīd

The cornerstone of Islam is monotheism or *Tawhīd* [Arabic], believing that there is only one God, all-powerful and merciful, and that associating any human being or any thing with God is tantamount to *shirk* – false worship. Prophet Muhammad clearly declared that it is God's right that we should worship Him, and Him alone. Central to *Tawhīd* is belief in the absolute mercy and clemency of God. There are many Prophetic traditions or *Hadith* that testify to this, among them the Prophetic dictum: 'when Allah created the creatures, He wrote in the Book, which is with Him over His Throne: "Verily, My Mercy prevailed over My Wrath"' (Bukhari, cited in Al-AlShaykh 2000, p.506). The manifestation of God's mercy upon humans is to send messengers and prophets to guide them to that which will gain them felicity in this life and the next. Prophet Muhammad, the Qur'an proclaims, was 'sent as a mercy to the worlds'. In addition to the rights of God, Islam strongly emphasises the rights of the creation of God, humans, animals and other creatures alike. These rights are clearly defined and articulated in a legal and moral code known as *Sharia*, which literally means a way to the watering place or a path seeking felicity and salvation (Kamali 2006, p.2). *Sharia* is defined by Muslim scholars as 'the canon law of Islam', 'the injunctions revealed to the Prophets of Allah related to law or belief', or 'following strictly the injunctions of Allah or the way of Islam'. In summary, *Sharia* deals with three major aspects: beliefs (such as belief in God and the hereafter), morals and ethics (truthfulness, etc.) and actions of individuals and their relations with others.

Islamic law

Islamic law originates in two major sources: divine revelation (*wahy*) and human reason (*'aql*). The *Sharia* provides general directives, whereas detailed solutions to particular and unprecedented issues are explored by *fiqh* or jurisprudence, which is the utilisation of human reason to interpret the *Sharia*. *Sharia* is the divine revelation contained in the Qur'an and the teachings of the Prophet Muhammad, or his *Sunnah*, and has a closer association with the dogma of Islam. *Fiqh*, on the other hand, is a 'rational endeavour and a product of speculative reasoning which does not command the same authority as that of the Sharia' (Kamali 2006, p.37). While *Sharia* concerns itself with legal and moral codes, it also deals emphatically with the purification of the self as a whole – otherwise known as spirituality, a central concept of the teachings of Islam. The purification of the self or heart is an aspect of Islam that is often neglected or disregarded in academic literature, or misrepresented altogether. Interestingly, this aspect of Islam has a long-standing tradition and is quickly being revived in many parts of the world.

Spirituality in Islam

In the Arabic and Islamic contexts, spirituality is commonly known by the term *rūḥāniyya*, which is 'derived from the adjective *rūḥānī* according to a well-known mode for the formation of abstract nouns' (Chodkiewicz 2009). But the usage of this term was commonly confined to the description of the unseen world of spirits and also the practice of magic and the like. For our own purposes, however, spirituality is a science (*'ilm*) that deals with the cleansing of the heart of all spiritual diseases such as malice, envy, hate and arrogance, to name just a few. A more accurate name for the purification of the self in Arabic and Islamic contexts is *tazkiyat al-nafs*.

The purification of the self (or heart, depending on how one defines *nafs*) is inherent in the Qur'an and the traditions of Prophet Muhammad, as the following illustrates. In the Qur'an, God says that on the Day of Judgement, nothing will be of any use to us, except a sound heart – *qalbun salim* (Qur'an 26:88). According to the famous classical commentator of the Qur'an, Ibn Kathir, a clean heart means 'free from any impurity of *shirk* [false worship]'. Others such as Ibn Sirin state that it means a heart that 'knows that Allah is true, that the Hour will undoubtedly come and that Allah will resurrect those who are in the graves' (Ibn Kathir Tafsir 2000, p.244). Likewise, in a famous *Hadīth*, the Prophet Muhammad says that: 'Verily in the body there is a piece of flesh. If it is sound, the body is all sound. If it is corrupt, the body is all corrupt. Verily, it is the heart' (Muslim, cited in Al-AlShaykh 2000, p.955). According to Islahi, the purification of the self can be defined as 'checking ourselves from erroneous tendencies and leanings and turning them to the path of virtue and piety (fear of God's displeasure) and developing it [the self] to attain the stage of perfection...' (Zarabozo

2002, p.72). Essentially, spirituality means the cleansing of the self from all evil traits and 'a genuine realignment of the soul' (Murad undated). At the heart of Islamic spirituality is the 'seeing of the One, uttering the Name of the One, and knowing the One who is God in His absolute Reality beyond all manifestations and determinations, the One to whom the Qur'an refers as Allah' (Nasr 1997, p.xiii). The central doctrine of *Tawhīd* is in fact the essence of spirituality, whose aim is to allow the seeker to acquire 'the experience and knowledge of this Unity and its realisation in thoughts, words, acts, and deeds, through the will, the soul, and the intelligence.' Ultimately, Islamic spirituality is 'to live and act constantly according to God's Will, to love Him with one's whole being and finally to know Him through that knowledge which integrates and illuminates and whose realization is never divorced from love nor possible without correct action' (Nasr 1997, p.xiii). While Islam demands of its followers the observance of external practices such as prayer five times a day, fasting during the month of Ramadan and performing the *Hajj* or pilgrimage once in a lifetime, it is the 'inner dimension that one must turn to in order to see, utter and know the One'. This dimension of 'inwardness is the domain *par excellence* of Islamic spirituality, and in fact the Spirit (*al-Rūh*) is defined with this dimension, which is at once beyond and within the macrocosm and the microcosm' (Nasr 1997, p.xiii). Islamic spirituality has become well known as Sufism, defined by classical Muslim scholars as:

> ...knowledge through which one knows the states of the human soul, praiseworthy or blameworthy, how to purify it from the blameworthy and ennoble it by acquiring the praiseworthy and to journey and proceed to Allah Most High, fleeing unto Him. (Keller 1994, p.861)

Sufism started during the early periods of Islam and later developed into different *tariqas* or orders, the most universal of these being the Qādiriyyah founded by 'Abd al-Qādir al-Jīlānī. Other Sufi orders include the Shadhiliyyah, Mawlawiyyah, and one of the most widespread and influential of the Sufi orders, the Naqshabandiyyah. While these orders differed in their approach, their aim was to know the One, Allah.

Sufism has been defined and explained in many ways and forms, but according to the famous Sufi, Maliki[1] scholar and Hadith specialist, Ahmad Zarruq (d. 1493) all of these are:

> ...reducible to sincerity in turning to Allah Most High [and that]...there is no Sufism except through comprehension of Sacred Law, for the outward rules of Allah Most High are not known save through it, and there is no comprehension of Sacred Law without Sufism, for works are nothing without sincerity of approach. (Keller 1994, p.862)

The founder of one of Sunni's four schools of thought, Imam Malik, declared that 'He who practices Sufism without learning Sacred law corrupts his faith, while he who learns Sacred law without practicing Sufism corrupts himself. Only he who combines the two proves true' (Keller 1994, p.862). Therefore, in Islam, spirituality without an understanding and an implementation of the sacred law is not possible. Essentially, Sufism is concerned with the purification of the self and, according to the great classical scholar, Nawawi (d. 1277), is based on five principles: to fear God 'privately and publicly, living according to the Sunna [example of Prophet Muhammad] in word and deed, indifference to whether others accept or reject one, satisfaction with Allah Most High in dearth and plenty, and returning to Allah in happiness or affliction'. As for the methods of the purification of the soul, there are five principles:

> lightening the stomach by diminishing one's food and drink, taking refuge in Allah Most High from the unforeseen when it befalls, shunning situations involving what one fears to fall victim to, continually asking for Allah's forgiveness and His blessings upon the Prophet (Allah bless him and give him peace) night and day with full presence of mind, and keeping the company of him who guides one to Allah. (Keller 1994, p. 862)

The above description of what constitutes Sufism or Islamic spirituality is brief and oversimplified. Sufism is a 'vast and complex subject, and one which contains many traps for the unwary', and it is not possible, according to Seyyed Hossein Nasr, to 'do justice to the wholeness of the Islamic tradition and its immensely rich spiritual possibilities by putting aside its inner dimension. In speaking about Sufism, therefore, in reality we shall be speaking about the Islamic tradition in its most inward and universal aspect' (Eaton 1994, p.226). A failure to correct the inward leads to superficial following, and the outcome is nothing but disaster.

Islamic spirituality and modern Islamic movements

Some Muslim scholars argue that the crisis within the Muslim world today and Muslim movements is the neglect of Islamic spirituality. It is their belief that the teaching of the sacred law without the purification of the self has led to a state of failure in approach and implementation. Modern scholars such as Abdal-Hakim Murad argue that the essence of the failure of modern Islamic movements is the absence of spirituality. He states:

> It is true that we frequently hear the Quranic verse which states that 'God does not change the condition of a people until they change the condition of their own selves.' But never, it seems, is this principle intelligently

grasped. It is assumed that the sacred text is here doing no more than to enjoin individual moral reform as a precondition for collective societal success. Nothing could be more hazardous, however, than to measure such moral reform against the yardstick of the *fiqh* [jurisprudence] without giving concern to whether the virtues gained have been acquired through conformity (a relatively simple task), or proceed spontaneously from a genuine realignment of the soul. The verse is speaking of a spiritual change, specifically, a transformation of the *nafs* of the believers – not a moral one. (Murad undated)

Murad argues that at least for the last six decades, Islamic movements such as the Muslim Brotherhood of Egypt failed to achieve leadership and establish an 'Islamic' state – this being the movement's ultimate aim – despite having millions of followers and supporters. Meanwhile, 'a man like [Jamal Abdul] Nasser, a butcher, a failed soldier and a cynical demagogue, could have taken over a country as pivotal as Egypt, despite the vacuity of his beliefs' (Murad undated). The reason for this failure, Murad contends, is the absence of spirituality that resulted from the 'increasing radicalization' of Islamic movements. To find a solution to this problem, it is essential to revive 'the spiritual life within Islam'. Furthermore, Islamic movements need to recognise that they are in a crisis and that 'the response to this must be grounded in an act of collective *muhasaba*, of self-examination, in terms that transcend the ideologised neo-Islam of the revivalists, and return to a more classical and Indigenously Muslim dialectic' (Murad undated). This requires a substantial paradigm shift in attitudes, and recognition that a change will not occur simply through outward conformity to the sacred law, but rather by proceeding 'spontaneously from a genuine realignment of the soul'. For the Qura'nic verse which states that 'God does not change the condition of a people until they change the condition of their own selves' (Qur'an 13:11) is 'speaking of a spiritual change, specifically, a transformation of the *nafs* [self] of the believers – not a moral one'. This is particularly true given the already stated fact that Islam as a *din* is not 'a manual of rules which, when meticulously followed, becomes a passport to paradise. Instead, it is a package of social, intellectual and spiritual technology whose purpose is to cleanse the human heart' (Murad undated). This package needs to be utilised mostly for the service of the weak, oppressed, downtrodden and those who cared most for us – the elderly. When a young man asked Prophet Muhammad's permission to join a military campaign (or take part in *Jihad*), the Prophet responded by asking whether his elderly parents were alive. When the young man responded in the affirmative, the Prophet of God instructed him, 'Go and serve them, this is your Jihad' (Bukhari, cited in Al-AlShaykh 2000, p.506).

Spirituality and the issue of ageing

As stated above, an essential feature of Islamic spiritualty is the purification of the self and the cleansing of the heart by cultivating inward and praiseworthy qualities (such as love and mercy) and eliminating blameworthy attributes (such as envy and malice). An essential manifestation of this is the way we are meant to treat old age, and to honour and respect the elderly. The prophetic dictum clearly states that 'He is not one of us who shows no mercy to younger ones and does not acknowledge the honour due to our elders.' 'Does not belong to us' means that a person who does not honour the elders is failing to follow the example of the Prophet Muhammad. For a devout Muslim who seeks the pleasure of God, this is a matter to be avoided at all cost. Since a devout Muslim is concerned about how God will deal with him in this life and the next, he is also aware of the Prophet's teaching: 'If a young man honours an older person on account of his age, Allah appoints someone to show reverence to him in his old age' (At-Tirmidhi and Abu Dawud, Hadith no. 359). Here, there is a prophetic promise of divine assistance for those who help the elderly or ageing. There are clear injunctions in the Qur'an regarding benevolent treatment of the elderly, especially if they are one's parents:

> Your Lord has commanded that you worship none but Him, and be kind to your parents. If either or both of them reach old age with you, do not say '*uff*' to them or chide them, but speak to them in terms of honour and kindness. Treat them with humility, and say, 'My Lord! Have mercy on them, for they did care for me when I was little.' (Qur'an 17:23–4)

The strain of caring for one's parents in this most difficult time of their lives is considered an honour and a blessing, and an opportunity for great spiritual growth. In Islam, it is not enough that we only pray for our parents, we should also act with limitless compassion, remembering that when we were children, they preferred us to themselves:

> And We [God] have enjoined on human (to be good) to his parents. In travail upon travail helpless did his mother bear him, and in two years was his weaning. Show gratitude to Me [God] and to thy parents; to Me is thy final return. (Qur'an 31:14)

According to the above verse, gratitude to God and gratitude to parents, especially when they reach old age, go hand in hand. Gratitude to God is incomplete without showing gratitude to one's parents. Since being grateful to God is a form of worship which earns heavenly rewards, it can be said that being grateful to one's parents also earns heavenly rewards. Mothers are particularly honoured, as expressed in sayings of the Prophet. For example, someone went to Muhammad and asked him, 'Who has the first priority to be well treated?' Prophet Muhammad answered him, 'Your mother.' He asked, 'Then who?' He answered 'Your mother.' Asked again, 'Then who?' 'Your mother,' answered the Prophet. Asked 'Then who?' The Prophet answered, 'Your father' (Sunnan AbuDawud, cited in Al-AlShaykh 2000, p.1599).

When Muslim parents reach old age, they are supposed to be treated mercifully, with kindness and selflessness. In Islam, serving one's parents is a duty second to prayer, and it is their right to expect it. It is considered despicable to express any irritation when, through no fault of their own, the old become difficult. The reverence and consideration afforded to the elderly is evident in the manner Prophet Muhammad has instructed of dealing with parents and the elderly. The respect that the Prophet instructed us to show to the elderly, even in the prayer itself, which is one of the pillars of Islam, is evidence of the respect and consideration that are due to them. We are to feel sympathy and concern for the elderly while we are performing the prayer. We should not extend or prolong the congregation prayer, especially if there are elderly among the faithful. In one Hadith the Prophet said: 'So whoever leads the people in prayer should shorten it because among them there are the sick the weak and the needy' (Bukhari, cited in Al-AlShaykh 2000, p.56). It is, then, reasonable to expect similar consideration in other everyday, mundane activities. In fact, caring for parents, especially in old age, is considered superior to military *Jihad*, as mentioned in a number of statements by Prophet Muhammad.

The great value Islam has placed on caring for the elderly has become an integral part of Muslim societies through the passage of time, and in many cultural contexts. As caring for the old is a religious duty and an honour, the idea of nursing homes for the old is seen as inconsistent with the dictates of Islam.

Services for the elderly

Typical in all Muslim countries is the absence of old people's homes, whether nursing homes or retirement villages. It is taken for granted that the elderly are to be cared for by their kith and kin, and the idea of old people's homes is inconceivable in countries with majority Muslim populations. That said, in many instances this scenario is slightly different, particularly in countries where Muslims are a minority, and services for the elderly are the option – retirement villages for the able-bodied, and nursing homes of varying degrees, based on the medical needs of the residents. As Islam plays a significant role in everyday practice, it is therefore vital for service providers to consider the cultural and religious values of their residents. Spirituality and religious beliefs have been a common coping mechanism for many Muslims. The divine decrees in Islamic beliefs help them to think that everything is in the 'hands of God'. In these circumstances reliance and trust in God become second nature, and this aspect of a person's spirituality may sometimes be overlooked or trivialised. It is usually the case, for example, that when someone prays there is some relief, and with faith there is hope. It is important for service providers to value these religious beliefs and cultural norms.

Prayer

In Islam, prayer is compulsory five times a day for all male and female adults who are sane and conscious. These prayers have set times and a Muslim must face in the direction of Mecca whilst performing them. While the prayers must be done standing and involve bowing and prostration, they can be performed in a sitting position, or while lying down, if the need arises. This need usually arises if a Muslim is unwell, old or injured. As an exemption, prayer can be performed in whatever position is suitable to the person in need. In very few cases one will come across Muslims who do not offer their prayers. To facilitate the performance of these prayers, service providers can provide suitable space for their Muslim clients. The Friday congregational prayer is also compulsory for men who are not travelling and who are able to attend. While Islam does not prohibit women from going to the Mosque, based on the Prophetic order 'do not prevent the female servants of God from attending the Mosque', the Friday prayers are optional for them.

Personal hygiene

As a condition for the validity of prayer, Muslims are also required to maintain a certain standard of personal hygiene. As an essential requirement of remaining clean, Muslims need to wash themselves after urinating or defecating. This is a practice that is religious and not cultural, for it has been taught by Prophet Muhammad. Usually, in Muslim countries or countries that have a substantial Muslim presence, such as Singapore, lavatories have provisions for washing with water. As this is not found in other countries, some Muslims take their own water bottles to fulfil this requirement. Additionally, in preparation for the prayer, Muslims are required to perform *Wudhu* or ablution, a practice where Muslims wash their hands, face and feet, and rinse their mouth and nose. This practice of *Tahara*, or purity, is essential for the purification of the bodily limbs and is also pertinent for spirituality – for there is no spirituality without adherence to the sacred law. As some Muslims may be unable to perform the ablution on their own due to illness or old age, they will require assistance. If this assistance is not available, a Muslim may perform dry ablution, called in Islamic law *tayammum*. Whenever possible, it is essential for Muslim women to be cared for and assisted by female staff.

Fasting

Fasting during the month of Ramadan, the tenth month of the Islamic lunar calendar, is also obligatory for every male and female Muslim, provided they are mentally and physically able to do so. Islamic sacred law exempts the sick, old, children, pregnant women and travellers from fasting. If the sickness is permanent, then there is no need for the missed fasting days to be made up, otherwise it is necessary. For those who are exempted from fasting permanently, compensation in the form of feeding someone needy will do.

Muslims begin their fast at dawn and end it by sunset. So, they wake up before dawn to have *suhur*, or a pre-dawn meal. While this meal is not compulsory, it is recommended, as it was the practice of the Prophet and assists in fasting. Breaking of the fast is done immediately after sunset. In terms of spirituality, fasting is known to be one of the best practices. Its rationale is the purification of the self and to gain close proximity to God through abstinence from food, drink and sexual relations with one's spouse during the day. Fasting also aims to purify the self by abstinence from harbouring malice, hatred, ill-feelings or envy, and to be in a continual state of *muraqaba* or God-awareness.

Halal food

Other specific needs are in the areas of *halal* food. For Muslims, it is important that only food that is deemed *halal* be consumed. In Arabic, the word *halal* means permitted or lawful, and these are foods that are consistent with Islamic guidelines. There are clear injunctions in Islam's Holy text, the Qur'an (6:145; 16:114–116; 5:3–5; 6:118–119; 6:121), to eat that which is good and pure. This means that Muslims should abstain not only from pork and its derivatives, but also from any meat that is not slaughtered according to sacred law (animals that were dead prior to slaughtering, animals not slaughtered properly or not slaughtered in the name of Allah), blood and blood by-products, carnivorous animals, birds of prey, and intoxicants and any substances that befog the mind, such as illegal drugs. Most cities have *halal* butchers, and so it is no longer an excuse for service providers that *halal* meat is not readily available. In addition, there are *halal* guidebooks and organisations in Australia, such as the Australian Federation of Islamic Councils (AFIC) and the Australian Halal Food Directory, which provide important guidance in these matters.

Medication

Some elderly people will be on some type of medication, therefore it is essential that, as far as possible, such medications meet the *halal* requirement stipulated above. Medication that may have alcohol as a base should be avoided. *Halal*-based gelatine should be used for capsule casing where possible. When there is no alternative and a prescribed medicine does contain non-*halal* ingredients, Islamic sacred law (*Sharia*) allows its consumption. This is based on the Sharia premise that 'necessity allows the prohibited'.

Death and burial

Additionally, service providers need to be aware that issues associated with death, preparation of wills and provision of Muslim burials are vital knowledge when caring for elderly Muslims. Before death a Muslim is required to write a will and distribute his or her inheritance based on the dictates of *Sharia* law. In addition, in the event of death a Muslim's body needs to be washed according to Islamic teachings. Islam also recommends that the body of the deceased be buried as soon as possible, and that there should be no delays unless there are strong grounds for this. Islam is also against autopsy, unless required by law for such reasons as to determine the cause of death. Finally, while there is allowance in *Sharia* for organ donation, the matter is complex and the advice of an imam or Muslim religious leader, or medical doctor familiar with Islamic issues, should be sought.

Communication

Another important factor in dealing with the elderly is communication. There are more than 70 languages spoken within the Culturally and Linguistically Diverse (CALD) community in Australia and the vast majority of elderly speak very little English, or not enough to express themselves clearly. So, language as a tool of communication becomes an essential element in appropriate service delivery. The local Muslim communities themselves have become a valuable source of support for clients. Community assistance can include community consultation, continuous contact and support, training for staff and other service providers, and an education campaign. Addressing the various levels of clients' needs – psychological and social – will provide crucial support. A holistic approach combined with impartiality and neutrality can be useful. When migrants get older they revert to their own mother tongues, so there is an added complication in caring for Muslims. For service providers, community resources can provide additional and special assistance.

Conclusion

The topic of Islamic spirituality is being revived in many parts of the Islamic world, and in the Western world. After 11 September 2001 Muslim scholars recognised the importance of the spiritual dimension of Islam in the nurturing and development of Muslim communities. The absence of this facet of Islam has been a determining factor in the rise of radicalisation in some parts of the Muslim and non-Muslim worlds. Since Islamic spirituality concerns itself with the purification of the self and the cleansing of the heart, any attempt to practise Islam without it will lead to serious deficiency. A Muslim who seeks the pleasure of God cannot do so without adherence to the sacred law while making consistent efforts to reform his inward self. Such a Muslim recognises the importance of honouring and respecting the elderly and endeavours to provide all necessary facilities for their comfort. The elderly, on the other hand, are supposed to increase in their spiritual attainments and become nobler in their conduct.

Traditionally Muslim societies care for the elderly in their homes, but in Western countries there is a need at times to place elderly Muslims with care service providers. The experience of both clients and providers can be positively enhanced if certain aspects of Islamic practices and teachings are recognised, and Muslim clients given the opportunity to practise these in a friendly environment. In such a context it is hoped that the spiritual experience of the elderly will be enhanced and not inhibited.

Notes

1.   Maliki is the name of one of the four Sunni schools of thought. It is named after its founder, Imam Malik b. Anas.

CHAPTER 9

The Spiritual Needs of the Aged and Dying: A Buddhist Perspective

Subhana Barzaghi

As we age and walk the labyrinthine path between birth and death, we face many physical, psychological, emotional and spiritual challenges. Buddhist teachings focus on practices that liberate and heal the suffering and dissatisfaction woven into the fabric of our lives. These teachings are profound in the sense that they help us to face and meet the challenges of sickness, old age and death with calmness and serenity. Buddhist practices foster deep acceptance and peace of life itself and promote a wise, compassionate response to our own departure.

Most families want the best possible care for their loved ones facing the vagaries of old age, such as dementia, chronic illness and pain. Although the physical or medical aspects of care play an important role, whether caring for someone at home, in a hospice or in hospital, it is equally important to recognise the emotional, psychological and spiritual needs of the person in providing a quality of care. Babacan and Obst (1998) have explored cultural perspectives on death and dying and have provided a valuable understanding about the beliefs and practices of different cultural groups and faiths; however, it is incorrect to assume that the same practices are uniformly appropriate for everyone within a particular faith.

A variety of Buddhist traditions have taken root in Australia, reflecting both national and sectarian differences. Therefore, it is not only important to establish whether a person is a Zen, Theravadin or Tibetan Buddhist, but also if they practise, for example, Korean, Chinese or Vietnamese Zen, as each has their respective Asian cultural heritage. Amongst the different Buddhist traditions, however, there are some common principles, which transcend differences in individual beliefs and culture. It is essential in spiritual care to work cooperatively and respectfully with an individual's belief system and worldview, and this also applies for people who have no religious affiliations.

The philosophy of spiritual care that has been adopted by the health professionals, pastoral care workers and helpers at the Karuna Hospice Service in Brisbane is summarised by (Tenzin) Chodron (2001, p.1) who states that 'spiritual care goes beyond the boundaries of any particular religious system yet incorporates and values them all'. Karuna is a Buddhist home-based support service for clients faced with terminal illness wishing to spend their final months at home. Karuna Hospice aims to provide a compassionate response to a wide range of predominantly non-Buddhist patients. Spiritual needs are considered important throughout life, but are particularly important in preparing for death (Chodron 2001).

This chapter will explore eight general principles of spiritual care for the aged, sick and dying, which are outlined below.

1. **The need for spiritual care and guidance** – the need to be treated with respect and kindness, to be given support and guidance to transform whatever is holding the person back, to finish and tidy up affairs so that they can let go and die at peace.

2. **The spiritual need to deeply connect and understand oneself** – through meditation and contemplation practices, turn the attention inwards and study the self.

3. **The need to cultivate and express the deeper qualities of the heart** – to cultivate loving-kindness, compassion, generosity, patience, joy and equanimity.

4. **The spiritual need to deeply connect with others** – to develop meaningful, honest, loving relationships and connections with others, to reduce the sense of aloneness and isolation in times of acute need.

5. **The spiritual need to recognise and express the deeper qualities of one's true nature** – the need to connect with something greater than our ordinary mind or ordinary self, to connect with the 'profound', whatever a person understands this to be.

6. **The need to find meaning and purpose in life and in death** – to put our life into perspective and recognise the value of our

experiences and the opportunities for growth and change, especially in times of crisis and intense suffering.

7. **The spiritual need to prepare oneself for death** – for most people death is a frightening prospect and an intense time that amplifies our experiences, and we can either attain deep peace and acceptance, or experience fear and despair. To let go and die a peaceful death is a worthwhile goal for most Buddhist practitioners.

8. **The need to express one's spiritual faith** – either through prayer, meditation, other rites, rituals or services or through a more scientifically orientated contemplation.

The need for spiritual care and guidance

No matter what a person's beliefs, Buddhists hold the view that everybody should be treated with respect and kindness. Spiritual care is especially appreciated when a person is vulnerable, sick, distressed, agitated, dying or in pain. Emotional and psychological support or a simple, open, non-judgemental listening ear can allow a person to transform at their own pace and move through the stages of grief from shock, through adjustment and resolution, to understanding and acceptance. Empathetic guidance can help to resolve whatever is holding a person back from completing their life's journey, to tidy up unfinished business so that they can let go and die at peace.

The spiritual need to deeply connect and understand oneself

One of the primary needs of many Buddhist practitioners is to deeply connect and understand oneself by focusing the mind within, meditating and exploring one's inner life to develop wisdom and compassion. A famous quote from Zen Master Dogen encapsulates this point succinctly.

> To study the Buddha Way is to study the self
> To study the self is to forget the self
> To forget the self is to be enlightened by the myriad beings and things of the world. (Tanahashi 1985, p.70)

Contemplation and meditation practices are employed to study the self. These practices cultivate both wisdom, as the ability to see clearly into the nature of life as it is – the self-less nature of existence – and compassion – the quality of the heart that is responsive to the pain and suffering in one's own life and in others. These practices promote healing through the awareness of our potential for change and transformation. Turning the light of attention inwards, cultivating self-awareness and contacting the depth of qualities within us enables us to find meaning and purpose in life. This is especially important in preparing for death, when the emphasis is on cultivating a serene state of mind, so that the person can move towards acceptance and deep peace.

Mindfulness is an ancient practice originating 2500 years ago with Shakyamuni Buddha. One of the most significant talks ever given by the Buddha is known as the *Sattipathna Sutta* and sets out four foundations of mindfulness (Ñānamoli and Bodhi 1995). The four foundations of mindfulness are mindfulness of: the body, feelings, thoughts, and knowledge of the teachings that release one from suffering.

These profound, yet simple, practices have the capacity to cultivate clarity of mind, release one from grief, distress and despair and open a door to a deep peace and, ultimately, the joy of liberation. To live with awareness and observe the whole mind–body process from a place of stillness is the essential foundation of emotional intelligence and the foundation of wisdom. Through mindfulness practices, a practitioner learns to dwell more at ease in the present moment.

Over the last decade, there has been a growing scientific interest and research evidence on the healing effects of mindfulness meditation on the body and brain. Clinical trials conducted by Jon Kabat-Zinn (1990) reveal that mindfulness practices help patients to reduce anxiety, panic and psychological and emotional stress; to cope with and manage physical pain; and to enhance their general well-being.

Recent advances in neuroscience and emerging sciences like psychoneuroimmunology (the study of the interaction between the psychological processes and the nervous and immune system of the human body) provide significant evidence that beliefs, attitudes, thoughts and emotions can harm or heal. Candace Pert (1997) has demonstrated how chemicals inside our bodies form a dynamic information network, linking mind and body, establishing a biomolecular basis for emotions and how they affect health. Richard Davidson, a neuroscientist (cited in Goleman 1995), using brain scans and fMRI (functional Magnetic Resonance Imaging) has demonstrated that the brain is 'plastic' and that our quota for happiness can be enhanced through mental training. Kabat-Zinn (1990) summarises the numerous studies which provide evidence that our physical health is intimately affected by our patterns of thinking and feeling and is also affected by the quality of our relationships with other people. Kabat-Zinn (1990, p.216) specifically identifies negative thoughts, feelings and beliefs that appear to be particularly toxic and can predispose us to illness.

Conversely, positive patterns of thinking, feeling and behaving appear to be associated with robustness and health (Kabat-Zinn 1990, p.217). The relevance of this evidence is that it strengthens the importance of bringing awareness and mindfulness to the psycho-emotional and bodily experience of our behaviour, physical condition and social relationships.

As the ageing process sets in, bodily changes bring us into a direct relationship with impermanence and the transient nature of all things, especially the body. Mindfulness practice creates a calm space to witness sensations, pulsations, vibrations, movement, pain and tensions compassionately – the actual direct, felt experience of bodily life. Through mindfulness, we can learn to be with and accept our body as it is, without undue attachment, aversion, shame, judgement or fear. We can learn to cultivate a wise relationship to our body, one that fosters a compassionate attitude to the ageing body, even with all its frailties and idiosyncrasies.

Mindfulness training is helpful for patients suffering long-term chronic pain and is complimentary with pain relief medication. Mindfulness training involves directing a calm attention into the felt sense of the pain, to enter into the pain with a curious, open, non-judgemental attitude of mind. It is not the pain *per se*, but our attitude of mind, our reaction to the pain that often amplifies the degree of suffering we will experience. Our normal habitual reactions to pain may involve tightening up, avoiding it, hating it, suppressing it, distracting ourselves or trying to ignore it. Although it is counter-intuitive to focus on the pain, given our habitual reaction to pain, mindfulness practice cultivates detached observation in relation to the strong sensations of pain. 'It can feel as if you are completely detached from the sensations you are experiencing, as if it were not "your" pain so much as just pain' (Kabat-Zinn 1990, p.283). Under a steady and kind attention, the mind becomes still and calm and is less reactive to the pain; it just witnesses it, rather than endures it. The witness part of oneself, that part that is aware and can notice thoughts, feelings and painful sensations, is itself not in pain. Awareness, while intimately connected with the flow of life, is not ruled by our thoughts, feelings or painful sensations; it is free of them.

I have instructed many students who were struggling with pain on intensive meditation retreats to breathe into the painful, tender areas of their inner life, to direct the breath into the painful region, soften and relax into it.

Overall, this practice of cultivating a kind and steady attention to either the pleasant or the painful experiences enhances the quality of equanimity so that we can meet the joys, tribulations and difficulties of our daily life with greater ease and balance.

The need to cultivate and express the deeper qualities of the heart

Within all of us lie the seeds of extraordinary qualities and potential, such as love, compassion, kindness, joy, generosity, forgiveness, patience and equanimity. The more we cultivate and express these wholesome qualities, the more beneficial and positive our life becomes. Cultivating these qualities and expressing them creates an opportunity for spiritual growth and transformation.

Buddhist practices on loving-kindness and compassion are grouped under the teachings of the *Brahma-Viharas,* known as the four divine abodes (Salzberg 1995). The four divine abodes are; *Metta* – love, *Karuna* – compassion, *Mudita* – joy and *Upekkha* – equanimity. These four states of consciousness are said to be the most beautiful, powerful and sublime states of consciousness we can experience as human beings. Through consistent, dedicated practice, they can become our natural abiding place. The other root meaning of *metta* is 'spiritual friendship'. The healing power of *metta* loving-kindness has similar qualities to having a good friend. A good friend is consistent also through times of difficulty and trouble. They will support and care for you when you are lonely, sick or depressed. They provide refuge for you when you are afraid and rejoice in your successes and achievements. The art of *metta* is to be a good friend to oneself and others.

There are three dimensions to an open and loving heart: cultivating platonic love, learning to receive love, and learning to embody unconditional love in its fullest measure for all beings. *Metta* practice works to restore this lost connection to the heart. The loving heart has the power to deeply heal and transform our lives from the inside out and gives deep meaning to our life.

The Buddhist practice of loving-kindness begins with directing loving energy, kind thoughts and feelings towards oneself, just as you would naturally wish your loved ones to experience ease, happiness and good health. Self-love is a very misunderstood term; unfortunately, it is usually associated with 'selfishness', being 'self-centred' or self-indulgent, or with self-importance. Petra King, in her book *Quest for Life* (2004, p.3), suggests 'that you might find it easier to think of it as self-care rather than self-love'. In teaching numerous workshops on loving-kindness, I have discovered that many people find it quite challenging to direct loving-kindness towards themselves. People are often plagued with negative feelings about their own self-worth. The power of loving-kindness directed inwards towards oneself burns away these feelings; it helps one let go of all the non-deserving thoughts, drop one's fears and to let the heart soften and melt through its radiance. Through the practice of *metta* we uncover the possibility of truly respecting and valuing ourselves as an equal part of the universe of flowers, ants, stones and clouds. To open the heart to receive what is on offer, to trust and not fear love's wounding, but to hold the door of your heart open to life's fierce grace is to engage with life and love at a profound level.

When the mind has become calm and steady, strong positive feelings of love *metta* are more easily evoked and are directed towards loved ones and friends and extended to people from all walks of life. This practice has the effect of breaking down the artificial divisions created in our mind between oneself and others. Directing loving-kindness to someone who has hurt us or caused us harm is challenging. Yet by purposefully forgiving them, we can let go of feelings of anger, resentment, hurt and righteousness. Loving-kindness practice comes to maturity when we notice it has changed from a preferential love, that is, just loving those who are dear to us, to an all-embracing, unconditional love for all beings regardless of whether we like them or not, regardless of their race, class, status, personality or disposition. Encouraging a person to practise loving-kindness, generosity, goodwill and forgiveness in times of difficulty cultivates strong positive emotions which help them to let go of deep hurt, ill-will and resentment.

The following prayer of loving-kindness is a variation on a traditional verse that I wrote, which I use regularly in my own practice.

May I (you/they) be free from harm, anger and ill-will,

May I (you/they) be free from fear and the causes of fear,

May my (your/their) heart and mind be filled with the power of loving-kindness.

May I (you/they) be well in body, heart and mind,

May I (you/they) be protected from inner and outer harm,

May I (you/they) learn to take care of myself (themselves) joyfully,

May I (you/they) learn to live in harmony with others,

May I (you/they) be peaceful and happy in this life.

May I (you/they) find freedom and liberation in this life.

The spiritual need to deeply connect with others

Having meaningful, honest, loving relationships and connections with others helps to reduce the sense of aloneness and isolation in times of acute need. When we are ill, sick or in pain, isolation and loneliness tend to exacerbate our suffering. A warm hand, a kind word, a soothing touch helps to ease a person's discomfort. The Pali Buddhist word for compassion is *karuna* – which literally translates as 'experiencing a trembling or quivering of the heart' in response to another being's pain. Compassion arises when our heart is open to the suffering in the world. The experience of illness, pain and suffering is seen by most Buddhists as an opportunity to reflect on the universal nature of suffering. It is an opportunity to generate compassion. Ven. Thich Nhat Hanh actively invites his students to keep the door of their heart open by reflecting on the precept: 'Do not avoid contact with suffering or close your eyes before suffering in the life of the world' (Ven. Thich Nhat Hanh 1987, p.34). Learning to feel compassion for other beings' suffering puts our own discomfort into perspective and it reduces our sense of alienation, self-pity and self-centredness.

Paul's story is an example of the power of cultivating compassion for others and how it can touch a person's life in profound ways. Paul is a dear friend, an internationally respected architect and a long-term Buddhist meditator. Paul has lived with cancer for the last 18 years. Recently, Paul decided to undergo major surgery to remove a malignant tumour that had eaten through the bone at the base of his skull and was spreading rapidly into the outer envelope of his brain. This was a very delicate, complex and potentially life-threatening operation. Paul realised that he had to come to terms with the fact that no-one, not even his leading brain surgeon, could guarantee the outcome of the operation – whether he would be blind, lose his speech, perhaps lose partial motor movement, or if he would ever walk again. On the morning of the operation, Paul calmly meditated, and when he reached the operating theatre all his vital signs, blood pressure and heart rate were, to the doctors' great surprise, stable and perfectly normal. Before the anaesthetic was administered, Paul visualised his favourite meditation rock in the bush and calmly entered into meditation. On awakening and emerging out of the anaesthetic many hours later, Paul found himself physically lying in intensive care but mentally still meditating calmly on his favourite rock. It was a very successful operation and Paul's surgeon felt he was a living, walking miracle. After only a week's recovery in hospital, Paul returned home better than he had been for more than a year. But what really touched Paul profoundly was the enormous loving-kindness and compassion that he felt he had received from his family, spiritual community and dear friends all around the world who had sat and sent prayers of loving-kindness and compassion to him. Paul was overwhelmed by the tender gravity of kindness and felt it infuse his body, heart and mind and radically change his life forever. Paul strongly believes that the successful outcome of the operation was a combination of the alignment of these many positive forces:

having one of the best brain surgeons, his strong meditation practice, being surrounded by his loving family, and the compassion and loving-kindness that flowed from his friends and spiritual community.

The spiritual need to recognise and express the deeper qualities of one's true nature

As we approach the end of our life, there is a strength of urgency to connect with something greater than our ordinary mind or ordinary self, to connect with the 'profound', whatever a person understands this to be. For some this refers to God, or to a higher consciousness; for Buddhists it refers to the awakened heart-mind. The 'profound' is often revealed through an experience of interconnectedness with nature that is beyond any formal religious beliefs.

Contemplating the impermanent nature of all life is considered by Buddhists to be one of the keys to developing wisdom. This stimulates a deep appreciation for the richness and preciousness of each and every passing moment, each relationship, each situation and circumstance. Impermanence highlights that each person, each fingerprint and every blade of grass is utterly unique and unrepeatable. If we deeply appreciate this human life as a precious gift, a valuable opportunity for awakening, then we will not waste our time and vital energy in denial or superficiality. A beautiful reminder of the teachings on impermanence is found in the Diamond Sutta (Price and Mou-Lam 1985), verse xxxii:

> Thus you should think of this fleeting world: a star at dawn, a bubble in a stream, a flash of lightning in a summer cloud, a flickering lamp, a phantom and a dream.

One of the sublime insights that is enhanced by meditation is the experience of interconnected oneness, also referred to as *inter-being* by Ven. Thich Nhat Hanh (1991). Inter-being is an opening of the heart and mind to that which is greater than our small ego-self; it is a recognition of the interconnected seamless totality of life. The world of inter-being opens our heart-mind to a deep experience of ourselves as the wind in the trees, the sound of the kookaburra, the mountains and rivers, and all other fellow beings. With this insight, we learn to live in greater harmony and reverence with all of creation, as none other than our very own great body, our true nature.

When we contemplate the changing universe it begs deeper questions. Is there anything that does not change – that can endure, even death? What is the changeless, timeless reality that the great spiritual teachings point to? When our senses reveal a world in flux, what then is true and real? Who am I, whose days, pleasures and adventures are drawing to a close? It takes spiritual insight to perceive that within this universe of ceaseless movement and transformation, there is that which is untouched by the passage of time, that which is ageless and deathless. In Buddhism, 'deathless' refers to our enlightened nature or our unborn, empty essential nature. A Buddhist meditation teacher who has worked extensively with the dying, Stephen Levine (1987), observed that those who face the challenges of preparing for death reach subtle and profound states of wisdom, compassion and peace. As they approach the portals of their physical dissolution, those who meet the stark face of impermanence, who let go of all that is unnecessary in their life and focus on what is healing and most meaningful, find peace.

> Entering healing beyond ideas of life and death, we become who we have always been, that which preceded birth and survives death. Recognising that healing never ends, our life becomes whole, each step so precious, each moment approaching the grace of the ever-healed, the always uninjured, the deathless. (Levine 1987, p.290)

The need to find meaning and purpose in life and in death

In workshops that I have conducted on death and dying, I invite participants to contemplate the following questions: 'If you had six months to live, what would you do, how would you spend this time?' 'What shall you do with your precious life?' 'Imagine yourself sitting on top of your own grave, looking back over your life; how or what would you like to be remembered for?' While doing this contemplation, I ask each person to write their own epitaph. These questions and exercises clarify in a matter of a few short paragraphs what is truly important to us in this life. And it is evident that people rarely find much significance in their financial achievements or how many credentials they have after their name. All these concerns pale into insignificance in the final analysis. What most people value is: learning how to love well, how to walk in peace, how to work with integrity, how to live in harmony with others, or having contributed something worthwhile and beneficial for this world.

Most people want to be remembered for having a good soul; being a kind, generous, loving person.

The spiritual need to prepare oneself for death

Death is a sensitive subject because there are a lot of different beliefs and views about it. It can be a very difficult time for families who are experiencing the death of a loved one. Death is a poignant, harsh teacher: it sharpens the truth of impermanence, it confronts all beings with their vulnerability and mortality, and it lays bare the mystery at the heart of all things. For most people, death is quite a frightening prospect, it is a time when our thoughts, feelings and experiences are intensified – and we can approach death with fear and despair, or attain deep peace and acceptance. Providing spiritual guidance to those who are dying helps them prepare for a peaceful death, which is considered to be a very important goal for most Buddhists. To die well means to die with peace and to be as conscious as possible through the various final stages.

Death is taken up as a subject of contemplation in the Buddhist tradition. Some of my first teachers were the Tibetan lamas of Kopan Monastery in Nepal. At the ripe age of 20, the initial meditations were contemplations on death, which were given to beginners specifically to motivate students to dedicate their lives to spiritual practice and face the inevitability of death. The four traditional contemplations are:

1. Death is certain.

2. The time of death is uncertain.

3. Given that death is certain, and the time of death uncertain, what is the purpose of your life, or what truly matters?

4. What will help you at the time of death?

These contemplations were not as morbid a matter as you might think; in fact they had quite the contrary effect. Tibetan Buddhists believe that if we prepare ourselves for death, if we release our deep fears about the dying process, then we are more likely to die with grace, ease and peace in our hearts. Contemplations on death can help a person face the sharp claws of impermanence and foster a profound enquiry into that great mystery which is timeless and deathless.

Zen Buddhist teachers often ask students questions about their understanding about death to check the depth of their insight and practice. Any deeply authentic spiritual experience should, in many ways, resolve some of our fears about death. Yamada Koun Roshi, a Japanese Zen teacher, asked Anne Aitken, 'What do you think about death?' Anne replied, 'Why, it's like when a bus stops before you, when the time comes you just get on the bus and you go' (Aitken 1999). The old teacher approved of her response, and this is how Anne lived her life and approached death, with no fuss, no drama, a straightforward departure with grace and ease. When Anne was admitted to hospital following a massive heart attack, her husband and Zen teacher Robert Aitken Roshi and close friends were in her room discussing with the doctor about whether Anne should be put on a life support system to prolong her life or not. It was well known that Anne hated the idea of being dependent on a life support system and wanted to die naturally. In the midst of the discussion, Anne opened her eyes and looked at Aitken Roshi with utter resolve in her face, pursed her lips in a most definite way, as if to say, 'No thank you!', and breathed her last breath. Anne recognised that her time was up and simply got on that bus and left. Anne's response, along with others of remarkable insight, shows us how to embrace the moment of death and to let go with a clear, peaceful heart.

This is not limited to Zen teachers. Mona Wurtz, a Sufi teacher and Jungian analyst, had gathered her close friends around her before her death. Generous with her material things, she invited the women to try on her clothes, shoes and jewellery, and we adorned ourselves with her elegant wardrobe and then paraded around her as she lay on her bed. Mona was an exceptionally generous, loving and spiritually passionate woman, who practised how to let go and walk through this life with a sense of freedom and lightness of being. She died serenely from stomach cancer in 2005, at home, surrounded by loved ones. Her departure was a graceful exit, a fearless testimony to the spirit of letting go. I wrote this verse in honour of her beauty and grace.

> On that day,
> you took my hand in yours
> and stroked your thin translucent cheeks
> that receded peacefully into those bare bones of light.
> But it did not end there,
> the loving mysterious presence
> that held us both,
> that holds us all in an effortless palm,
> is the psalm that is still with us now.

Death is a very charged moment, just like the extraordinary miracle of birth; it is stepping towards the edge of the precipice where the veils of ego start to fall away, where we have to let go of all our roles, responsibilities, joys, precious things and connections with loved ones. We have to let go of all that we think, know and believe about ourselves. Death is sometimes termed 'the great remover', where we are stripped down naked to the bone. Tibetan Buddhists believe that at the time of death there is a unique opportunity for insight, a possibility of awakening to the clear light nature of mind. The only way to prepare for the true nature of mind when it reveals itself spontaneously at the time of death is to practise the art of letting go here and now in this life.

The need to express one's spiritual faith

Buddhist practitioners place great importance on preparing the mind for death and making the process of dying as peaceful as possible. The family usually prefer to care for the loved one at home rather than in a hospital, so that they can provide a quiet, peaceful and calm environment for the last stages of their life. These are some general helpful reminders for pastoral care workers and health professionals to support Buddhists at the time of death (Khadro 1997).

- Help the person find deep meaning in life by encouraging them to remember positive, kind and helpful things one has done in this life.

- Help the person create a calm, quiet environment to meditate, to read Buddhist teachings – or read to them. The person may request to have Buddhist images in the room.

- If requested, provide access to a Buddhist teacher (monk, nun) or a meditation teacher.

- Allow the person to express regrets for past mistakes; encourage the person to resolve any unfinished business, emotionally and psychologically, that may hinder them from letting go.

- Encourage the practice of mindfulness and awareness of the present moment, as most people will want to keep the mind as alert and calm as possible.

- Provide empathy and spiritual guidance so that the person can move through the stages of grief towards acceptance and deep peace.

Conclusion

Generally most Buddhists will focus on addressing their spiritual needs throughout their life so that they will have the tools to meet old age, sickness and death with greater ease and serenity. The following is a summary of some of the healing and spiritual practices that are important for Buddhists generally.

- Cultivate mindfulness, serenity and self-awareness that leads to the development of wisdom and compassion.

- Through mindfulness develop a wise, healthy relationship to the body and mind.

- Cultivate and express the qualities of the heart – loving-kindness, compassion, joy, generosity, patience, forgiveness and equanimity towards oneself and others.

- Live a wholesome life of integrity and ethics, that has value and meaning.

- Contemplate the teachings on impermanence and prepare for old age and death.

- Develop wisdom through meditation and contemplation into the deeper truths of one's being – our interconnected, vast, timeless, self-less true nature.

Spiritual care becomes particularly relevant for those who are suffering long-term chronic illness and pain, the frail aged and those preparing for death. If families and patients are given the appropriate support and spiritual care that is sensitive and responsive to their needs and traditions, they will be more able to find peace and comfort in the final days of their precious life and die a graceful exit.

CHAPTER 10

Dying: An Approach to Care from Hindu and Buddhist Perspectives

Amy Rayner and Purushottama Bilimoria

Introduction

In both the Hindu and Buddhist traditions, death is not looked upon as a final end to one's life, but as a journey from one life to another. In the words of the celebrated *Bhagavadgita* (often recited at Hindu funerary services): 'As a person casts off worn-out garments and puts on new ones, so the embodied soul casts off the worn-out body and enters other new ones.'

Because a Hindu or Buddhist will spend a good part of their life not just preparing for peaceful death, but also looking toward a new life (which may or may not entail re-embodiment in a physical body), the practices and rituals at the time of dying are of particular importance. This chapter provides an instructional insight into the dying process of two particular religious traditions, Tibetan Buddhism and popular Hinduism.

We will begin by examining the particular practices, mental attitudes and rituals that contribute to a positive outcome in death and rebirth in the Tibetan Buddhist tradition. There are countless practices that may be recommended by a teacher to a student of Buddhism, of varying levels of complexity. In this case, we have included advice, prayers and rituals commonly used in the Gelugpa tradition of Tibetan Buddhism, of which His Holiness the Dalai Lama is recognized as the lineage holder, and to which Kyabje Lama Zopa Rinpoche, Spiritual Director of the Foundation for the Preservation of the Mahayana Tradition (FPMT) belongs. We have selected these particular practices and advice for their adaptability into the context of a Western medical care facility, hospice or home for the aged. They include: talking about death, managing meditation and medication, the power of listening to prayers, setting up an altar, making time for meditation, and ways for the family to support a peaceful death. We will then outline some practices for the ageing and dying, including Medicine Buddha, White Tara and *tong-len*, the practice of giving and taking. We shall conclude this section by suggesting what is beneficial to do at the time of and after death for a Buddhist in your care, such as offering *pujas* and prayers.

Hinduism comprises a number of ancient, classical and contemporary traditions and sects with their origins in the Vedas, Puranas and epics, as well as customary and Indigenous practices. In this religious tradition there is emphasis on proper attitude, certain mandatory rites and ritual preparations for the soul (*jiva*) in the period before and after the last breath is taken, and when the soul has left on the onward journey to a destiny hereafter. In this discussion we shall focus on the more popular Vedanta tradition as practised in modern-day Hinduism. We shall also note the particular practices and ceremonies associated with cremation – or burial, depending on the status of the person – and the reasons for their continuing importance in the Hindu life-world. The mystic power of mantras (syllabic sound-forms) recited during the service and upon lighting the funeral pyre will also be considered, as well as the modifications that such rites may have undergone as Hinduism has spread around the world.

When death, modern Western medical paradigms of treatment and care, and religion interact, there are always questions. As both Hinduism and Buddhism assert continuity between life, death and a life hereafter, there are particular questions that are often raised. In this section, we seek to respond to the most frequently asked and relevant questions on dying from a Hindu or Buddhist perspective.

The aim of this chapter is to give you an insight into the way in which an 'ideal' journey from life to death and rebirth could be undertaken from the perspective of two religious traditions. We hope that this practical insight, underpinned by the religious and philosophical ideas explored in the earlier chapters, will help you to support the spiritual needs of those in your care with greater awareness and sensitivity. In the *Bhagavadgita* it is stated that the last thoughts one has as the life-breath leaves the body more or less sum up one's psychological and psychic constitution – to which otherwise the gods alone are privy. So what thought one has at the moment of death is highly important. This is also the case in Buddhism, where it is said that the mental state of the dying person has a powerful influence on the type of rebirth, positive or negative, that he or she takes. For this reason in both traditions much care, compassion and confidence has to be extended to the dying in order that they may be helped toward cultivating the correct and most benign frame of mind – free of feeling angry, hurt, or resistant to the inevitable. We have outlined a range of traditional practices and their modern adaptations that are commonly used to create a calm, peaceful and spiritually comforting environment for practicing Buddhists and Hindus.

Part one: An approach to dying, from the bedside of a Tibetan Buddhist of the Gelugpa tradition

Talking about death, managing meditation and medication

Many Buddhists in your care will feel comfortable to some degree in talking about their own death with you. Feel at ease and be open with them about what they can expect. If you are managing a sickness or health condition, let them know how this may impact them and what medications they might need to take, with particular emphasis on how their state of mind may be affected. This will allow them to prepare for their passing, knowing what lies ahead; and will give them an opportunity to plan practices that they will be able to do during this time.

You may find that Buddhists will try to minimise the amount of medication they take, because having a clear mind that can meditate and pray is very important to them. Some patients will try to balance physical pain with mental clarity for as long as possible. An open and trusting relationship between the caregiver and patient therefore becomes very beneficial. If initially you support a Buddhist's wishes to minimise medication so that they can continue to pray and meditate in the early stages of their illness, you will find that many patients will then listen to your advice and accept medication closer to the time of death when you recommend it. On this matter the Dalai Lama advises that it is best to keep one's mind as clear as possible: 'Nevertheless, if the dying person is in great pain and there is nothing that inspires them with a positive outlook, it is preferable not to die in a fully aware state. In this case, it is helpful to give tranquilizers and medication' (Dalai Lama 2001, p.113).

The power of listening to prayers

A Buddhist in your care will probably genuinely wish to practise their faith daily to the best of their ability, no matter what state of health they are in. A central aspect of this practice may be listening to prayers, teachings and mantras on CD or portable music players. Even when a person is in a coma or has suffered a major debilitating stroke, this is a way in which you can still enable them to connect with and practise their faith.

Simply listening to Buddhist chanting, prayers and mantras is a hugely beneficial practice. To be able to hear the *Dharma*[1] will often give someone who is in distress or physical discomfort, or is mentally struggling with depression or fear, great comfort and support. An effective way to support a

Buddhist patient would be to have available some different Buddhist chants and prayers, or, as many Buddhists will have their own, making available CD players in aged facilities and hospitals. The spiritual power of the prayers is not solely dependent on the medical consciousness of the person. You might like to arrange to play a CD continuously for a patient during medical procedures, surgery or even the dying process.

Setting up an altar

Altars with pictures and statues of the Buddha and one's teachers provide immense spiritual support for a practitioner. Many Buddhists will find an altar a positive object just to gaze at and have close to them. It is the centre of their meditation practice, and (no less important), it is a way to help them feel safe and at home.

If an older Buddhist, who has spent his life practising devotion to the Buddha, found himself in an unfamiliar environment such as a hospital, and saw his altar, prayer beads or *Dharma* books being treated as ordinary objects, he could become quite distressed. Here are a few tips on how to treat an altar and *Dharma* objects with care and respect.

The person's bed should not have their feet pointing towards the altar. Try to keep in mind that the objects are precious and are usually best placed on a raised box or a cloth. *Dharma* books should be kept up high if possible, or wrapped in cloth. They should never be placed on the ground or stepped over. Some Buddhists may want to offer small flowers, wrapped lollies and fruit, lights or cups of water on their altar. Making offerings is a spiritual practice of generosity and has an uplifting effect on the mind. It's best not to tidy them away as if they are just ordinary clutter; rather discuss it with the person and try to find a working solution. A conducive and supporting environment will mean a great deal to any student of Buddhism in your care. This will greatly improve their outlook and overall well-being.

Making time for meditation

What with meals, doctors, visits, showers and so forth, an elderly person's day in an aged care home, hospice or hospital can be quite busy. It is important to try and make time in the morning and early evening for meditation and prayer. One of the basic practices of Buddhism is the practice of refuge. This involves reciting a prayer three times and making three prostrations at the beginning and end of each day. A prostration involves placing one's palms together in the prayer posture at the crown, throat and heart, kneeling down and rising again. If a person's mobility is affected it would be kind to offer to assist them in their prostrations. If a patient has suffered a severe stroke or has paralysis and is unable to perform prostrations, you can help them by simply placing their palms together in the prayer position and touching their palms to their crown, throat and heart while they are still in bed. The person can mentally visualise himself or herself performing the prostrations. Many Buddhists will have prayers or mantras they have vowed to recite a certain amount of times each day. It is vital to try and support them in this practice by making a structured time where they know that they will not be interrupted.

Ways for the family to support a peaceful passing

The family of a Buddhist may have a different faith, and be unfamiliar with the religious wishes and considerations of a Buddhist approaching death. For example, a 'Western' Buddhist's family may be predominantly Catholic or have no set faith. In this situation, to help the person in your care, it may be helpful to speak to the family about what you have done to support their loved one.

Encourage a calm, peaceful environment. The Dalai Lama advises that if family come to visit older people it is important not to squabble, but through gentle talking allow them to revisit positive times in their life. This will help them to feel content, and that all their loose ends, old arguments and worldly affairs have been laid to rest.

Encourage the family not to show distress or cry excessively around the person in the immediate time before passing. Dramatic outpourings of grief increase the fear, anxiety and suffering of their loved one. This advice is emphasised in almost every teaching given on death by the Buddhist masters. If a family member needs to cry, express emotion or intense sorrow, kindly ask them to sit in another room and come back when they are calm. You can explain to them that the best way to help their beloved is to create a feeling of warmth and support, not fear and emotion.

Two practices for the ageing and dying: Medicine Buddha and White Tara

There are two particularly powerful meditation practices that are associated with healing and longevity. These may be performed by the patient, their family or *Dharma*-friends. Medicine Buddha, the manifestation of the healing energy of all enlightened beings, is represented as a blue Buddha holding a bowl filled with nectar. Medicine Buddha is associated with healing and overcoming obstacles. The practice promotes peace, calmness and tranquility in a person's heart. White Tara, a female Buddha, is frequently associated with nurturing energy. White Tara grants long life and wisdom to living beings. Both practices involve generating a compassionate motivation, prayers, mantra recitation and visualisation of warm, gentle light emanating from the Buddha that washes away any darkness, negative karma and worry in the mind, followed by a dedication of the positive karma to the happiness of other beings. Students of Tibetan Buddhism may be familiar with these, or similar practices, and will generally bring their own prayer books and Buddha images so that they can complete their individual practices.

Tong-len: the practice of giving and taking

Tong-len is a way to generate compassion through meditation. You take on all the suffering of living beings and, transforming it, offer all your happiness and positive energy to them. For a Buddhist who has trained in this technique over the course of their lifetime, the results can be very great when practised at the time leading up to death. The person is encouraged to think, 'By my experiencing this cancer/illness/pain, etc., may all other beings in the world be free of this, and may they have good health, happiness and long life.' The person uses their sickness as a way of opening their heart to others who are in a similar situation. An even more advanced technique is to include breathing and visualisation. The person visualises taking on the suffering of all other living beings in the form of black smoke, which is taken in on the in-breath. Then, on the out-breath, all of our health and happiness and all positive qualities are sent out to other living beings in the form of white light, and we visualise them receiving everything that they want (Hawter 1995).

Many Buddhists who are preparing to pass away won't want their family to suffer grief and sadness. This worry may have an unsettling effect on their state of mind. You can encourage them to practise *tong-len*, first on themselves, and then their family, strongly concentrating on taking away their suffering and grief and placing them in contentment and peace; then expand this compassion to a much wider field by doing the practice for all beings who are experiencing sickness and loss.

What to do at the time of and after death for a Buddhist in your care

A calm and peaceful environment is the best gift you can offer to a dying person of any faith. If you have arranged to read prayers, such as the traditional King of Prayers, do so, speaking in a soft, warm and reassuring way. Playing CDs mantras and chanting is good to do if this has been pre-arranged. Try not to do anything that might agitate or distress the patient.

The time of death is not necessarily when the person has stopped breathing. Death in a Buddhist context is when the consciousness leaves the body. This can take some hours or days to happen. Try to leave the body for as long as possible, and when you do move it, act in a gentle and respectful way, as the mind of the person may still be aware of what is happening.

Pujas, *prayers and offerings, coming to peace with losing a loved one*

It is common for a Buddhist family to make offerings to commemorate the death of a loved one. This can take the form of sponsoring a *puja*, an elaborate prayer and offering ceremony performed by ordained monks and nuns, making an offering annually for prayers to be recited in temples, sponsoring the publication of *Dharma* books, and the production of holy objects such as statues and stupas.

It is important to come to peace and acceptance about losing a loved one. While there are extensive explanations on the death and rebirth process, these may not necessarily provide comfort to a Buddhist's grieving family. Sogyal Rinpoche, when talking on grief and letting go, teaches that for up to about 21 days after a person dies, they are more connected to the previous life than to the next one. So for this period in particular the loved ones can be encouraged to continue their (silent) communication with the deceased person – to say their goodbyes, complete any unfinished business, reassure the dead person, encourage them to let go of their old life and to move on to the next one. It can be reassuring even just to talk to the dead person, and at some level to know that they are probably receiving your message. This practice can also play an important part of the healing process for those grieving (Rinpoche 1992).

Part two: An approach to dying, from the bedside of a practising Hindu

Showing gratitude and giving thanks for life

As we explained earlier, death is not considered as final. Rather, the act of dying is seen as a continuation of the life-process. In many ways dying also marks the completion of a person's embodied life in the social world she came to be part of. Hence it follows that in marking this moment certain exchanges have to take place between the dying person and the community of people she shared her life with. The foremost among these acknowledgements is that of gratitude.

The act of gratitude extends to the gods and ancestors as well. Apart from the usual gifting of flowers, the family and other members close to the dying will also bring with them water (preferably from the holy rivers in India or elsewhere), incense and scriptures sacred to the tradition, from which chants, hymns, prayers and devotional music will be recited and played at the bedside. Everyone present or calling by will express the genuine wish that the one they are about to lose will be received with gracious embrace by the gods and those who have gone before, and be guided to a safe place as she makes the transition to the other side. (The dying can participate in ceremonious observances within the confines of the modern hospital environment, if the process cannot take place at home.) These observances end with silent meditation and incantation (*japa*) of mantras that are supposed to embed mystic powers and awaken the buried unconscious mind, so that upon death the dying will retain full consciousness of her identity as she makes the transition.

Prana: *Travelling freely without fear*

Hindus believe the subtle awareness of life-breath *(prana, qi)* only becomes awakened when the current body is discarded. Leaving behind the body, all the traces of the senses and the intellect, memories and experiences, the *prana* travels freely without fear of death or the eventual encounter with the god of death (*yama*). The *prana*, ideally, should not be tied to attachments to this life or to any excessive doubts that might hold the soul back.

To bring this about, the person acknowledges the care he enjoyed in the cradle and the family home. He also begs for forgiveness, if perchance he has in any way injured or caused harm and insult to any members of the family, or the human and animal worlds at large. This act of forgiveness is a recognition of the burden of karma and the understanding both that one is a product of, and that one can be totally free of, all karma. The process of forgiveness and giving thanks is reciprocated by the family and attending friends. They express gratitude for all that the person has brought into their lives and into their larger world. They may also beg forgiveness for their weaknesses and, in this instance, perhaps the failure to prolong the life of the person. In some instances, of course, prolonging life would cause more suffering, so a mutual understanding is arrived at – that their loved one's passing is the wish of the gods, that human beings have little control over destiny at some points in their lives, and that it is time to lovingly let go.

Last rites (antyesthi): *Cremation in the Hindu tradition*

Once death has occurred (or, from the Hindu point of view, the life-breath of the dying has completed its exit from the physical embodiment in which it temporarily resided), the process of preparing for the final rites begins. Let us explain what this process entails.

Hindus have a name for the final rites that mark the end of the life-cycle process. These are known as '*antyesthi*' – literally, the 'end rites'. Hindus believe that the deceased should be cremated, not buried. The two exceptions to this rule are holy men (*sannyasins*) who have renounced the material world and are therefore outside the sphere of social norms, and stillborn foetuses and infants who have not yet been initiated. In both these instances, the bodies are buried. Cremation signifies offering of the body to the gods as the ultimate sacrifice, through the medium of fire and smoke (*agni*). If death has occurred away from home, the body of the deceased is not allowed to be returned back home, unless special arrangements have been made.

People will try to avoid touching the corpse, as it may pollute the body. It is usually bathed and dressed in white, traditional Indian clothes. If a wife dies before her husband, she is dressed in red bridal clothes. If a woman is a widow, she will be dressed in white or pale colours. Markings are made on the deceased's forehead to indicate gender, caste and the sect the person belonged to. This is followed by a memorial service at which a Hindu priest will perform seven *pujas,* or prayer rituals, to request the mind of the deceased to move peacefully onwards on their journey. The following mantra is recited 108 times by the principal mourners:

> Om Tryambakam Yajamahe
> Sugandhim Pushtivardhanam
> Urvarukamiva Bandhanan
> Mrityor Mukshiya Maamritat.

> We meditate on the three-eyed reality
> Which permeates and nourishes all like a fragrance.
> May we be liberated from death for the sake of immortality,
> Even as the cucumber is severed from bondage to the creeper.

Traditional last rites then involve placing the wrapped body beneath a wooden pyre smeared with ghee or clarified butter and covered with scented flowers or sandalwood paste. At the funeral site, in the presence of mourners and close relatives of the deceased, the eldest son or equivalent takes charge of the final rites and lights the funeral pyre to the accompaniment of Vedic mantras and aligned chants from sacred texts. The entire ritual is believed to facilitate a smooth journey for the parting 'soul' (*atma*) onwards to the celestial regions. On or after the third day of the cremation rite, the ashes are scattered in one of the holy rivers, preferably the Ganges.

Fasting and prayer: Family rituals after the death of a loved one

A period of 13 days is set aside for mourning, even though the scriptures sermonise that one should not grieve for the parting of the deceased, as all life is indeed transitory, and another birth will ensue. Most grieving ones observe a period of seclusion, because, until the soul of the deceased has fully transited, the likelihood of spiritual pollution through association with the world outside, or consumption of wrong items, could hinder the process. Fasting is observed and the day ends with devotional chanting and meditation in remembrance of the deceased. Some families will also follow a regime of scriptural recitations in larger groups, which ends with sharing sacredly prepared offerings of food or distributing gifts to the poor.

The fourteenth day marks a time of celebration, when the soul of the deceased is thought to have been freed entirely from all earthly bonds, suffering or pleasures. To be cremated on the banks of the Ganges in Banares, India is an ideal shared by many Hindus. A particular feature of the Hindu ritual during the deceased's memorial service, which is often revisited on the anniversary of the death for several years thereafter, is the preparation of rice balls (*pinda*). These are offered to the spirit of the deceased. In part, these ceremonies are seen as contributing to the merit of the deceased, but they also pacify the soul so that it will not linger in this world as a ghost but will pass through the realm of Yama, the god of death.

Cremation in Australia

We will say a little about *antyeshti*, or the 'end rites', in the Australian context. The practice reflects changes so as to adhere to local health regulations. In the early days cremation was neither popular nor encouraged in Australia. The first recorded cremation in Australia took place in March 1895, when a Mrs Henniker of Richmond in Melbourne was cremated on a beach on the outskirts of Melbourne. Chalmers reports that it was 'bad enough when Europeans turned bayside beach into crematoria, but when Hindus followed their ancestral customs on a nearby beach later that year, mayhem was unleashed' (Chalmers 2001, p.79). Only very gradually were proper facilities for cremation introduced. In the early stages the cremation facilities used wood pyres. It was not until 1936 that the first modern (furnace-style) crematorium appeared. Despite the availability of such facilities, some Hindus chose to bury their deceased, although increasingly, cremation is practised. The practice is becoming popular among non-Hindus as well.

Part three: Buddhist and Hindu responses to frequently asked questions

How can we reconcile religious belief with medical practices such as life support machines, 'Do not resuscitate' and organ donation?

Buddhist teachers generally do not recommend euthanasia (even for animals). This is because of the belief that euthanasia is not an end to suffering and its karmic causes, but is simply the end of suffering in this body. It is often advised to try and support a living being with as much compassion and loving-kindness as possible through their illness. Helping to make a Buddhist practitioner's suffering as bearable as possible gives the patient the opportunity to experience the ripening effect of their negative karma,[2] so that it cannot ripen again. Also, sickness is an opportunity to transform their suffering into compassion and positive spiritual attainment (Zopa 2008, p.115).

However, when a patient is in a coma, or the person's breathing continues without awareness, and there is no hope of reviving them, the Dalai Lama suggests that we must act accordingly and with skilful means. He advises, 'When there is no hope left that the person will regain consciousness, or when such hope is unrealistic because what is required to bring this about is too expensive, then it is best to simply say "goodbye"'(Dalai Lama 2001, p.117).

On the topic of organ donation, the usual answer given by Tibetan lamas is that if the wish to donate one's organs carries the motivation of compassion, then any disturbance to the death process that this causes is far outweighed by the positive karma that is created by this act of giving. It is another way in which one can die with a positive and compassionate mind (Hawter 1995).

Hindus believe that life has sanctity. They do not believe that life can be forfeited or made short without due considerations to other concerns. There is a purpose in life that has to be fulfilled. However, by the same token life is not considered to be interminable to the point that the ailing body has to be kept alive by enforced resuscitation, or other artificial means such as life support. In extreme cases, where there is some possibility and promise of life continuing in a dignified form, Hindus will accept an organ donated from another person's body to repair or replace their own. For example, a healthy, living brother may donate his kidney to his sibling who has suffered a kidney failure.

Hindus believe that cremating the body vacated by the deceased retains or re-establishes connection with the released and reconstituting astral body[3] in another realm, where the soul has been taken for a period of rest and healing. Any radical damage caused to the earthly counterpart, such as by harvesting organs for donation or medical research, would affect the constitution of the astral body. An organ removed moments before death would suddenly appear to the astral body as conspicuous by its absence. This would be a cause of some confusion to the spirits attending to the astral body in their attempt to heal any remnant scars or disease from the life just completed. Generally, then, Hindus will not wish to donate their organs, as having a whole corporeal form to be cremated is a key element in the healing process that occurs in the afterlife.

How can we support the spiritual needs of patients suffering from Alzheimer's, dementia or stroke?

As with any suffering person, their moral and spiritual needs and wishes must be supported and enhanced. Most often this is done through keeping prolonged company with the suffering patient and attending to their physical needs, as well as the spiritual practices they are familiar with.

From a Buddhist point of view, there is a clear difference between a person's brain and their mind or consciousness. Inviting members of the Buddhist community to visit the individual, speaking gently with them and engaging in Buddhist practice in close proximity to them, is very beneficial for the patient. Although the gross consciousness of the person is no longer fully functioning, the karmic imprints of hearing the *Dharma* will be retained in the person's subtle consciousness, which is largely unaffected by biological symptoms, such as Alzheimer's or dementia. You can also continue to support the patient by playing CDs of chanting. A Buddhist with Alzheimer's, dementia or stroke can also generate positive karma through engaging in simple acts of rejoicing or generosity. Lama Zopa teaches, 'If you live by cherishing others, when you die you can die with a smile on your lips and a smile in your heart' (Zopa 2008, p.49). The practice of rejoicing may include acknowledging and rejoicing in the kindness of others; if their long-term memory is still clear, rejoicing in the positive deeds they have accomplished over their lifetime; and wishing that all living beings may have happiness and the causes of happiness.

In terms of generosity there are many ways for a patient to generate positive karma, and also improve their well-being. This may include, but is not limited to, simple acts such as the offering of affection and giving food to a 'Pets as Therapy' trained animal; offering flowers to others, or at their own altar. If you have the time or resources you can assist the stroke or Alzheimer's patient to 'dedicate' the positive merit at the end of the day, or after a particular activity, by saying a short prayer together: 'By the merit of these virtuous actions, may I quickly attain enlightenment in order to benefit all sentient beings.'

From a Hindu approach, where cognitive processes are intact or responding sufficiently, efforts are made to introduce the patient to regular exercises (yoga), breathing techniques and mantra recitation that are believed to energise the body. Yoga has been known to yield beneficial results to patients who have suffered from stroke and are trying to regain mobility. It may be a little more difficult and challenging to extend the same to Alzheimer's disease and dementia. The traditional healing system of Ayurveda recommends various herbal and physical remedies, even for advanced illnesses such as these.

What do we need to take into consideration when handling a body after death?

In Buddhism, it is believed that if the consciousness leaves the body of the dead person through the crown or from a higher part of the body, it is likely to result in a good type of rebirth. Conversely, if the consciousness leaves from a lower part of the body this is likely to result in rebirth in one of the lower realms. For this reason, when a person dies it is believed that the first part of the body that should be touched is the crown of the head. To rub or tap this area or gently pull the crown hair after a person dies is regarded as very beneficial and may well help the person to obtain a higher rebirth. There are also special blessed pills that can be placed on the crown after death, which help facilitate this process. Once the consciousness has left the body (which, as mentioned earlier, can take a number of days), it doesn't matter how the body is disposed of or handled, because in effect it has just become an empty shell. However, if the body is disposed of before the consciousness has left, this will obviously be very disturbing for the person who is going through the final stages of psychological dissolution.

Hindus, by and large, do not touch the body of the deceased, more out of fear of polluting the body, or perhaps recalling the soul back to the body, due to attachment. However, there are medical experts, nurses, artisans and experts from certain classes who are allowed, and indeed assigned, the tasks of handling the deceased body, just as our paramedics and funeral home employees or undertakers are trained in preparation toward the final rites.

If there are no Buddhist or Hindu pastoral care workers, monks, nuns or gurus available at the time of death, how can we support a dying Hindu or Buddhist in the best way?

The Dalai Lama offers very simple advice on this subject. He suggests that if you are a religious person, you can sit by the bedside of the Buddhist, reconnect with your own faith and quietly pray. Encourage the patient, if they are able, to generate feelings of faith or loving kindness in their heart. Faith, hope and compassion are qualities each living being has within them, regardless of which religious tradition they follow, if any. These positive states of mind have the power to give strength and spiritual support to the dying person, pacify their mind and open their heart.

Similarly, Hindus are not exclusionists and are welcoming of help, support and spiritual succour from anyone who has the capacity and willingness to offer the same, regardless of their faith or creed, or even non-belief. In such a case, as was experienced by one of the authors of this article, equivalent personnel from other faith traditions can be called in to provide the same kind of support. In the case in question, since the cancer hospital was operated by a Christian-based order, there was a chapel and pastor at hand, who was asked by the family to make regular visits to the patient's bedside. In addition, a Chinese *Qi-gong* master steeped in the Daoist tradition came every day to provide brisk massage, followed by Shinto incantations, after entering into a meditative state himself.

Notes

1. *Dharma*: from Sanskrit root 'dhr' meaning 'to uphold; that which sustains order and balance. More technically, *Dharma* (*Pali dhamma*) refers to the code of social conduct appropriate to one's 'station in life'; also teachings conducive to correct action, norms and universal harmony among all sentient and living beings, and things and non-beings alike.
2. 'Negative karma' is the Indian analogue for 'sin', where the consequence from an untoward action leaves traces that will in time bear negative results.
3. It is the spiritual, ether-like counterpart of the physical body and said to be composed of etheric substance that simulates the physical form that it embodies. This energetic body is attached to the physical body, usually at the chakras, energy centres. The astral body leaves with breath upon the death of the physical body.

Further reading and resources

Bilimoria, P. (1989) *Hinduism in Australia. Mandala for the Gods.* Melbourne: Spectrum Publications with Deakin University Press.

Bilimoria, P. (1997) 'The Australian South Asian Religious Diaspora.' In J. Hinnells (ed.) *A New Handbook of Living Religions.* Oxford/Cambridge, MA: Blackwell Publishers.

Fremantle, F. and Trungpa, C. (1975) *The Tibetan Book of the Dead: The Great Liberation through Hearing in the Bardo.* London: Shambala.

Rinbochay, L. and Hopkins, J. (1979) *Death, Intermediate State and Rebirth in Tibetan Buddhism.* London: Rider & Co.

Rinpoche, S. (1992) *The Tibetan Book of Living and Dying.* London: Rider & Co.

On multicultural palliative care approaches, see the guidelines by Palliative Care Australia, 1999: www.palliativecare. org.au/Portals/46/resources/MulticulturalGuidelines.pdf.

On palliative care approaches for Hindus: http://hinduism.about.com/od/deathdying/a/approachdeath.htm.

For extensive advice on Buddhist practices to complete for the very sick and dying (including prayer books) visit the FPMT website, a worldwide Buddhist organisation affiliated with Lama Zopa Rinpoche. Australian Foundation for the Preservation of Mahayana Tradition (FPMT) centres hold hospice and palliative care courses: www.fpmt.org.

The Buddhist organisation Rigpa, of which Sogyal Rinpoche is director, has an active spiritual care programme in Australia. Visit www.rigpa.com.au/sp_care.htm.

CHAPTER 11

Orthodox Faith: A Lively Spirit for Older People

Rosalie Hudson[1]

Old age is often associated with a diminution of the spirit. Nowhere is this more apparent than in the world of dementia, where people are labelled as 'lost souls' or even 'non-persons'. 'The lights have gone out' is a common metaphor, or 'There's nobody upstairs', or 'Dementia is a living death'. In an age and a culture where rationality reigns supreme, orthodox Christianity reminds us of the spirit which enlivens all who are made in God's image. Writing from the perspective of a son caring for his mother who has Alzheimer's disease, Keck affirms his confidence in orthodox Christianity, where orthodoxy means 'that which seems good' (Keck 1996, p.75). He states further: '*Orthodoxy*, defined broadly as being faithful to the Creeds and Ecumenical Councils, is crucial because it *describes the framework within which we can proceed confidently with faith, hope and love*' (Keck 1996, p.92).[2]

In this chapter the focus is specifically on the frailest of older people and whether faith, hope and love can find a place in the midst of the mysterious malady of dementia. The discussion is grounded in the belief that at the heart of the orthodox faith is the lively spirit of the Trinitarian God whose love enfolds us all, regardless of age or physical or mental capacity. These issues will be explored, particularly from the theological framework of Eastern Orthodoxy, in order to identify some of the implications for the church's worship and pastoral care of older people. The stories of Annie and Bert (fictitious names) challenge us to find within the orthodox faith a way of understanding the location of the spirit and thus the true meaning of persons.

---

1 This chapter is published in extended form as 'Dementia and personhood: a living death or alive in God?' in *Colloquium: The Australian and New Zealand Theological Review 36*, 2, 123–142. It is published here in amended form with the permission of Colloquium: Copyright © 2004.

2 Unless referring to the 'Eastern Orthodox church', 'orthodox' (in lower case) is used throughout this chapter in its general sense of 'correct, in keeping with established tradition'.

In the nursing home it was the evening of our masquerade ball. There was considerable debate as to whether Annie should attend; her behaviour was often inappropriately antisocial, some staff were worried she would become too tired, others were concerned she would become overstimulated. 'She should not miss out' was the opinion that won the day. During a pause in the band's playing and when the wheelchair dancing had stopped, Annie's plaintive cry was heard: 'Where am I? Will somebody please tell me where I am and who I am?'

Annie's quest would not be solved by the most patient repetition of her name and location. Her search for identity could not be equated with a missing article, or her search for meaning with a deficit of information. Through the plaques and tangles of Alzheimer's disease Annie seems to be rehearsing an ontological plea – and who will answer? The first clue is found in the opening chapter of Vladimir Lossky's *Orthodox Theology*, which begins:

> The theologian does not search for God as a man seeks an object; he is seized by Him as one is seized by a person. And it is because he has initially been found by God, because God, one might say, has gone forth to find him in the encounter of revelation, that he can then search for God. (Lossky 1978, p.27)

Translated into the everyday practical realities of Annie's world this means the relationship Annie seeks is personal rather than therapeutic; a yearning for someone to hear her story. To enter her story is to engage with her history; to encounter the mystery of knowledge not dependent on intelligence, rationality or verbal expression. Annie's quest finds its place in the context of everyday lived experience, and is therefore ripe for a lively encounter of her spirit with the spirit of her carers.

Another vignette from the world of dementia sharpens the issue of where a person's spirit is to be found:

Bert has remained in his nursing home bed, mute and immobile, for nine years. No longer able to recognise or to respond to his family in any meaningful way, unable to engage with friends, he is now almost totally deprived of visitors. An old photo, sitting askew on the wall beside his bed, points to a time when he served his country at war. Some faded artificial flowers are the only remnants of the last gift he received. Now, his past means little, as busy nurses clang the bedrails up and down, not infrequently (although unintentionally) tearing his frail skin in the process. Leaking urine and faeces, legs contracted tight together, Bert does not exemplify wholeness or dignity, and many nurses question the value of his existence.

What right to life does Bert have, what is his claim to care? Is he there merely as a recipient of our compassion? What passes between the nurses and Bert as they attend to his needs? Who is this person? When Bert's life is weighed on the scales of quality and dignity he defies logical measurement; he serves no useful purpose, neither does he exhibit any potential. In terms of the health dollar he may be more readily expendable than a 14-year-old awaiting a kidney transplant. Those who are old and suffer the double jeopardy of dementia score very low on the autonomy ladder; they cannot articulate their rights and they have no part in decision-making about their own lives. Furthermore, they show us no gratitude for all our care, so how do we judge whether it is worth it?

Bill Hayden, former governor general of Australia, in his well publicised remarks about people with dementia in nursing homes stated, 'succeeding generations deserve to be disencumbered of some unproductive burdens' (Hayden 1995, p.15). Sadly, the vocabulary of many professional carers is similar: 'Shoot me if I ever get like that!' Bert's family exemplify the common response, 'I can't bear to visit him any more. He's no longer a person. It's just a living death.' And what do *we* say, reflecting our cultural preference for productivity, the glorification of youth and abhorrence of any burden? 'Hope I can just pop a pill when my time comes.'

In response to the view that we should be disencumbered of unproductive burdens, Stanley Hauerwas reminds us how odd it is 'that in the name of eliminating suffering, we eliminate the sufferer', for in so doing we are actually removing our *own* suffering (Hauerwas 1986, p.34). He contends:

> We especially fear, if not dislike, those whose suffering is the kind for which we can do nothing. They are not self-sufficient, they are not self-possessed, they are in need. Even more, they do not evidence the proper shame for being so... It is almost as if they have been given a natural grace to be free from the regret most of us feel for our neediness... We do not like to be reminded of the limits of our power, and we do not like those who remind us. (Hauerwas 1986, p.176)

For Alan Lewis, these realities of infirmity, disability and mortality expose an illusion:

> The truth, which humanity at large is busy denying, is that we all have a *proper* inability to be persons alone, and need others to be our own, free selves. Such freedom entails the risk that others will try to own – or disown – us... And when we banish the dependent to a sub-world of their own, the guilt and fear they expose in us are proof enough that they belong with us in ours. (Lewis 1982, p.16)

What does incapacity, usually measured in terms of deficits, mean in the light of the Son of God assuming human flesh? Can there be a hopeful future for those unable to articulate their faith as present reality? Can life flourish in the presence of this 'living death'? And, when we cease to breathe, are we fully alive in God? The discussion begins with the stories of Annie and Bert, not to exalt them to some special status of the manifestation of the human spirit, but to enquire about the nature of human encounter with God, especially in the absence of coherent thought. Sadly, as the end of the chapter shows, the world of dementia and what it represents is all too often remote from our ecclesial life, theological education and pastoral practice. A lively spirit seems therefore anathema to this particular 'sub-world'.

Annie and Bert prompt us to consider the relationship between those who have become forgetful through disease, and those of us who have 'forgotten' it is the work of the Holy Spirit to bring all things to our remembrance. To explore the question of a lively spirit for older persons is to pursue the ontological question and ask what it means *to be* a person.

Personhood

Maximus the Confessor tells us that God does not know us according to our nature, for that would be to impugn God's freedom; God knows us through God's will (Zizioulas 1975, p.414, n.1). Our *being persons*, therefore, is not dependent on our qualities or capacities. For Zizioulas, personhood is identical with being.

> Personhood is about hypostasis, i.e. the claim to *uniqueness* in the absolute sense of the term, and this cannot be guaranteed by reference to sex or function or role, or even cultivated consciousness of the 'self' and its psychological experiences, since all of these can be *classified*.... (Zizioulas 1991, p.45)

In other words, qualities and capacities can be defined; uniqueness cannot. On this understanding of 'person' we cannot know Annie and Bert by gathering information about them – defining, describing and classifying their individual characteristics. Hence, holistic, 'person-centred' care, despite the well-intentioned claims, remains an illusion. That is not to say individual characteristics are unimportant; rather, we are to see them in a relational context.

Personhood, understood theologically, goes beyond the concepts of 'personalism', 'personal identity' and 'personality', to the relational aspect of who each person is for the other, in freedom. In each person we see not only a part of humanity; we see the whole. This corporate humanity does not detract from the utter uniqueness and unrepeatable nature of each person. Zizioulas puts it more concisely: 'Thus communion does not threaten personal particularity; it is constitutive of it' (Zizioulas 1975, p.409). In another place Zizioulas says, '…nobody seems to recognize that *historically* as well as *existentially* the concept of the person is indissolubly bound up with theology' (Zizioulas 1985, p.27). Furthermore, he says:

> Belief in creation *ex nihilo* – biblical faith – thus encounters belief in ontology – Greek faith – to give to human existence and thought its most dear and precious good, the concept of the person. This and nothing less than this is what the world owes to Greek patristic theology. (Zizioulas 1985, p.65)

The deepest meaning of personhood finds its life in the Triune God, who *is* only in communion. Humanity is not decided *first,* humanity is decided communally in God. Through the personhood of Jesus Christ the communion of all human nature is restored. Through the power of the Holy Spirit we are invited into the Son's communion with the Father. In this Trinitarian drawing near, as David Hart so beautifully expresses it, 'there can be no exile' (Hart 2003, p.323). This is indeed good news for Annie and Bert, for whom a lively spirit is not immediately evident; their spirit can, however, be enlivened through relationships. According to orthodox theology, the nature of our relationships is grounded, not in ourselves, but in the Trinitarian God.

Once separated from the source, a relational understanding of person*hood* can become mere ideology. Alistair McFadyen, who came to study theology from a background in psychiatric nursing, where he developed a concern for the dehumanising way disabled, vulnerable patients were treated, warns against romanticising this analogy through to a model for social relations. The complex world of persons requires much more than a mere relatedness of all things and all people to each other, for mere relatedness offers no basis for ethics or the transcendent factor which constitutes relatedness (McFadyen 1990, p.54). As 'personhood' is not a characteristic of the persons of the Trinity, for they are not 'parts' of God, so personhood is not a 'part' of who we are. As Fatherhood is not a mere property but who God is as Father in Himself, so personhood is not one property of our being (Hart 2003, p.183). And for the Son, Jenson says: 'To speak simply of Jesus the individual as by himself the second identity of God, is an abstraction. For it belongs to the individuality of this someone not to be without others…' (Jenson 2003, p.12). Similarly, to separate the Spirit from the Father and the Son is to relativise and depersonalise the triune relationships. Personhood, separated from who we are in the body of Christ, may therefore be too readily equated with the singular, rather than with the whole of humanity, losing the catholicity of the 'person'. Similarly, to try and locate an older person's 'spirit' apart from their relationships with others is to reduce the human spirit to a mere objective, component part.

Individual

Beginning my nursing research for this subject of personhood some years ago I was interested to note that the databases have no entry under 'person' but refer the researcher to 'individual', indicating that prior to 1988 the reference was under 'personhood'. The subtlety of this change exposes the cultural shift to individualisation; and the implications of this move can only be briefly mentioned in this discussion. One example will suffice.

In the reductionist, bureaucratic world of residential aged care, each individual is compared to every other individual, their deficits and incapacities calculated according to a sophisticated scoring system designed to keep a director of nursing bound to her computer and away from any interpersonal engagement with residents and families, in order to do the sums to maximise the funding to provide the staffing to give the care. Funding is based on the relative care needs of each person. Such a departure from the meaning of person can only be characterised by the architects of this system, who call the residents of the institution neither person nor individual but 'care recipients'. The intention is certainly not to dehumanise; it is, however, a far cry from the understanding of each person being discussed here. As unique persons, our spirits fully alive in God, we are no longer defined by our idiosyncratic differences or similarities; we are the *recipients*, not merely of care but of glory and grace. We are made whole not merely by therapeutic intervention; we are created anew. That is why, says Alisdair MacIntyre, benevolence is insufficient as a means to care, for it generally presents us with a generalised other – 'one whose only relationship to us is to provide an occasion for the exercise of *our* benevolence' (MacIntyre 1999, p.119). When we regard any person as the recipient even of our compassion or charity, we also regard their existence as a *cost* to the community and not a *benefit*; they forever remain apart from us in the artificial distinction of 'them' and 'us'. This compromises for us all, the true locus of a lively spirit – our being alive in God. Being classified as 'recipients' also presumes a one-way relationship where the person receiving care has no reciprocal capacity to contribute to the relationship.

Image and likeness

To be fully alive in God is not to make ourselves at one with ourselves or at one with the world – a state which the person with dementia finds impossible to achieve, appearing *not to be at one* with any one or any thing – but to be distinguished from the cosmos and likened to the Creator (Lossky 1978, p.119). To attain this likeness is to be crowned with grandeur and beauty; to become *one* as God – Father, Son and Holy Spirit – are one. This is to be clothed in a way that covers even the confusion of not knowing what our own clothes are for. This takes us into a mystery, where nature and grace are not divided but interpenetrative. Lossky says:

> The image of God in man, as far as it is authentic, is, according to St Gregory of Nyssa, necessarily unknowable, for, reflecting the plenitude of its prototype, it too must possess the unknowability of the divine being… What corresponds in us to God's image is not a part of our nature, but the person including nature in itself. (Lossky 1978, pp.123, 127)

Can the image be lost? This is a pressing question, not only in relation to the person with dementia who seems to have lost everything, but for those of us who so often 'lose it' or simply 'don't get it'. To enjoy the plenitude of God's love and grace is to rest assured in the knowledge that this gift of God's image in us is indestructible (Lossky 1978, p.128). Thus, orthodox faith provides us with some clues about how an apparently diminished spirit may be enlivened. While the source of our spirit lies beyond our human capacity to know and understand, the mystery is enfleshed in the way we relate to one another. As Jenson says:

> I am dependent for my humanity on yours. And that is a risky bet. There is not only risk here; there is mystery. For if I am dependent upon your humanity for mine, on whom are you dependent for yours? On me… We wait endlessly for the word of love: each of us from the other, for none of us dares to speak it first… And so I wait, and so do you, and the word of love is not spoken, to which our humanity would be the response. (Jenson 1995, pp.29–30)

To live out this image towards those unlike ourselves is a challenge to our natural proclivities, for as Lossky says, 'The love that God claims is not physical magnetism, but the living tension of opposites' (Lossky 1978, p.72). We may not be drawn instinctively towards Annie or Bert; the spirit that enlivens us comes from another place. Hart sees an 'unsettling prodigality' in the way God 'takes pleasure' in affirming difference and otherness, even in the most unattractive and even atrocious of settings (Hart 2003, p.15). Furthermore, he says:

every face becomes an icon: a beauty that is infinite. If the knowledge of the light of the glory of God is given in the face of Jesus (2 Corinthians 4:6), it is a knowledge that allows every other face to be seen in the light of that glory. (Hart 2003, pp.343–344)

A lively spirit, therefore, is not located in some ethereal world of unreality, but in the concrete presence, the face-to-face encounter of everyday life, where we also find those least like ourselves. How do we respond when confronted by an 'other' who seems totally strange and with whom there appears to be no common language?

David Malouf, in *An Imaginary Life*, fictionalises the journey of the Roman poet Ovid who, in exile, encounters a wild boy, brought up among wolves in the snow. Gradually, the role of protector and protected are reversed as the two form a touching alliance. Ovid wrestles with the problem of befriending this boy, unattractive in every sense. How can he relate to this strange child with no language? How can he share a meal with this creature who, like many a person with dementia, fails to distinguish between fork and food? Ovid says:

> I think and think. What must the steps be? How should I begin? Kindness, I know, is the way – and time. To reveal to him first what our kindness is, what our kind is; and then to convince him that we belong to the same kind. It is out of this that he must discover what he is. (Malouf 1978, p.77)

Ovid, choosing never to return to the familiar, distinctive, defining language of Rome, must now find a new language.

> The language I am speaking of now, that I am almost speaking, is a language whose every syllable is a gesture of reconciliation. We knew that language once. I spoke it in my childhood. We must discover it again. (Malouf 1978, p.98)

'Kindness' is a word suggestive of a lively spirit. As Malouf implores us to rediscover this language of kindness, orthodox Christianity reminds us to receive the gift of love, in freedom. 'This state obviously can only be realised from outside human existence. The whole of Christian doctrine ought to be precisely about this' (Zizioulas 1975, p.433).

A lively spirit for older people does not reside in our usual understanding of time and place. So the question about when the spirit has left the person or when 'the lights went out' is, in the light of orthodox faith, put in a different context. We are already enlivened by the Holy Spirit who, in very personal terms, knows our weaknesses and encourages us to live in a new reality. In the light of these images can we tell the time, particularly to those for whom a clock no longer has meaning – but also to ourselves, for whom the clock assumes *all* meaning? It seems that to tell the time afresh is to live a life of love, not in the moral sense but the ontological. This renewed state of being is not of our making, but comes from God, with whom and in whom we are formed anew.

> For we do not merely meet God face to face, but are formed by God's hands in ineffable proximity; embraced by word and spirit. God does not merely talk and appear: he touches, grasps, shapes and models. (Osborn 2001, p.92)

Perhaps it is this touching, grasping, shaping and modelling that allows us to engender a lively spirit of faith, hope and love in our relationships with the older people in our care.

Rationality and a lively spirit

In *Dependent, Rational Animals* MacIntyre makes a correction to his earlier works in acknowledgement of his failure adequately to treat the subject of vulnerability and dependence on others. He claims the history of Western moral philosophy has also been negligent:

> From Plato to Moore and since there are usually, with some rare exceptions, only passing references to human vulnerability and affliction and to the connections between them and our dependence on others... And when the ill, the injured and the otherwise disabled *are* presented in the pages of moral philosophy books, it is almost always exclusively as possible subjects of benevolence by moral agents who are themselves presented as though they were continuously rational, healthy and untroubled. So we are invited, when we do think of disability, to think of 'the disabled' as 'them,' as other than 'us,' as a separate class, not as ourselves as we have been, sometimes are now and may well be in the future. (MacIntyre 1999, pp.1–2)

Peter Singer would argue, however, that rational capacity is essential to personhood. By these criteria Annie and Bert would fail the test; along with the foetus and the fish; according to Singer, they meet the definition of *non-persons* (Singer 1994, p.183). Such a view not only kills the spirit of relationships with frail older people; it can quickly lead to the involuntary killing of the people themselves. As Swinton argues:

> This leaves us with the rather odd situation wherein human beings can be persons for 60, 70, 80 years, and live under the protection of this particular notion of personhood, only to find themselves living out their final years as non-persons who suddenly (or gradually) become less worthy of moral attention and protection. (Swinton 2008, p.25)

Similarly, Stephen Post argues that in this 'hypercognitive' culture dementia is an affront to our values. Is this really 'life unworthy of life'? Are those who are deeply forgetful mere 'shells' or 'husks' of humanity; does forgetfulness dissolve the autobiographical narrative of our lives (Post 2004, pp.12–14)? Does our ability to think really constitute who we are? If we follow the Cartesian dictum ('I think, therefore I am'), where does that leave those who appear incapable of rational thought?

The Psalmist here corrects our perspective: 'How precious to me are *thy* thoughts, O God, how vast is the sum of them' (Psalm 139:17–18; emphasis added) Waking or sleeping, conscious or unconscious, even in Sheol, the place of forgetfulness and dust, God remembers us. Meilaender warns against exaggerating our ability to be the authors of our own lives, and recalls St Augustine's famous discussion on memory: 'How great, my God, is this force of memory, how exceedingly great… Who has ever reached the bottom of it? Yet this is a faculty of my mind and belongs to my nature; nor can I myself grasp all that I am' (Meilaender 2003, p.24).

This very brief excursus into memory and time takes us now to the eschatological and doxological world of worship.

Worship

Christians at worship practise 'who we are becoming' and in so doing 'engage in a variety of practices that are constitutive of and normative for the identity of Christian persons and communities… Thus, the church imprints upon its people the memory of who and whose it is' (Anderson 2003, pp.31, 41). What practices are appropriate for those who do not know their own name, let alone have the necessary forms of words to give praise to God? What does belonging to the body mean for the person who has forgotten how the body functions? What does it mean to be offered the body and blood of Christ in the service of Holy Communion when the person has forgotten how to eat or drink? What does their involvement in worship mean, when the person lacks liturgical etiquette? Here, recalling the instruction of Gregory of Nazianzus, 'Thy attuning teacheth the choir and the worlds to adore Thee in musical silence', Dietrich Bonhoeffer reiterates: 'Teaching about Christ begins in silence… We must study Christology in the humble silence of the worshipping community' (Bonhoeffer 1966, p.27). For orthodox faith this is the true meaning of doxology or 'right praise'.

In the church's worship, and supremely in the Eucharist, we rehearse that adoration, to be shared with the whole world, including those whose tangled brain cells prevent them from remembering what it means. Perhaps we would welcome the voiceless and the forgetful to the Lord's Table if we remembered that the Eucharist is a sacrament of remembrance, not for the purpose of providing a personal, subjective experience but to unite us, in all our differences and personal alienations, into one body. In this unique body the suffering of one is the suffering of all. The *anamnesis* (remembrance) of the Eucharist is no mere psychological recollection, but an ontological transformation, independent of our fragile memories, made possible by the gift of the Holy Spirit. When the Holy Spirit aids our remembrance we are truly remembered. This signifies profound hope for those who are *de-mented*; who may now in Christ become *re-mented, re-minded* and *re-membered*.

To remember who we are, with and for one another in the *koinonia* or fellowship of the church, is to remember also our baptism, of which Lathrop says:

> It is a great leveler. The learned are welcome, so are the unlearned. The adults are washed as if they were children, to be carried and clothed. *Infantes,* they are called 'speechless,' the 'newborn,' the 'sucklings'. And the children are baptized as if they were adults, addressed, asked questions, given great promises. In some communities, the children are even regarded as models of faith since they so utterly rest in the arms that carry them and are given the words that surround them. (Lathrop 1993, p.60)

To be given the words that surround them removes from those who have no words or memory, the burden of individual recollection. Lathrop's description of speechless infants is not intended to suggest that people with dementia are to be infantilised. This recollection on the part of the whole body of Christ remains a hopeful sacrament for the voiceless of any age. When the pastor who encounters such people is at a loss for words, he or she can do no better than to recall the continued work of the Spirit, present at the time of the person's baptism and no less present when all memory has faded, or even in death. This attitude requires of those of us who consider ourselves healthy and whole, to recall not only the times when as infants we were totally dependent (and at other times also); but to recall that in all the sacraments of the church we come as sinners along with the most needy, in total dependence on the one whose grace alone sustains us.

There are other elements of worship (which can only be briefly alluded to here) appropriate for people with dementia and their families. The ministry of confession, absolution and forgiveness is surely not confined to those who can speak? And what of the sacrament of healing? For Schmemann, the 'sacrament of oil' is to be understood neither as the 'last rites' nor as a 'useful "complement" to secular medicine'; it is a *passage* not into supernature but into the 'very reality of this world and its life as redeemed and restored by Christ' (Schmemann 2003, pp.105–106). However, these ministries are seldom offered to those in nursing homes, with or without dementia.

Within such ministries the place of music, and of prayer, is also important. Carers of older people are familiar with the phenomenon of those who cannot utter a lucid sentence, yet will join in singing hymns, or reciting words of the liturgy. On the subject of prayer for and with these persons, I recall one confident and creative chaplain who was not afraid of attracting surprise, incomprehension or even ridicule, as she would boldly repeat the prayers of the church at the bedside of those who did not appear to offer a flicker of response. On the other hand, I recall a chaplain in similar circumstances who voiced his own lack of confidence when asked by the family to pray: 'Well, of course she can't hear and she doesn't understand but I suppose it can't do any harm.' Thus the 'spirit of the age', in giving priority to cognition and rationality, fails to express adequately the true spirit of ageing (Hudson 2004, p.91). An enlivened spirit will encourage us to welcome more intentionally into our ecclesial life those who are inarticulate, or incapacitated in other ways.

In a Trinitarian understanding of personhood, we are free for each other, not merely as those who choose to relate to one another on grounds of natural magnetism, but as those who are *unlike* each other. As the Son of God comes to earth to unite his perfect humanity to our proud and rebellious existence, we as mere creatures are enfolded by the power of the Spirit into the life and love of the Father. To share this life is to bear the burden of our neighbour. To belong to Christ's body is to share God's purpose for creation, where all distinctions between weak and strong, first and last, patient and healer are turned upside down, where relating to each other is the unself-conscious consequence of the life we all receive as a gift. And so, the natural outworking of worship is a lively spirit of pastoral care.

Pastoral care

Schmemann calls for a recovery of the *pastoral* dimension of theology, which, together with the missionary and prophetic dimensions, has always signified the essential link, particularly in Eastern Orthodoxy, between dogma and experience, church and life. When theology becomes pastoral it becomes 'attentive to the real needs of man, when, putting aside the academic "straining at a gnat" which has never prevented anyone from "swallowing a camel", it accepts, in humility and with courage, its proper function in the Church' (Schmemann 1979, p.122). Ritschl also calls for a renewal of the inseparable tasks of worship and pastoral care: what we need is 'a new search for the correlation of prayer and thinking and a more radical

understanding of the priestly or vicarious task of the Church for others…
for it is obvious that *nature and grace, reason and faith, scholarship and piety,
theology and doxology, historical past and existential present have been separated from
each other*' (Ritschl 1967, p.xiii).

It is necessary here to draw a distinction between *kerygma* (proclamation)
and therapy. The latter, says Alan Torrance, is typified by the culture of
narcissism. 'It is to make man's concern with his own existence the ground
of one's proclamation of the kerygma when it is precisely this "attitude" of
self-concern from which contemporary man needs to be freed' (Torrance
1987, p.495). Similarly, Helmut Thielicke's cogent comment: 'When the
final authority resides in me, or more precisely, in my intelligible ego, I no
longer need to receive the Word which binds and looses me, because I now
speak that word myself' (Thielicke 1960, p.13). Perhaps the person with
dementia is already freed from this kind of narcissistic self-concern; the
propensity to psychologise and the attempt to find wholeness through self-
justification. Perhaps the person with dementia can teach us the meaning of
grace: the wholly unmerited love of God.

The person with dementia is usually excluded from the ubiquitous
verbatim, which finds its place in some CPE (Clinical Pastoral Education)
programmes as the ultimate test of meaningful pastoral care. Again, the
spirit of the age makes the pastoral encounter dependent on words. We
are encouraged, nevertheless, by Bonhoeffer's comments in *Spiritual Care*,
that many a true pastoral encounter occurs through our hesitant words and
imperfect actions (Bonhoeffer 1985, pp.36–37). 'The church's pastoral care,
in all its frailty, bears witness to the transcendent reality that we are not
our own; we are not alone' (Hudson 2000, p.12). There is no body/soul
division here; prayers for healing of the body are accompanied by prayers
of confession and forgiveness of sins. The kerygmatic truth of pastoral care
is therefore not to be confused with superficial comfort or psychological
therapy.

Associated with aids to remembrance is the ministry of *reminiscence,*
described by Elizabeth MacKinlay as an enjoyable experience for those
who engage in such supportive presence with older people (MacKinlay
2006, pp.81–95). The spirit of liveliness is evident as the process moves the
conversation to a deeper level, enabling an exploration of life's meaning,
even for those whose ability to communicate is compromised by dementia.

One can hardly focus on the orthodox faith as a lively spirit for older
persons without discussing death. Comments here are of necessity confined
to a very few; nevertheless they are intended to follow logically from the
previous discussion on worship and pastoral care.

Death

For the Eastern Orthodox church, resurrection and ascension are already 'in' death. What is communicated in the silence of Christ's descent to death is the glorious hope of resurrection, the time when we will truly be ourselves. Gregory of Nyssa reminds us that in the death of Jesus Christ, an unbroken communication occurred:

> He knitted together again the disunited elements, cementing them, as it were, together with the cement of His divine power, and recombining what has been severed in a reunion never to be broken. And this is the Resurrection. (Guroian 2000, p.128)

What does a pastor have to say in response to Bert's daughter who, at the funeral of her father, said: 'This funeral commenced for me nine years ago when the dementia was diagnosed'? Can a lively spirit be found in such seemingly deathly circumstances? Schmemann warns against the sentimental nonsense we hear at so many funeral services where an all-out effort is made to convince people that suffering and pain are now over because the loved one is now in a better place, an 'other world' where, in contrast to this vale of tears, all is well. Recalling Christ at the tomb of Lazarus, Schmemann says:

> Christ does not say all those things we do in our pathetic and uncomforting attempts to console. In fact he says nothing – he weeps. And then, according to the Gospels, he raises his friend, that is, he restores him into that life from which we are supposedly to find liberation toward a higher good. (Schmemann 2003, p.25)

Christ, in his weeping, 'reveals his own struggle with death, his refusal to acknowledge it and to come to terms with it' (Schmemann 2003, p.30).

By contrast, and in the spirit of the age, we want to come to terms with death; hence the burgeoning grief and loss industry, the renewed interest in thanatology and the recent inclusion in tertiary palliative care courses of a subject called 'death education'. Death, as the last enemy, is not a natural part of life; it is not therefore to be welcomed, as a mere slipping from one room into the next, as some sentimental funeral poetry indicates. 'God did not make death, and he does not delight in the death of the living' (Wisdom 1:13). Schmemann asks why the world has become 'a kind of cosmic cemetery, a place where a collection of people condemned to death live either in fear or terror, or in their efforts to forget about death find themselves rushing around one great big burial plot' (Schmemann 2003, pp.11–12). A 'living death' is a universal phenomenon; not confined to those suffering from dementia. 'Get a life,' we urge one another, not recognising the fatal flaw of our desire. Then, if that fails, and in order to console ourselves, we construct a world where we can find a new spirit within ourselves. Orthodox faith reminds us that a true and lively spirit is not of our own making; it can, however, be claimed, by grace, as a reality both in this life and the next.

Conclusion

Returning to Annie's question: *Where am I? Will someone please tell me where I am and who I am?* I suggest we cannot rely on a common pastoral premise that the starting point must always be where the person is 'at', for we have no idea where Annie is 'at'. So, how on earth do we help her? Perhaps it's to heaven we should look, to the risen and ascended man, Jesus Christ, who alone knows where any of us is at, and in that knowing stands beside us in all the frailty of our forgetfulness. This does not mean our 'heavenly gaze' is divorced from the realities of everyday, practical care. It means that, for Christians, our calling is to be 'in Christ'; this *being* is grounded in *doing* the Father's will, which is nothing less than standing alongside our neighbour – whoever and wherever that person may be – in solidarity and with compassion. We do this, not in our own strength, but by the power of the Holy Spirit. True neighbourliness comes to expression in the unself-conscious *doing* through which we meet Annie and Bert as one human *being* to another.

So, what is the basis for hope when words and memory fail? We remember it is the Holy Spirit who takes to the Father all our feeble, half formed utterances. From this perspective, the pastor or professional carer is no more capable than the person with dementia, for we are all prone to forget *whose* we are – to whom we belong. The poverty of our own spirit is enriched by the overflowing love and grace of God, manifest in Jesus Christ through the power of the Holy Spirit. Orthodox faith reminds us that we are enfolded into the abundant fellowship of love which is the Holy Trinity; not for God's sake, but for the sake of the world. In the context of older people and particularly those with dementia who are so often forgotten because they cannot remember, this is indeed good news. Rather than enduring a 'living death sentence', Orthodox faith embodies a lively spirit of hope for the frailest of the frail. This is good news for the whole of humanity, where no one is considered less worthy than another.

CHAPTER 12

Cultural Diversity in Aged Care: A Showcase of Services Tailored to Meet the Physical, Cultural and Spiritual Needs of People of Greek Origin

Robyn Simmonds and Nicholas Stavropoulos

History of St Basil's Homes

St Basil's Homes is named after St Basil the Great, Bishop of Cappadocia in Asia Minor, who founded a town for the aged, orphaned and infirm in the fourth century. He is recognised as setting the prototype for highly organised social welfare provided by the church, in the spirit of early Christian charity as Christ intended. Our organisation has St Basil and his work as a role model.

St Basil's Homes is an Aged Care Provider that has operated in Sydney since the late 1960s under the Greek Orthodox Archdiocese of Australia. Our services began with a nursing home in Wentworth Falls and two boarding houses. In 1972 we were allocated 220 beds by the Commonwealth Government and soon afterwards, in 1976 and 1980, we commissioned our first two hostels. Whilst we accommodated many Greek residents, we also provided care services to the mainstream community. In 1989 we built the first Greek culturally specific nursing home in Sydney, which now provides high care residential accommodation for 110 frail aged residents, including a 19-bed dementia unit. Today we also provide a centre-based respite programme for Greek clients, offering culturally appropriate meals and activities. In addition, we provide community packages for frail aged people living in the community, offering them the opportunity to receive all levels of care in their homes. In all these services we are catering to general, culturally specific and special needs groups. The organisation operates out of Sydney's Inner West, South West and South East, where the majority of residential and community services are situated. These areas have been identified as having higher densities of people of Greek descent.

Our newest facility, 'Hellenic Village', is at Miranda in the Sutherland Shire. This project provides 40 self-care units and a 100-bed residential aged care facility, facilitating ageing in place and dementia-specific care.

So why is it important to provide culturally appropriate residential aged care and services?

In developing our residential and community care services to meet the needs of the Greek community, and other culturally diverse populations, we have been conscious of the cultural barriers in our community regarding access to such services. Historically, the culture of caring for one's parents was written into ancient Greek law, with significant penalties within most of the city states for those failing to fulfil this obligation. To this day, within the Greek community, there is an ongoing expectation that families will care for their parents as they age. This was evident in the initial response and resistance when we commissioned our nursing home, in 1989. Frail aged people of Greek descent living in Australia felt that they should be looked after at home by their families, and that by going to a nursing home, they were being turned out of their homes. Furthermore, it is our experience that the families of the clients feel anxious and guilty about placing their parents in a nursing home. We have also found this to be the case for other migrant groups, such as the Italians and the Chinese, as indicated by these groups in consultation with St Basil's.

Providing a culturally appropriate environment and a culturally sensitive approach to care services, right from the start, broke down these barriers. We facilitated opportunities for family members to be actively involved in the care of their parent or loved one. The quick result was a significant waiting list for our residential care, which remains to this day. St Basil's current waiting list times for the nursing home ranges from six months to three years, depending on sex and care needs.

What do we mean by providing culturally appropriate aged care?

We have created an environment in our nursing home that reflects the cultural and religious experiences and values of our residents. At St Basil's we have used many strategies, in particular in our nursing home, to create and nurture a comfortable and familiar environment and home for our residents.

Familiar colours, light and outdoor spaces

The first special feature is the design of the nursing home as a built environment. With the assistance of an interior designer of Greek heritage, we have planned a homely interior, with large windows and plenty of light, bright Mediterranean colour schemes and warm, inviting lounge rooms. Residents and families love the outdoors, and reflecting on the summers in Greece where everyone loves to live outside. So we include in the nursing home many outside spaces, with shaded courtyards and colourful garden beds. We create a familiar and enjoyable environment where our residents can sit and relax. In our dementia unit we have a lovely olive grove and a sensory garden, providing pleasant outdoor surroundings. For many older Greek people, especially men, being able to tend the earth and grow plants is important; some courtyards have been designed with raised garden beds and pots, so that residents can tend their own plants.

A central gathering place

We have a number of small, intimate lounge rooms throughout our nursing home. However, the focus of the home is a large lounge room. It is a pleasant, relaxing space for our residents and their families. This room is a hive of activity. It is the central hub of our home – familiar like a village plaza. It is the central area of activities each day, where there is the aroma of freshly brewed coffee, delicious food, music, chatting and lively activity with people. It is a sharing place where families, grandchildren and friends gather with residents and enjoy each others' company. Family and friends often bring in food to share, not only with residents, but with each other too. In the adjoining kitchenette they make Greek coffee or just sit around and chat, listening to music or watching Greek TV together. It is a place where family and friends feel welcome, and where residents feel they are still part of a community.

Familiar sounds

Traditional Greek music is a key part of life in the lounge room. On many days there are cultural activities, entertainment, live music and dancing. We have regular groups who volunteer to come in and entertain our residents – these range from children from Greek schools in Sydney, to professional singers and dancers.

Familiar special events

Within our nursing home, the observation and celebration of cultural and religious days with prayers and celebrations is an important part of regular life. Easter is a particularly significant part of the Greek Orthodox faith, and residents participate actively in church services, prayers and festivities. For example, during Lent, there are multiple weekly opportunities for worship in the chapel with hymns, prayers, colours and smells that awaken the mind and stir the soul of residents and their families as they prepare for Easter.

One of the activities which residents enjoy is to paint and crack the traditional red eggs at Easter. We also enjoy celebrating Greek National Day and Australia Day. On Greek National Day we take a number of residents into the city by bus for the annual celebrations at the Opera House. We celebrate saints' days, namedays, birthdays and other traditions, such as Mother's Day and Father's Day.

Such opportunities for reminiscence are effective only if they are culturally and spiritually appropriate. Placing a resident in a situation where they are exposed to unfamiliar traditions and activities leads to a sense of loneliness and alienation.

Familiar food

The food we provide is paramount in creating a familiar and enjoyable living environment for our residents. All our meals are freshly cooked and culturally specific, using authentic Greek recipes. We have our own kitchen on site, which means that while food is being cooked, the aromas drift around the home. This stimulates the appetite of residents (and often the staff!). In this way our residents enjoy not only healthy and nutritious meals each day, but also meals that are tasty and familiar to them. Many of our residents have indicated that the tastes, textures and smells rekindle memories of happy times in their past. Apart from giving sustenance, culturally appropriate meals offer pleasure and comfort within their home, which is now St Basil's. People gather together to share meals and each meal starts with a prayer. This, again, reflects their life-long traditions and values.

It is not unusual, at Christmas or Easter, for there to be a barbecue with lemon- and oregano-scented lamb. The tables are decorated with traditional sweetened breads. The predominant and very familiar colours at this time are red and white. Shortbreads dusted with icing sugar are brought in by visitors and are offered to anyone caring to satisfy their sweet tooth.

Interestingly, seafood is not a traditional food at these times for Greek people, as it might be for people of other cultures. Seafood is eaten by Greek people during the Lenten fast, as an act of discipline and cleansing, so the last thing our residents would want is seafood at the time when they are meant to break the fast and eat meat for the first time in 40 days.

One of the challenges we face at St Basil's is persuading the elderly not to fast when it is detrimental to their health and well-being. In these situations, it usually takes the intervention of the priest to convince them that in their case they are not expected to fast.

Some of the menu items one might observe at meal times at St Basil's include:

1. *spanakopita* (spinach and feta in pastry)

2. lentils, beans and other legumes

3. *youvarlakia* (meatballs cooked in a white, lemony egg soup)

4. moussaka (baked aubergine, mince and potato layers)

5. *souvlaki* (marinated lamb pieces on skewers)

6. *pasticcio* (mince and pasta and bechamel sauce, layered and baked)

7. *loukoumades* (deep-fried honey puffs)

8. *yalaktobouriko* (custard and filo pastry steeped in syrup)

9. taramasalata (caviar dip) – and of course

10. olives and feta.

Needless to say all our food is cooked using olive oil.

Familiar entertainment

St Basil's provides access to 24-hour Greek satellite TV in every resident's room, as well as in the lounge areas. This means that all our residents can watch TV beamed directly from Athens at any time. This includes news services, documentaries, church services, chat shows and golden oldies from the Greek film industry of the 1950s.

We have weekly sing-alongs with volunteer musicians playing Greek songs of the 1930s, 40s and 50s. It is not unusual for staff to stop their work and join in with singing, and even dancing. What a sight is it to see residents, staff, visitors and performers all belting out a favourite old song!

During major festivities, student choirs from the schools of our church and other choirs, such as those of other Greek community groups, take turns in sharing performances of choral and dramatic entertainment. Afterwards, these guests move through the home talking with residents and exchanging stories. The atmosphere is one of excitement and laughter. Residents' sincere gratitude and emotions overflow, and some will go over to the microphone and offer a vote of thanks to the performers.

Familiar language

We have a large number of Greek staff who are able to communicate with residents and families. In the words of one of our residents, 'It's very important to have someone who speaks my language.' These staff include domestic, nursing and maintenance staff. Some of our nursing staff are not of Greek descent, but through learning and familiarity can now communicate with residents in Greek. In our dementia unit we ensure that all staff working directly with residents are Greek-speaking. As is commonly known, most residents living with dementia have lost a substantial part of the English language that they may have acquired. In addition, to ensure further that our residents are comfortable and do not feel isolated, we have organised Greek lessons for new non-Greek-speaking staff. In this way, they can at least communicate everyday greetings and process simple requests in a language that is familiar to our residents. The take-up rate by staff has been high. Speaking Greek enables staff to respect and reinforce the cultural values at St Basil's. Understanding Greek helps them in their endeavour to observe the old traditions that are so important to our residents; in the words of one of our long-term staff members, 'this is their home; we just work here'.

Everyone should join in!

We encourage spouses, children and other family members and friends of our residents to be involved and join in our celebrations and special days. To allay their anxieties about having one or both of their parents in a nursing home, many are actively involved in the life of the home, visiting regularly and for many hours. We have a small number of relatives who stay with their loved one all day, from early in the morning until after dinner.

The church in our life

At the heart of St Basil's is our on-site, centrally located Greek Orthodox chapel, where we hold regular services for residents and families. In the Greek community, daily life goes hand-in-hand with the church. By having an on-site chapel, with regular services and extra services on special days, we have merged the physical and spiritual world of our residents and families within the home. The familiar sounds of our singing, readings and prayers, the smell of incense during our services, the taste and feel of the blessed bread, and the traditional words used are a comfort to all. In particular, for many of our residents with dementia the familiar words, songs and aromas in our services trigger a cognitive response. Residents who have lost verbal skills in other contexts often join in the familiar words and prayers in our chapel services. In addition, the on-site chapel provides a quiet place where people can sit, reflect, pray, light a candle, as is customary in our culture, just as some of them would have done in their youth in Greece.

Residents at St Basil's have 24-hour on-site access to presbyters of the Greek Orthodox faith. Father Nicholas Stavropoulos, the Chief Executive Officer (CEO), is also appointed on the executive, so that the organisation meets not only the care and service needs of the residents, but also their spiritual needs. Father Nicholas is very visible in the nursing home amongst residents, visitors and staff. As part of the executive, he manages administrative tasks in the operation of the services, conducts services in the chapel and spends valuable time walking around the home, greeting and speaking to residents and their families several times each day. He also provides spiritual support for residents, their families and our staff. This pastoral and spiritual care has been crucial in building the trust of residents and their families in the organisation and all that it stands for. It has also built trust and confidence in the management and operation of the home in providing a quality care service for residents, and meeting physical, emotional and spiritual needs.

Residents in palliative care often prefer to remain in their home with their family around them

At St Basil's we have made available a palliative care room, to enable residents to be cared for in the home, if they do not need or want to be in the unfamiliar and clinical surroundings of a hospital. Again, this is an important cultural initiative, nurturing traditional family values and choices, where loved ones would prefer to die in their home. This palliative care room provides privacy and a quiet space for family members to come and go as they need, with the provision to stay all night. Often, after a resident has died, the family chooses to have their funeral service in our chapel. When funeral services are held in the chapel, staff who have cared for the resident often request to attend the service, where they form a guard of honour, escorting the deceased resident from the chapel and their 'home' for the last time.

What has all this meant for our residents?

Overwhelmingly our residents feel that they are in a comfortable, familiar home environment, well cared for physically, emotionally and spiritually. The provision of centre-based respite care, hostel and nursing home care on one site means that many residents are able to move from one level of care to the next as necessary, all within a familiar environment. This has enabled a more comfortable and smooth transition for clients and families, from community-based care into residential care.

The words of the daughter of one of our residents, Marianthi, sum up best what St Basil's is about. Marianthi died at 87 after living with dementia. Marianthi's daughter wrote that she found it a great comfort to watch her mother settle into a lifestyle in which she was totally at ease.

> Each day is full of joy, laughter and a sense of connection with all those around her. She has grown familiar with her surroundings and has become part of the extended family at St Basil's. St Basil's offers Marianthi all that she had lost over the past few years of her illness. Once again she can experience being part of a family unit within a Greek framework. She can communicate all her needs and requests, she can comprehend all that is said to her and appreciate a joke... Her day is full of common practices to Marianthi, which were very much part of her daily life: like prayer before meals, listening to church services on the radio, chatting to fellow residents while in the lounge room, visiting the hairdresser, who speaks Greek (as personal grooming has always been important to her)... The stimulating, friendly and caring environment has been a great contributing factor to Marianthi's assimilation into life at St Basil's and to the even nature of her temperament. She no longer expresses anger and frustration... But the chapel at St Basil's is where Marianthi likes to be most of all, especially participating in the services. She recalls all hymns and recites verses out loud, reliving what was near and dear to her heart. For Marianthi, being part of a church community and celebrating the Orthodox faith fulfils her greatest needs and makes life meaningful and satisfying.

Our management supports culturally inclusive service

Our service is supported and guided by management and a Board which understands culturally specific needs and the values that underpin our programmes. The Board's leadership has supported and contributed to our success in providing a culturally appropriate residential aged care home. Our Board members, all of Greek heritage, bring a depth of understanding to the St Basil's philosophy of culturally appropriate care. They fully understand and are completely committed to the responsibility of providing culturally relevant care and services to the frail aged and their relatives. This commitment requires a passion and energy over and above the responsibilities of being a quality aged care provider. These qualities are evident throughout the organisation.

In addition, St Basil's management is well supported by the Greek Orthodox Archdiocese of Australia and the Archbishop, who is the president of St Basil's Homes in Australia. In addition, St Basil's is well supported by other Greek organisations in Sydney, including St Andrew's Theological College and the Greek Welfare Centre. Referrals to our services come from 35 parishes all over Sydney, as well as from organisations within our community.

In fact, St Andrew's Theological College students participate in a recognised clinical pastoral education programme with St Basil's as part of their undergraduate and postgraduate studies, which provides emotional and spiritual support to both residents and families. The students of St Andrew's visit each week, supervised by their lecturer/mentor, and participate in practical pastoral interaction with residents in the home. The success of the programme is evident in the close relationships developed by students and residents and the fact that these relationships continue even after the course has been completed. Residents have been greatly encouraged and nurtured through many different experiences, some joyful and some tragic. Not only have the students and residents built relationships of trust and faith, but life values have been recognised and honoured from both perspectives.

In addition to attaining additional qualifications in their college education, students also have the opportunity to learn from residents about the challenges and joys of ageing, within a wide realm of practical and spiritual dimensions. These life lessons are invaluable to them as they prepare to enter parish work within the wider community and within an ageing population. As young priests they are better equipped to communicate and understand the situations facing the elderly in their parishes, where they will have more confidence in dealing with issues of isolation, depression and illness. Many colleges prepare students for work in many areas of youth and social ministry, but there is often a lack of specific training for students to work with the elderly, and particularly those of culturally specific background.

What are the key lessons from our experience at St Basil's for other communities?

The main lessons from our experiences in working with the Greek community concern the developing, maintaining and nurturing of the traditions of that same community. At the same time we have to meet the care needs of people in ways they understand, appreciate and value. It is so very important not to disregard what has been important to people all their lives. We are obliged to provide for them surroundings with which they are familiar, activities which they appreciate and values with which they identify.

We have been able to bring our residents and their families together as a whole community. We have done this through the warmth and vitality of life in our homes, the love of family and friends, music and good food, the opportunity for spiritual counsel, common worship, and the comfort derived from all of these.

Another lesson is to develop and maintain close association with the Greek community in Sydney in our services, working closely with churches, community groups and schools. This is what we have done for three decades, and this length of time has facilitated a proven track record, which in turn imbues trust within the Greek community.

St Basil's is completely focused on the way people think about and appreciate the services: we like to try to emulate what people would have experienced in their own homes. In addition to providing the appropriate environment, St Basil's Homes regularly trains our staff to think about how to bring 'the Greek home' into all aspects of their work.

Conclusion

Our success has been based on not only meeting the physical needs of those for whom we care in a culturally appropriate environment, but also looking after their spiritual needs at the same time. In our culture, daily life unfolds hand-in-hand with the church. We have reflected this in the way we run our services.

In an Orthodox setting, the provision of spiritual care is emphasised by the following:

1. Use of regular worship rites – regular Holy Communion is of paramount significance to the residents.

2. The visual presence of the priest on a daily basis.

3. The sensory stimulation of worship in Orthodox life through sight, smells, tastes, sound, colour and textures.

In this respect, our *residential* programmes can offer more for elderly residents than for those elderly out in the community, via the presence of the chapel and regular worship opportunities, which are always within walking distance; the constant presence of the people as the body of the church; the priests, visitors and families sharing together in the home.

On the other hand, our *community* programmes meet the need for families to care for their loved ones at home, within a familiar setting, with full acceptance of all relevant moral obligations amongst family and friends within the community. Culturally appropriate support services are provided, and we ensure that carers are able to communicate and understand specific needs of clients and families.

We have long recognised the significance of spiritual care and support provided to residents within the home and our chapel, as it is evident in their response, particularly those living with dementia. These residents need to be prompted in many daily tasks of living, yet in the chapel they are able to follow the formalities of their faith and offer prayers and hymns in a way that is truly amazing. We have seen many residents who are not able to lift a spoon to their mouth or a cup to their lips, which are life-long tasks taught to them so many years ago; staff need to assist residents in every aspect of daily living, including hygiene, grooming and feeding. These residents go into their beloved chapel and immediately begin to respond appropriately – reciting verses, interacting appropriately with the physical environment (for example, with icons) and signing themselves with the cross. These have also been life-long traditions taught to them at the same time as their life skills, and are only ever witnessed in the chapel. Once out of the chapel, the residents again become fully dependent on staff for every action. One resident is able to receive and consume the blessed bread from the priest in the chapel, yet when she is taken outside into the lounge room and is offered bread, she is unable to respond.

St Basil's would particularly welcome involvement and participation in research into the link between spiritual care and resident outcomes and cognition, particularly in relation to those living with dementia.

As part of our philosophy of care, we seek every opportunity to provide a standard of care and service to our residents and clients that reflects excellence, relevance and respect. Our objective is to provide the maximum quality of life to each resident and client in a truly holistic way: physically, socially, culturally, emotionally and spiritually.

Research into spirituality and cognition will enlighten, inspire and motivate us to recognise and revere our faith more fully, to benefit our residents and clients in quality-of-life outcomes, and to share our knowledge and experiences with others.

We believe we have created and nurtured a way of life for our residents and clients which is an extension of how they have lived and loved their whole life. We know that in the future we will need to adapt this to meet the needs of the younger generations, and that what we provide now may not necessarily be what we need to provide in the future. In any case, we know that there will be ongoing need to provide culturally appropriate care for the Greek community, and this need will probably peak by 2016.

St Basil's has made a commitment to its clients and residents that physical, cultural, emotional and spiritual needs will be equally met and nurtured within a culturally appropriate framework. It is this sensitivity to client needs that would well serve any aged care provider in the pursuit of excellence, providing an atmosphere which allows peace, dignity and respect.

CHAPTER 13

Spiritual Well-being for Older People

Ann Harrington

Introduction

Society is facing an ageing population, with the United Nations claiming that 'the proportion of older persons is projected to more than double worldwide over the next half century' (United Nations Population Division DESA 2009, p.12). They estimate by 2050 throughout the world, more than one in five persons is projected to be aged 60 or over. When people age, existential questions become more prominent and include questions of spirituality.

The terms 'spirituality' and 'religion' are often used interchangeably; however, the majority of the literature 'differentiates spirituality from religiosity' (Burkhart and Hogan 2008, p.928). For the purpose of this paper, spirituality is defined as a search for meaning, linking spirituality to the provision of meaning in/of life. On the other hand, religious practice (including human expression of the rites and rituals of a particular faith tradition) may be included as an expression of spirituality (Burkhart and Hogan 2008; Harrington 2006).

Of interest to health care providers is the link between spiritual health and illness, first proffered by Jourard (1971). Bown and Williams (1993) argue that 'illness, suffering and death...challenge personal meaning systems and intensify the search to make sense of life' (1993, p.50). Therefore it is of importance for health care providers to be involved in spiritual caring. Burnard (1986, 1987) goes further, claiming that failure to invest life with meaning can lead to spiritual distress. This distress, he claims, is similar to, or may be part of, clinical depression. The link between spiritual health and illness is often discussed under the rubric of 'spiritual well-being'.

Therefore, to guide those offering spiritual care, including the care of older people, this paper will discuss the importance of 'spiritual well-being', define the concept, clarify what is meant by 'older people', give guidelines for assessing spiritual well-being for older people, highlight barriers to the implementation of spiritual care and offer suggestions to assist in the removal of those barriers.

The importance of spiritual well-being

Age-related changes affect our physical, psychological and spiritual well-being. Wooding Baker, McLean Heitkemper and Chenoweth (2008, p.68) argue that 'the age at which specific changes become evident differs from person to person and within the same person'. Some people appear to have a capacity to manage physical and psychological changes with few life disruptions, while for others, the gradual decline in physical and psychological abilities presents a challenge to their well-being.

It is argued here that *spiritual* well-being becomes more important when physical and psychological decline occurs, such decline leading older people to questions of meaning, a remit of spirituality (Baldacchino and Draper 2001; Harrington 2006; Miner-Williams 2006). What is central to an individual's life-meaning is critical to a sense of well-being, as out of this core, hope and a will to live can flow (MacKinlay 2006). The term 'spiritual well-being' was coined in the USA in 1971, following the White House Conference on Ageing (O'Brien 1999).

Defining spiritual well-being

American psychologist Ellison (1983, p.330) claims there were attempts to measure what was then termed 'subjective well-being' of Americans for some 20 years prior to the 1971 conference, but these were couched in survey terms, such as 'economic indicators' (1983, p.330). Over time it became evident that economic indicators alone were not sufficient for an understanding of Americans' 'quality of life' (1983, p.330) and that measurement of 'spiritual well-being' would be a better reflection of this quality. Further, Ellison points out that within psychology, 'behaviourism', which offered an 'exteriorising' (i.e. objective) concept of human beings, had lost some of its impact as it became evident that an objective approach was an insufficient measure of life's quality. Consequently, a movement developed that was termed 'the social indicators or quality of life movement' (Ellison 1983, p.330).

This quality of life movement regarded subjective measures of well-being as important and essential if the 'true welfare of people was to be known' (Ellison 1983, p.330). It is interesting that, despite claims that well-being was a *subjective* experience (and therefore immeasurable and unique to each individual), a tool with set 'objective' responses that included the 'spiritual' dimension was developed to measure this phenomenon. Called the *Spiritual Well-being Scale* (see below) its development originated from David Moberg, a sociologist and major figure in the developing of 'ageing and spirituality in the United States of America'. Following the 1971 Conference on Ageing, Moberg published a seminal text in spirituality, *Spiritual Well-being: Sociological Perspectives* (1979). Within this text he defines *spiritual* well-being as:

> the wellness or 'health' of the totality of the inner resources of people, the ultimate concerns around which all other values are focused, the central philosophy of life that guides conduct, and the meaning-giving center of human life which influences all individual and social behavior. (Moberg 1979, p.2)

From this definition he developed a two-faceted model with both vertical and horizontal axes. Ellison explains the model, claiming that the horizontal dimension relates to 'a sense of life purpose and life satisfaction', and the vertical to 'our sense of well-being in relation to God' (Ellison 1983, p.331). Others have extended this model, where the horizontal typifies spiritual well-being derived interpersonally (among other sources), and the vertical transpersonal (a relationship with a higher being [or God]) (Edwards 1995; Harrison and Burnard 1993; Relf 1997). Others now include an intrapersonal (within) component (Reed 1992). The *Spiritual Well-being Scale* (Paloutzian and Ellison 1982) that is purported to measure religious and existential well-being has been used extensively. Following its development, studies of spiritual well-being have been published (Ellis and Smith 1991; Hungelmann *et al.* 1989; Mickley, Soeken and Belcher 1992; VandeCreek and Smith 1992). Its use within the nursing literature has been cited by many authors (Carson *et al.* 1990; Edwards 1995; Harrison and Burnard 1993; Reed 1992; Stoll 1989), with Paloutzian (2002) claiming that 'approximately half of the research done with the [Spiritual Well-being] scale comes from the field of nursing' (2002, p.16).

Efficace and Marrone (2002) reviewed publications from 1990 to 2001 which showed that quality of life for cancer patients was closely related to spiritual well-being. A nursing study that attempted to link spiritual well-being with illness was conducted by Millison and Dudley in 1992. Surveying hospice caregivers, they found that 71 per cent (n=117) strongly agreed that 'a patient's spiritual well-being has a major impact on his/her health and illness' (1992, p.56). Moreover, studies of hospice patients themselves by Derrickson (1996), Harrington (2004) and Irion (1988) claim that spirituality increases as patients face death. Baldacchino and Draper (2001, p.833) assert:

> Research suggests that spiritual coping strategies, involving relationship with self, others, Ultimate other/God or nature were found to help individuals to cope with their ailments.

This demonstrates that, as people age, questions surrounding death and dying become more prominent, leading to discussions of spirituality. Nevertheless, within the literature, the definition of an 'older person' is evasive.

Defining older people

The terms 'older people', 'old age', 'aged care services' are used frequently in the literature. According to Woods (2008) in 1950 there were fewer than 131 million 'older people' in the world, representing 5.2 per cent of the population. By 2025 the projections for older people are that they will form 10.5 per cent of the global population, representing 839 million people.

Within Australia, 'those over 75 years are the most rapidly increasing age group and since the 1960s they have increased generally by 250 per cent' (Wooding Baker *et al.* 2008, p.63). (It should be noted these figures do not include Australia's Indigenous population, who have a higher mortality rate).

Anticipating a change in ageing demographics and different expectations, the Australian government in its interim report *A Healthier Future for All Australians – Interim Report* (Commonwealth of Australia 2009) claims that there will be a 'huge growth in demand for aged care services' (p.161) and suggests that 'aged care services need to become more responsive to the needs of older people and their families' (p.161).

A definition of 'aged persons' becomes clearer when the discussion centres on periods of time. Healey (2008), citing data from Aged and Community Services Australia and Department of Health and Ageing, argues that the 'baby boom generation' (people born between 1946–1965) will be 'the main driver of the increased number of people 65 years and over' (p.3). He contends they will enter older age with different aspirations and expectations than previous generations, demanding both a greater range and higher quality of services. He states further that they will 'experiment with ways of experiencing older age' (p.3). Therefore, it is argued here, our current understanding of the 'older person' will need to change.

Currently, three classifications of 'older people' have been proposed in the literature (see Table 13.1) and are offered here. They can be classified as *chronological* (Healey 2008), *Australian Bureau of Statistics* (McCrindle Research 2008) or *functional* (Woods 2008).

Table 13.1 Comparison of three classifications for older people

Chronological[1]	Australian Bureau of Statistics[2]	Functional[3]
85+ years (oldest-old)		Fourth agers – those who are older and frail, unable to live independently.
75–84 years (old-old)	Builders – those born before 1946	
65–74 years (young-old)	Boomers – those born between 1946 and 1964	Third agers – those who are older but living independently.
	Generation X – those born between 1965 and 1979	
	Generation Y – those born between 1980 and 1994	
	Generation Z – those born between 1995 and 2009	

Sources: 1. Healey 2008; 2. McCrindle Research 2008; 3. Woods 2008.

Chronological

The terms 'young-old adult (65–74 years of age) and old-old adult (75 years of age and older) were introduced in 1978' (Wooding Baker *et al.* 2008). The propensity of human beings to fit 'outside the square' recognises the difficulty in classifying people using their chronological age. A person constitutes more than a 'number' that tends to depersonalise the uniqueness of the individual. 'One size does not fit all', in that some classed as 'young-old' (65–74) may well be incapacitated to a greater extent than those classed as 'old-old' and unlikely to live very far into their eighth decade.

On the other hand, those who fit the 'old-old' or 'oldest-old' may be able to live independently, sometimes with community support, well past 85 years and retain their vestiges of autonomy. An age 'label' can be seen as limiting, promoting societal attitudes and expectations.

Australian Bureau of Statistics (ABS)

Offering a 'within social context' view and using ABS statistics with stated categories, McCrindle (McCrindle Research 2008) defines different populations. Presenting a background for each cohort, based on the beliefs of that particular generation, he contends that some 'labels' can assist in understanding each other.

His research relates to the current workforce and he argues for a category other than chronological. He proposes that 'older people' (whom he classes as 'builders' and 'boomers' – see Table 13.1), drawing from the values of their generation, have developed a different work ethic from younger generations (in this case Generation Y). Breaking down ageist notions, he makes his point that, regardless of age, all groups need to understand each other to work together. The workplace (he claims) is not about age or life stage but employers (today classed as boomers and/or builders) understanding their employees (today classed as Generation Y). It is only as each generation understands the other that age differences permit all to get the most out of generation diversity (McCrindle 2008, p.10). Such consideration leads to 'winners' on all sides.

Functional

The literature from Woods (2008) and MacKinlay (2006) shows a preference for a functional definition of old age. The benefit of using a 'functional' definition is that a person's capacity to live independently is scrutinised. By the use of a classification stated as 'third' or 'fourth' ages of life, chronological age becomes irrelevant as the emphasis changes to functional capacity.

Functionally, the third age reflects the period where the individual is older but living independently. The third age may well extend into an individual's eighth or ninth decade, providing independence and functional capacity remain.

On the other hand, the fourth age often entails disability and poor health, leading to dependency. Those in the fourth age are those who are frail and unable to live independently (Woods 2008; MacKinlay 2001). 'Fourth agers' may present at any chronological age, a functional definition permitting any degree of disability to become more evident and therefore capable of being addressed.

What is important, regardless of what classification for 'older people' is proffered, is that the ageing process inevitably leads to questions of life's meaning. When these questions arise, spiritual issues will emerge. As has been stated, research has shown that there is a positive association between 'religious faith' (i.e. faith in God) and 'well-being' (Koenig 1994; Koenig and Lawson 2004).

To return to the definition of spirituality including both the vertical and horizontal axes (Moberg 1979; see also page 179 above), once a vertical dimension is identified (i.e. a God dimension), it is likely to include issues of religion. As has been stated above, for those without a vertical aspect to their spiritual definition, 'religion' may not be part of their understanding of spirituality. Therefore, health care providers need to be aware of differences and alert to different expressions of spirituality. How, then, does the health care provider assess spiritual well-being for older people?

Guidelines for assessing spiritual well-being for older people

Culliford (2009), citing medical schools in the United Kingdom, claims that they provide 31–78 per cent of 'any teaching on spirituality' (p.22). Koenig (2007), writing from an United States perspective, offers that despite the American Association of Medical Colleges endorsing the need to train medical students to include spirituality into the care of patients '…only about 10 percent of physicians often or always take a spiritual history and nearly 50 percent never take one' (p.5).

Within the discipline of nursing, spirituality and its assessment has a higher profile and features in most nursing curricula. Literature from the United States identifies the North American Nursing Diagnosis Association's 'nursing diagnosis', which includes assessment and diagnosis of a patient's spiritual needs (Kozier et al. 2003). Further, competency 5.1 in the Australian Nursing and Midwifery Council (ANMC)'s 'National Competency Standards for the Registered Nurse', under the heading of 'evidence-based assessment', states that the nurse 'collects data that relates to physiological, psychological, spiritual, socio-economic and cultural variables on an ongoing basis' (ANMC 2006, p.6).

Therefore, from the discipline of nursing and based on the work of MacKinlay (2006), Anandarajah and Hight (2001) and McSherry (2000), a number of assessment tools can be used to determine the spiritual needs of older people. The three offered here are from an Australian author, with one each from a United Kingdom and United States perspective.

Within the 'spiritual tasks of ageing' (Appendix 1), MacKinlay (2006) offers 'Assessment of the spiritual needs of older adults: Levels 1 and 2' while McSherry (2000), from the United Kingdom, provides a case study to assist in determining spiritual needs. Anandarajah and Hight's (2001) 'HOPE Model of Spiritual History Taking' is a useful framework and, for the purpose of this paper, the latter is expanded below to guide in spiritual assessment.

It should be remembered that these tools require a conversation with people, as they are based on a dialogue. For those unable or unwilling to converse, these tools will have some limitations. However, they are a starting point and provide some guidance for the novice.

Adapting Anandarajah and Hight's (2001) model, and with the assistance of Massey, Fitchett and Roberts (2004) questions are posed around the following, based on the acronym 'HOPE':

Table 13.2 The 'HOPE' model of spiritual history taking (adapted from Anandarajah and Hight 2001)

H	Sources of hope, meaning, comfort, strength, peace, love and connection
O	Organised religion – Does this feature, and what aspects are helpful?
P	Personal spiritual beliefs and practices that are independent of organised religion.
E	Effects of medical care, or how illness has affected spiritual practices.

H – when considering sources of hope, strength, meaning, comfort, peace, love and connection, questions may be framed using the following example:

What are your sources of hope, strength, comfort and peace? What do you hold on to during difficult times? (Anandarajah and Hight 2001; Massey *et al.* 2004)

O – the purpose of this question is to determine if religious practice is of benefit when it comes to spiritual care. Whether or not a 'God dimension' is flagged in response to the first question, the following example may assist in determining the relevance of religion.

How important is organised religion to you? What aspects are helpful to you? (Anandarajah and Hight 2001; Massey *et al.* 2004)

P – for some people, spiritual beliefs may not fit around organised religion. Questions here are designed to assist in determining what other spiritual practices might be of assistance.

Are your spiritual beliefs independent of organised religion? What aspects of your spirituality or spiritual practices do you find most helpful? (Anandarajah and Hight 2001; Massey *et al.* 2004)

E – illness often limits an individual's ability to implement their spiritual practices. Here the emphasis is on where the limitations may lie.

> *Has being unwell affected your ability to do the things you usually do regarding your spiritual practices? Is there anything we (or I) could do to assist you?* (Anandarajah and Hight 2001; Massey *et al.* 2004).

The above is a useful guide to determining spiritual well-being. Once determined, it is important that the next step is taken, of conveying the information to those able to implement spiritual care. In the case of a nursing assessment, the data needs to be included in the nursing care plan and acted upon. If the individual wishes to speak to a member of the clergy, then chaplaincy or pastoral carers need to be contacted. Once these needs have been determined, there may be barriers to the implementation of spiritual care.

Figure 13.1 Barriers to implementing spiritual care (based on McSherry 2000)

Barriers to the implementation of spiritual care

At any age, the onset of illness may limit the extent of an individual's control over aspects of their life. It is at these particular times that spiritual coping strategies (or spiritual well-being) can 'enhance self-empowerment, leading to finding meaning and purpose in illness' (Baldacchino and Draper 2001, p.833).

Nevertheless, Benner Carson (2008) argues that the skills required by nurses or health care providers to undertake spiritual assessment and spiritual care are compassion, listening skills, kindness 'and all the things that make them unique and giving' (p.126). Within busy health care settings, however, these skills are often difficult to find. Consequently, barriers to the implementation of spiritual care emerge, which McSherry (2000) classes as 'intrinsic' or 'extrinsic' (here they are defined as 'internal' or 'external' (Figure 13.1)), and his framework is useful to consider when reflecting on the implementation of such care.

Internal barriers

For spiritual care to occur, not only does it depend on the nurse or health care provider's spiritual development (Harrington 2004, p.143) but also on the individual's receptivity to the implementation of spiritual care. Internal barriers, those that emerge from within either the individual or the health care provider, need to be recognised, otherwise an individual's spiritual needs (and therefore their spiritual well-being) may be overlooked and remain unmet. McSherry (2000) classes them as: *inability to communicate*; *ambiguity* (discussed here as *lack of knowledge*); a *'sensitive area'* (discussed here as *pluralism*); and the potential *emotional demand* for the nurse or health care provider.

1. INABILITY TO COMMUNICATE

People of any age may be unable to communicate because of illness or loss of senses. Aphasia (loss of speech), loss of sight or hearing may follow a stroke and can impede communication, so assessment may be difficult. It becomes a challenge to be able to determine exactly what an older person's spiritual needs may be. However, visiting relatives may be able to clarify by providing background information on any religious practices or specific spiritual needs; or, in the case of an individual's loss of speech, the use of picture boards may help with communication.

2. LACK OF KNOWLEDGE

Koenig (2007) points out from a medical perspective that 'many physicians don't know how to take a spiritual history' (p.103). As already stated above (on page 185), although spirituality has a higher focus in nursing curricula, with at least two levels of nurses (registered and enrolled) and different health care providers employed in Australia all offering care, it is possible, in nursing as well, to find lack of education in spirituality and therefore inability to provide spiritual care. There is a need for health care providers to be alert to 'spirituality' as a domain of care and to reflect on their own spiritual beliefs, so that they are attentive to the possibility of offering spiritual care.

3. PLURALISM

Multicultural Australian society reflects 'religious' pluralism in that nurses or health care providers may embrace different and sometimes conflicting ideologies, philosophies and creeds. Consequently, some health care providers consider spirituality closely aligned to religion and, therefore, it may lead to personal fears of misrepresenting a person's religious practice. Concerns here relate to the health care provider feeling 'out of their depth' and unable to answer potentially awkward questions. However, if religion is considered the 'vertical' arm of spirituality (as proposed earlier), then ascertaining the religious practice of another person may be an important aspect of spiritual care. It should be remembered that the care implemented, spiritual or otherwise, must take into account the other person's needs, not those of the health care provider.

4. EMOTIONAL DEMAND

In agreeing with Benner Carson (2008) that not only listening skills, compassion and kindness, but giving of oneself is necessary for the implementation of spiritual care, it can be understood that issues to do with spiritual care require some emotional cost. If the implementation of spiritual care is emotionally demanding, then the cost of extending oneself may be too high. However, it is accepted that at some point, all health *care* involves an emotional component, and acknowledging that fact will prepare the carer in this area.

External barriers

There are *external* barriers (classed by McSherry (2000) as 'extrinsic') – i.e. barriers that exist outside of the person – which have the potential to prevent the implementation of spiritual care. They are: *organisation and management; environment distractions resulting in loss of privacy; economic constraints on staff and time; educational issues; reduced length of stay in hospital;* and *not directly relevant to area of practice.*

1. ORGANISATION AND MANAGEMENT

It has been argued here that spiritual care involves dialogue. Speaking to people for any length of time in a hospital or nursing home environment where the underlying emphasis is on 'doing for' rather than 'being with' the person, requires support from the management of the organisation. Staff may be unwilling to offer such care when there is an emphasis on 'doing tasks' rather than 'being available' to engage in dialogue with others. When there is a lack of such support, the implementation of spiritual care may be difficult. However, educating managers about the importance of spiritual care, and of health care providers being alert for short periods to engage in a spiritual discussion, may be all that is necessary to overcome this barrier.

2. ENVIRONMENT DISTRACTIONS RESULTING IN LOSS OF PRIVACY

For people to divulge personal information, a quiet space with the minimum of disruption is required. The use of a private room is an important consideration, and one that needs to be addressed in the planning stage of both the design and the implementation of spiritual care. Drawing drapes around a bedspace may be insufficient to ensure privacy, and so a person's bed space might need to be moved to accommodate spiritual care. It is acknowledged that these requirements impact on time (discussed below).

3. ECONOMIC CONSTRAINTS ON STAFF AND TIME

Engaging in a dialogue with a person in interventions classed as 'spiritual' may include a discussion around issues of life's meaning, strength or hope in illness, or empathetic understanding of the whole person and not just the part (Harrington 2006, p.181). Therefore there needs to be recognition that spiritual care takes time and comes at an economic cost. That said, if spiritual care is considered an important facet of well-being, then it is imperative that caring for the spiritual domain be seen as part of overall good care.

4. EDUCATIONAL ISSUES

It is accepted that many health care providers feel inadequate to meet the spiritual needs of people, due in part to a lack of formal education. It is essential that courses are offered at undergraduate and postgraduate levels to provide guidance to those offering health care. More research in the area of spirituality and spiritual care is needed, so that education can be seen to be evidence-based.

5. REDUCED LENGTH OF STAY IN HOSPITAL

In acute settings, a high proportion of bed days are taken up by older patients. However, regardless of age, rapid turnover with more use of 'day only' wards means that, once admitted, some people do not remain in hospital for long periods. Further, there is an increasing emphasis on community-based care (Stein-Parbury 2000). However, if spiritual needs are identified by a health care provider or raised by a patient in an acute hospital, these needs could be followed up by community carers. Therefore, any spiritual needs that emerge from a 'day only' ward placement need to be met by health care workers at the point of discharge. (For those in long-term residential care, this barrier may not arise, except for an unexpected admission to hospital.)

6. NOT DIRECTLY RELEVANT TO AREA OF PRACTICE

While spiritual care may be perceived to be the sole remit of the chaplain, 'patients do not always wait until the chaplain is present to raise these [spiritual] issues – conversations happen when they happen…' (Benner Carson 2008, p.125). Nurses and other health care professionals need to be prepared to respond in a timely manner to an individual's spiritual concerns; therefore, regardless of practice, spiritual care should become part of all disciplines' remit.

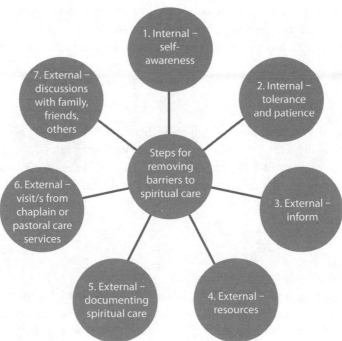

Figure 13.2 Steps for removing barriers to spiritual care (based on McSherry 2000)

To assist in moving spiritual care forward, the framework offered by McSherry (2000, p.111) is a useful starting point (see Figure 13.2). He proposes: *intrinsic* assets (self-awareness, tolerance and patience); and *extrinsic* assets (information; resources). Three additions are offered here: documentation of spiritual care; visits from chaplain or pastoral care workers; discussion with family/friends and significant others.

Steps to remove barriers to spiritual care

When it comes to person-centred care, Koenig (2007) identifies a professional boundary between health care providers and the individual, that is important to keep. However, he does acknowledge that with few exceptions 'spiritual assessment and support do not typically threaten boundaries' (p.97). Therefore the barriers discussed below are important ones to consider removing, when contemplating the implementation of spiritual care.

Internal

1. SELF-AWARENESS

As already stated, it is important for health care providers to reflect on their own personal beliefs and attitudes, values and spirituality. By addressing their own spirituality, they are more able to care adequately for the spiritual domain of others (Harrington 2004). It should be remembered that, following a spiritual assessment of older people, the health care provider should take their cue from the 'other' – that is, care for the needs of the other, not their own (McSherry 2000; Harrington 2004).

2. TOLERANCE AND PATIENCE

Health care, whether physical, emotional or spiritual, requires respect for those with different cultural, ethnic or religious principles. What should follow is a suspension of our own judgement, so as to permit any care to be instigated. For older people, there should be the recognition and acknowledgement that each generation will be different from the next (McSherry 2000).

External

1. INFORM

If staff, nursing home or ward design are barriers that inhibit spiritual care (e.g. a large bay of people with very little privacy), draw any obstacles to the attention of management. Provision of a quiet room and attention to adequate staffing levels are important for the implementation of spiritual care (McSherry 2000).

2. RESOURCES

Often, in many acute care wards or nursing homes, staff appear unaware of appropriate contact people or literature to support the implementation of spiritual care. For example, in some places there are no obvious leaflets directing staff to chaplaincy services and/or local church ministers. For patients or nursing home residents who request chaplaincy services, these resources are vital. Attention to the availability of leaflets or books regarding other religions/cultural beliefs is important, along with being cognisant of interpreter facilities. These resources can only assist with spiritual care (McSherry 2000).

3. DOCUMENTATION OF SPIRITUAL CARE

Once a spiritual assessment is undertaken, case notes need to reflect spiritual care as part of holistic practice, and documentation of individual requests for spiritual support should be noted. Further, during a 'handover' of information, requests regarding spiritual needs should be conveyed to those staff following.

4. VISIT/S FROM CHAPLAIN OR PASTORAL CARE SERVICES

On many occasions nursing staff are 'brokers' to chaplaincy services (Harrington 2006). In busy wards or nursing homes, the role of the chaplain may be minimised, or remain unrecognised. When it comes to the implementation of spiritual care, the chaplain's participation as part of the ward culture should be encouraged.

5. DISCUSSION/S WITH FAMILY, FRIENDS, SIGNIFICANT OTHERS

As family (however described) and friends may assist with the information required to instigate spiritual care, when appropriate they should be approached for information. As stated above, spirituality is more than religious preference, with the key to effective care showing respect to 'the person's belief system' (Schoenbeck 1994, p.22).

Conclusion

It has been argued here that spirituality (with or without a religious dimension) is an important component of a person's life. Moreover, as the ageing process occurs, questions relating to issues of spirituality will emerge.

Spiritual well-being, a concept in existence since 1971, represents the 'totality of the inner resources of people' (Moberg 1979, p.2), and therefore requires consideration by health care providers. As both illness and ageing can activate a spiritual quest, the provision of spiritual care should occur across the age span, with specific attention given to elderly people.

Within the next 50 years there will be a greater proportion of older people in the Western world. To assist in clarifying what is meant by an 'older person', three definitions have been offered here. However, regardless of age, the implementation of spiritual care is important. Although there may be barriers to its implementation, strategies to remove those barriers have been proposed, encompassing both internal and external considerations.

It has been argued previously within the context of health care (Harrington 2004) that to assist individuals with spiritual issues adequately, providers need to be attentive to their own spirituality. Issues surrounding spirituality will become more prominent as people age. Therefore the provision of spiritual well-being for older people can only be enhanced when health practitioners are self-aware and committed to its implementation.

CHAPTER 14

Integrated Support for Veterans in Aged Care Homes

Tracey McDonald

Introduction

Across the world countries with effective social support, education, health and care systems are experiencing demographic changes associated with increasing longevity. Countries with smaller proportions of children than of older persons are also a feature of demographic changes in Japan, United States of America, Canada and most European countries. Australia, in population terms, is a comparatively small country, but like so many other developed societies we take seriously our responsibilities for those among us who need care, protection, treatment and support. As in so many other countries, Australia's population is ageing as a result of sustained low fertility and increasing life expectancy, creating an emerging demographic pattern that requires strategies to manage an ageing population effectively; extended labour force participation; adequate housing and care services; and the supply of skilled labour (Productivity Commission 2005). Ageing veterans living in the community contribute to, and are also affected by, these emerging demographic changes.

Australians and others from comparable societies have benefited from a post-World War II period of economic prosperity which has generated an expectation of living longer and more productive lives than did previous generations. Currently Australian men are expected to live to around 77 years, and women to around 83 years, but both can reasonably expect longevity to increase in the future (ABS 2003). Long life is generally accepted as an indicator of a successful society that is cohesive in a way that supports a balanced population age structure, and provides appropriate care and support for those who are less able to be independent. The apparent success of assisting people to live full, long and enjoyable lives can give rise to public debates about the economic and social consequences of people living longer, despite experts in health economics in Australia and internationally (see for instance Cooper and Hagen 1999; Duckett 2002; Frankel, Ebrahim and Davey Smith 2000; Mullen 2000) predicting that any social or economic effects of long life will be small and easily managed.

Through astute planning and implementation of effective strategies for education, public health and provision for vulnerable groups, we now have a greater proportion of seniors in our midst, many of whom are veterans of twentieth-century wars. Every society that has been involved in past international conflicts remains grateful to the many men and women who placed themselves in harm's way during war, so that benefits from the democratic freedom and civil peace for which they strove are available to all. Our gratitude extends also to the families of these brave people in acknowledgement of the hardships they endured when family members joined the armed forces and other combat services; and for the ongoing support they give to those who returned, changed forever by their experiences.

A crucial part of returning home from war service is being able to reintegrate with communities and groups so that civilian life can once more become a source of spiritual and cultural inspiration that enriches the years following war service. Where poverty or social isolation undermine health and well-being, some older persons may feel compelled to rely on others for help in order to remain as independent as possible. However, for many adults in later years, ageing is not necessarily associated with ill health or disability, and they are able to participate as they like, within the general community.

Long life eventually leads to frailty involving diminished mental or physical capacity, or both, and when this occurs a small proportion of older people need considerable assistance to remain either in their homes or in residential aged care homes. Aged care services in Australia are regulated in such a way as to favour those with most need for care and support. In Australia, for instance, around 11 per cent of people aged over 70 receive some form of assistance and support, and relatively few (around 6%) go into residential aged care, known by various names such as 'care homes' or 'hostels' or 'long-term care'.

Experiences of war by one generation can shape the attitudes and cultural beliefs of several generations into the future. In some countries the influence of what occurred during war can influence national priorities around defence readiness, and these experiences can also shape a nation's cultural identity. The Australian Defence Force and armed forces of most countries undertake ongoing roles in war areas, civil unrest and other conflicts, as well as international peacekeeping activities. As a result, the generations following those directly involved with the two world wars of the last century must also live with their personal experiences of war service. As these people age, they too will need to be provided with services and supports that allow them to fare well and to access appropriate services as frailty increases.

The Australian Department of Veterans' Affairs (DVA), defines veterans according to individual and contextual terms related to their war service, and those deemed to be 'veterans' are issued with a health entitlement card and/or a pension card. War widows or widowers and dependants can also be issued with these cards. Under the Aged Care Act 1997 (as amended), a member of the veteran community is more broadly defined as 'a veteran of the Australian or allied defence force; or a spouse or widow/er of a person mentioned above'. Similar acknowledgements have occurred in legislation enacted by most countries with war history, and for the same reasons – that is, to ensure that veterans who have given so much are provided with the support and services they need in order to re-enter society and participate to the extent they are able.

According to the DVA website (2009) the Australian veteran population known to the DVA in 2009 is old and ageing faster than the general population. Across Australia there are approximately 300,000 known veterans and war widows or widowers with health cards for receiving subsidised treatment, and an additional 150,000 veterans who receive pensions or benefits but who are not entitled to DVA subsidised treatment.

The DVA website states that approximately three quarters of veterans and war widows or widowers with health cards are aged 75 or older, and over the next decade the proportion of DVA clients aged over 90 years will more than quadruple, to make up one quarter of DVA's treatment population, that is, those with health cards. While nearly half the Australian male population over 80 are veterans, most people would be unaware that female gold cardholders are expected by DVA to outnumber their male counterparts by 2013, if not before. Given the number of people involved in World War II, it is not surprising to DVA that the veteran population makes up around a quarter of the residents of aged care facilities.

Veterans as a group of older persons in aged care

While it is not the purpose of this chapter to canvass the similarities and differences between formal and informal arrangements made by various countries for their veterans, the basic thrust of policy and funding is generally consistent. The Australian experience, discussed below, provides an example of the types of strategies undertaken to support veterans, and in particular those who are now quite elderly.

Since receiving Special Needs status in 2001, under the Aged Care Act 1997, veterans living in aged care homes have had their care and support needs elevated to a prominence that is well deserved. For most of these people, the effects of war service include the establishment of deep and abiding bonds between comrades, while for others the consequences of this experience may have been less favourable. Whatever the individual outcome, sharing combat and service experiences forges a special identity for all involved. It is this shared identity that warrants acknowledgement of the special needs of veterans within the broader context of aged care services.

Several other groups within Australian society are deemed under the Aged Care Act 1997, section 11.3 as having 'special needs'. These are people:

1. from Aboriginal and Torres Strait Islander communities

2. from non-English-speaking backgrounds

3. who live in rural or remote areas

4. who are financially or socially disadvantaged

5. of a kind (if any) specified in the Allocation Principles.

When providing aged care services it is appropriate to acknowledge the special needs arising from the life-long effects on people who have served to defend Australia, or on those who support war veterans.

In considering the factors that warrant inclusion under the Aged Care Act as a group with special needs, it is worthwhile examining the culture and spirit of camaraderie that motivated so many Australians to serve in World War II. On their website, the DVA claims that one in seven of the total population of Australia enlisted. Those who stayed behind undertook unfamiliar roles and broke free of gender stereotypes to take on work essential to the survival of Australian society and to help the war effort. For all involved, life was fraught with difficulties arising from scarcity, loneliness, uncertainty and fear – but through persistence and mutual support Australians strove for the resumption of peace in Europe and the Pacific. It is not surprising, therefore, that these shared, intense experiences shaped the values and priorities of that generation and have resulted in the formation of a distinct cultural group within Australian society.

Observable attributes of the veteran culture can be seen across Australia in clubs set up by the Returned and Services League of Australia (RSL Clubs) which continue to provide a place of respectful commemoration of those who fell in war, and a social outlet for those who still remember. As part of their undertaking to comrades during dangerous times, veterans also contribute to the welfare and support of less fortunate or deceased veterans, as well as their partners and dependants. While not all veterans want to participate in public commemorative events, many do and attend various services with their families and friends on ANZAC Day (a day to honour members of the Australia and New Zealand Army Corps who fought at Gallipoli and in Europe in World War I) and Remembrance Day each year.

Despite increasing frailty among veterans and diminished capacity to participate in commemorative activities, there is no doubt that the unstinting spirit and commitment of older veterans to their comrades and the welfare of Australia remains strong. It is important, therefore, for providers of residential aged care services to understand why veterans have been given 'special needs status' and what this means in relation to provision of health and psychosocial support while in residential care.

Australia's government provides for the health and welfare of veterans as they age. For veterans living in a retirement village or in residential aged care, the known health problems listed below are highly likely to have prompted their and their family's decisions to access residential care services. Health information distributed by DVA (2009) claims that veterans:

- have higher rates of health risk factors compared to their non-veteran counterparts, including lack of exercise, obesity and long-term use of cigarettes and alcohol

- are more likely to experience a short- or long-term illness, develop cancer or suffer from diseases of the digestive, nervous, circulatory and musculoskeletal systems

- are also prescribed more medications than non-veterans, even allowing for disabilities

- have increased rates of mental health problems in the community. More than a quarter of the treatment population have mental health conditions, about half of which are accepted as being due to military service

- have much higher rates of conditions such as post-traumatic stress disorder (PTSD), although this diagnosis might not have been made in older veterans

- have war-related memories that may have a negative effect on those with dementia, and this issue should be considered in care planning for older veterans.

Understanding of veterans and their needs should also be based on an appreciation of individual war experiences and how these have shaped the person's opportunities and choices in life. Also needed is specialist understanding of specific chronic disorders such as PTSD and where to access information and resources to ensure that appropriate assessment, care planning, treatment and social support are made available.

Support and care for older veterans

A pivotal aspect of veteran care is that provided by the aged care system. In most countries veterans are integrated throughout the care and social support arrangements, where their needs as older persons are given prominence in resource allocations. Different societies also have veteran-specific services, mostly associated with rehabilitation and treatment services, and some long-term care services set up to cater to the cultural needs of a veteran community, for example the Royal Hospital, Chelsea in the United Kingdom (www.chelsea-pensioners.co.uk). Three centuries of service to veterans since 1682, driven by the goal to provide 'succour and relief of veterans broken by age and war', epitomises this proud service where 'the men in scarlet' make their home. Of course, different societies approach the task of providing such support to veterans in a range of ways, all related to providing a dignified and competent service that is acceptable to those who require it. In the sections below, examples from a veteran care service in Australia demonstrate the point.

Impairment of physical capacity is often considered to have negative consequences for older people and their quality of life. In research undertaken at the RSL LifeCare and ANZAC Village in Sydney, the question of whether life satisfaction is influenced by physical capacity has been examined in work ongoing since 2005. Measurements of physical capacity and quality of life are taken quarterly and compared on a sample of residents across all service areas, including high care dementia units. Results indicate that deterioration in physical abilities does not necessarily result in diminished quality of life, and vice versa. People with disabling disease do not necessarily have a low quality of life (McDonald 2006b). These findings at RSL LifeCare run counter to earlier research by Kendig, Browning and Young (2000), who state that the effects of diseases on well-being usually depend on whether disease effects are accompanied by functional impairment. In explaining the findings of the RSL LifeCare study, it is probable that quality of life in this group is enhanced, despite the presence of deteriorating physical capacity, because of the care environment plus feelings of social engagement and support within this community of veterans.

Further research undertaken at RSL LifeCare has focused attention on the effects of inclusion in activities programmes for veterans (and others) with cognitive deficits arising from a range of aetiologies. Two research studies examined the effects of active participation in physical, social and mentally stimulating activities on residents' sleep patterns and physical safety (Garrard and McDonald 2007; Hochkins and McDonald 2007). The results indicate that within the first few months of being admitted to a high care dementia unit residents experience increased quality (restfulness) and amounts of sleep (over six hours per night) without medication assistance; and their risk of falls and other accidents is significantly reduced.

The combined allied health, medical and nursing care efforts for this group of residents at RSL LifeCare in Sydney has established an environment where any negative effects of physical disability and mental confusion are minimised and they are assisted in remaining connected to an environment that acknowledges and respects the sacrifice made by veterans and their families for Australia.

Experiences of spirituality and expressions of culture in residential aged care

At the ANZAC Retirement Village in Sydney, Australia, the focus on providing services to veterans means that throughout the village the values and character of the environment, activities, events and lifestyle priorities endorse the special status of those who have served, while also working to ensure that veterans have opportunities to integrate socially with the general community. This objective is also prevalent in high dependency units where people with severe mental confusion are cared for in ways that optimise their potential for independence and ensure that their dignity is preserved along with their individual identity. In the two high care dementia units at RSL LifeCare, over half of the residents are veterans and their past service is acknowledged appropriately as part of their care and lifestyle plans.

The majority of people who choose to live in the retirement village are also veterans or have strong links with the services. Most choose to live in this village because of the acknowledgement given throughout the precincts to the contribution of veterans and those who made the ultimate sacrifice for Australia. Commemorative events include ANZAC marches and memorial services, Remembrance Day commemoration services and a range of interesting activities for war widows, ex-service nurses and other groups. The result is an environment in which people can freely interact and be acknowledged as a group with unique characteristics and interests.

Helping veterans in their search for happiness and peace

Since the end of World War II there has been an increasing recognition of war trauma and the effect it can have on individuals whose post-war goal is to return to their normal civilian lifestyle. The long-term psychobiological effects of trauma suffered during war may be mediated by individual responses and societal reactions, but researchers in America (Bracken and Petty 1998; Clipp and Elder 1996) argue that social and cultural responses such as commemorative events and social acceptance can help to mediate a person's individual traumatic experiences of war.

The single most significant threat to individual happiness and peace is war, which ravages the health and well-being of people and societies. Much depends on the individual's personal resources used to respond to trauma, but the role of war narrative and the limits that societies place on the telling of war stories also play a part in the psychological survival of veterans (Davies 2001). Social rejection of trauma responses as cowardice or weakness denies normal reactions to traumatising events and causes the traumatised person to feel alienated and alone. Such situations frequently occurred among World War II veterans, and again with veterans returning from the Vietnam conflict in the 1970s, who are now approaching an age where they may be considering residential care.

Throughout history post-traumatic stress disorder (PTSD) has been known under various names, but the symptoms are described in similar ways. PTSD is a psychiatric condition that can follow life-threatening experiences or witnessing events that directly threaten lives, such as in active military service. Nightmares, flashbacks, sleep disorders and feelings of alienation related to a past life-threatening event can persist long after the event and can erode the person's ability to cope with everyday life.

Studies of veterans of military service in Vietnam (Kulka *et al.* 1990) estimate that 15–30 per cent of those experiencing active service have had some post-war experience of PTSD. This level of incidence is comparable with veterans of other conflicts and also among United Nations peacekeeping personnel. A longitudinal study of PTSD among 576 Dutch veterans by Dirkzwager, Bramsen and Van der Ploeg (2001) found that PTSD symptoms persist long-term but are not necessarily aggravated by age stressors. Sher (2004) claims that PTSD is difficult to diagnose and quotes an Israeli study where 9 per cent of the sample had signs of PTSD, but physicians diagnosed only 2 per cent. Sher also refers to epidemiological studies indicating that in the general community a lifetime exposure to traumatic events affects from 40 to 90 per cent of people, whereas PTSD in the community ranges from 1 to 9 per cent. While not all people exposed to traumatic events develop PTSD, from the evidence it seems that it is much more likely to develop within those exposed to war.

Traumatising experiences can prompt a personal search for meaning, or at least a way to rationalise what occurred in terms of purpose or value. Psychiatric support and pharmacotherapy given to veterans following war service can assist them to investigate feelings of alienation, guilt and cynicism and reach a position where they understand their own responses to traumatic experiences. In their study of the effects of trauma on an individual's existential beliefs, Fontana and Rosenheck (2004) concluded that the issue of spirituality among veterans searching for reasons to explain what has happened to them could be more emphasised during psychotherapy for PTSD. Religious and spiritual rituals can be a source of comfort for people enduring the unendurable, and an environment that is set up to welcome and give solace should include opportunities for quiet reflection on some of the larger questions in life.

Dementia, the next battle

In later life, the effects of PTSD can be further compounded by mental confusion related to organic brain syndromes such as Alzheimer's disease, which can cause people to conflate flashbacks with normal memories.

Typical physical responses to PTSD emerge from a constant feeling of being powerless and threatened. When the person is also mentally confused, the symptoms can feel all the more real and the threats more imminent (Carlson 2001). Agitation, wariness and sleeping problems can combine with natural responses to adrenalin production, causing the symptoms experienced by the confused person with PTSD to be significantly exaggerated. In the elderly veteran population with dementing illness, manifestations of severe PTSD can result in challenging behaviours that do not respond to counselling, memory reconstruction approaches or relationship therapies that have been found to be effective in the non-confused PTSD population (Bryant et al. 1999). In most of these therapeutic approaches, the presence of dementia thwarts access to the cognitive and communicative aspects of therapy that are critical to symptom reversal. It follows that many cognitive therapeutic approaches used to relieve PTSD are rendered useless in the presence of dementia.

Nursing therapeutic interventions for elderly veterans with PTSD and dementia aim to reduce periods of physical agitation, relieve anxiety, stabilise sleep patterns, treat depression, if present, and promote normal body weight within an environment that is safe while promoting optimal independence. Within the high care dementia units at RSL LifeCare, just over half of the residents are veterans. While not all have evidence of PTSD around 30 per cent do. When PTSD is compounded by dementia symptoms, even families are sometimes unaware of the PTSD because the veteran has not spoken of it and has been able to override his or her responses prior to becoming confused. When dementia reaches a certain intensity, the ability to override responses to PTSD flashbacks, etc. is compromised and experiences of fear, loathing or aggression results in behaviours that can pose safety risks to the person or those nearby.

Ongoing PTSD and dementia research undertaken at RSL LifeCare since 2005 (McDonald 2006a) has identified the patterns of association between care needs, PTSD symptoms and strategies to reduce the incidence of flashbacks. This research has been incorporated into the assessment and care planning systems for PTSD, and a clinical pathway is now available to ensure that residents who have these special needs are not simply absorbed into general dementia care routines and protocols for managing behaviours that arise from traumatic experiences.

International trends in policy endorse a funding emphasis on care of older people with mental confusion and dementia symptoms, and it is not unexpected that aged care services will increasingly cater to a growing demand for dementia services across the general community as well as for veterans, who make up a large proportion of this group in most societies.

Connectedness and inclusiveness

Throughout aged care homes there is at least a general awareness that a person who has cognitive deficits is at risk of missing opportunities to undertake the many intellectual and emotionally draining tasks associated with healthy ageing. For people with dementia, it is even difficult for them to establish and maintain contacts in the early stages of the illness. Consequently, these people are at a disadvantage in any new situation where making meaningful connections with others is fundamental to accessing the benefits of social interaction. The task of establishing meaningful contact is equally difficult for those wishing to understand the needs and concerns of people with dementia symptoms.

Veterans in residential or social care environments have access to the unique culture of ex-service personnel, but it is important that they also remain socially and spiritually connected with the general community. Rowe and Kahn (1997) reported on a body of research that supports active engagement with life and community as playing a central role in life satisfaction among older people, even those with health problems. Successful ageing is affected by our ability to manage or maintain: (i) low risk of disease and disability; (ii) high functional capacity; and (iii) active engagement with life. However, the degree to which all three must be present to achieve high life satisfaction is unclear. Indeed, some people live a satisfying life despite severe disease and disability.

Social engagement, through interpersonal relationships and participation in social activities, promotes physical and emotional well-being and lowers mortality rates in later life (Lennartsson and Silverstein 2001), and it not only provides physiological benefits such as strengthening immune system function, cardiovascular reactivity and cardiopulmonary fitness, it also has psychological benefits such as promoting a sense of belonging, building self-esteem and giving purpose to life. Being socially engaged also promotes health-building behaviours such as no smoking, sensible diet and being alert to early signs of health problems. These, in turn, enhance physical and emotional well-being (Berkman *et al.* 2000).

As part of the process of ageing, certain spiritual tasks can emerge to cause changes in attitudes about many aspects of living within a community. Dalby (2006) reviewed research on spiritual change and concluded that while some aspects of spirituality remain stable into older age, emphasis increases on such spiritual tasks as integrity, humanistic concerns, changing relationships with others and concern for younger generations, relationships with a higher being or power, self-transcendence and coming to terms with dying. While cultural elements and individual differences play a part in the achievement of these spiritual tasks, there is little doubt that physical and mental health are linked to spiritual well-being and maintaining personal closeness with others.

Attempts to establish a connection between person and carers

In residential aged care contexts, it can be extremely difficult for care staff to build relationships with someone who is mentally confused. Aged-care staff spend long periods of time with their residents and, over the months and even years of an established caring relationship, it is possible to get to know each other very well, although the toll on care staff of long-term involvement with mentally confused older people is well known in the aged care industry.

Much has been written on dementia symptoms as stressors on caregivers in all contexts, and linked with negative caregiver outcomes (Donaldson, Tarrier and Burns 1997). There is also evidence that being associated over time with people with dementia who display aggression, significantly increases stress for nurses and carers in aged care settings (Rodney 2000) regardless of the socio-cultural context. Other research identifies care recipient outcomes as being linked to depression when relationships between carers and the recipient deteriorate, and there is no evidence to suggest that people with mental confusion are not similarly affected (see Burgener and Twigg 2002; Cohen-Mansfield, Marx and Werner 1991). It appears that the building of caring relationships under these circumstances can be impeded by risk avoidance attitudes of carers, and also by the limitations on communication endured by those with dementia symptoms (Rundqvist and Severinsson 1999).

Direct care staff in dementia care units often have limited information about the person they are caring for, other than their self-care problems, and interactions usually revolve around basic care needs. Within the context of contemporary aged care, opportunities for genuine relationships to build between staff and residents in dementia care units are reduced by the need for many staff to work in several locations around the organisation and the effects of staff turnover. Effective aged care work within dementia care units requires staff to get to know those in their care quickly, but often the social and more personal information gathered on residents is inadequate, or not easily accessible within a busy unit.

Some research has been done on ways to bridge the gap between carers and residents, and one approach in particular, life-story work, is commonly used in a number of health and social care settings, including those catering to residents with dementia. It has been defined by McKeown, Clarke and Repper (2006) as a 'biographical approach in health and social care, that gives people the opportunity to talk about their life experiences' (p.238). Several positive outcomes from using this approach are claimed by the researchers, including helping staff to see the person beyond the illness; viewing people as individuals; improving communication; and enhancing communication amongst staff, relatives and residents. Attempts using life-story albums have also been examined, in relation to carer and storyteller perspectives on the use of life-story work to establish a personal and spiritual connection between the person and their carers. Batson, Thorne and Peak (2002) found that while carers felt that the person with dementia became more animated during discussion revolving around their life-story album, this enthusiasm was not sustained, and no resultant difference in the carer's relationship with the person was noted. It was suggested, however, that person-centred care could be better promoted if carers develop greater knowledge of the person with dementia. More recently, it has been shown that life-story work can promote person-centred care, if care staff learn more about the individual with dementia, and as a result the potential to strengthen relationships between staff and family is enhanced. Further, Clarke, Hanson and Ross (2003) found that as the carer learns more about the person with dementia, their attitude towards the person positively changes, because they are better able to understand why the person is as they are now.

The benefits of life-story work, albeit limited, have become widely known, and many aged care service providers have introduced elements of social histories, and even photographic representations of the person at an earlier time of their life. In the example given below, the benefits of undertaking a culturally appropriate strategy to foster connectiveness are provided as a basis for consideration against different social contexts.

The RSL LifeCare Positive Connections project

Drawing upon research and the experiences of nurses and care staff at the ANZAC Retirement Village (McDonald 2007), all residents receive individualised care and experience social interactions that generate a feeling of security and comfort. The usual approaches to collecting social histories and having nostalgic photographs in residents' rooms go some way toward establishing their 'real' identity; but the information contained in care files is often not easy to read, especially if care staff also have to overcome personal difficulties with the English language.

In terms of special acknowledgement of residents' veteran status and needs, particular attention needs to be given to communication approaches that reinforce the values that have guided their lives. Best practice in this regard involves being aware that a person with dementia is at risk of becoming disconnected from their social and family contacts and even their own identities.

The 'Positive Connections' communication enhancement strategy implemented within high care dementia units draws together various aspects of known social history with the addition of personal elements gleaned from family interviews. The result is a simply worded, short overview of the person, their values and their life histories. The resident's story or 'bio' is written simply and concisely and placed on the front of case files, where all staff and visiting professionals to the unit can access it.

As part of the integrated approach to veteran care it is necessary for the biographies to be short, clear and readable by all involved. In writing the biographies the following elements need to be incorporated to maintain the integrity of the person's story:

1. Family involvement in constructing the story revealed some of the family dynamics with different members wanting to emphasise or downplay different elements. In some family contacts, siblings or their parent's previous marriage were not mentioned, but were later revealed by other members of the family.

2. The 'easy to read' nature of the story is essential to enable care staff and others to quickly become familiar with any resident's story. In this way each staff member can engage residents in conversation without having to focus their attention on a folder of pictures or photographs. Over time, staff gained deeper understanding of the person behind the symptoms, and genuine relationships between these residents and care staff began to build.

3. Placement of the biography on their private care file and not on doors or walls was a decision based on respecting residents' privacy and dignity. The location of the file in the office also allows staff discreetly to revise their knowledge of particular residents before speaking with them.

4. All staff are provided with in-service orientation to the Positive Connections strategy and the goals of forming genuine relationships with a person, notwithstanding their dementia symptoms. Individual coaching is provided to those staff who find conversations with seriously confused residents to be particularly demanding.

The examples below have had particular details altered to protect identity, but provide an indication of the content and style of biography used in the Positive Connections strategy at RSL LifeCare.

Who is Harry Mansell?

Harry was born in 1913 in Oberon and lived at Dee Why and Manly. He had two sons, Mack and Ian, with his first wife, Janice, and is now married to Ruby, whose daughter Margaret is from a previous marriage. Harry has a brother Jim and sister Jane, and his friends are Warren, Peter and Vince, a previous neighbour. Harry married his second wife when he was 77 and enjoyed what she describes as a 'fairytale' time together, Harry being 'what any woman would want in a husband'.

Harry was educated to Intermediate Certificate level at Fairlight Village School and later studied business management which helped him in his office management work. His war service was in the 9th Division in Tobruk, Syria, Egypt, the Holy Land, El Alamein, New Guinea and Borneo.

Before coming to RSL LifeCare, Harry was involved in the Dee Why RSL and National Retirement Association. He enjoyed sport – cricket, tennis, bodysurfing, golf, swimming, hiking, fishing and gardening. Harry was a committed and fit walker, enjoying walking groups when in his nineties. He was a keen reader, especially of business management, and enjoyed radio music, particularly 2CH (an easy-listening radio station in Sydney). He has travelled in Australia and overseas.

He now enjoys light orchestral music, classical vocals and sing-alongs. Ruby adores Harry and describes him as someone who never said a bad word about anyone, although more recently Harry struggles with the concept that Ruby must leave him in the hostel and go home without him.

Feedback from families, staff and visiting professionals has been positive, mostly because of a perception that contributions made by veterans are acknowledged in a way that brings their life values and character into the present, rather than relying on patchy reminiscences about the past. Topics of conversation can be based on real understanding of what the person has endured and achieved in their lives. Interpersonal connections that are genuine and respectful between veterans and staff are made possible and are a source of joy for all concerned.

The RSL LifeCare Positive Connections strategy draws upon international research around effects of dementia on relationships and health, of a diminished social circle or opportunities to relate with others in meaningful ways. Staff interviews following implementation of the strategy indicate an increase in staff comfort level in approaching residents and interacting with them, confident that they know the residents' preferences and understand the values by which they lived their lives before dementia. Conversations occurring within the unit between staff and residents are more personal and less activity-focused than before. The result is a more relaxed and inclusive environment, despite residents having symptoms of advanced dementia.

Who is Edie Smith?

Edie was born in 1924 in Chatswood in Sydney and is now a widow. She and her husband Jack had five children. Her daughter Jill with her two children and two grandchildren, her son Bill with one child and one grandchild both live locally. Edie is very proud of her nine grandchildren and four great-grandchildren.

Edie left school after primary school and worked as a cleaner in public schools for 16 years. Her husband Jack served in the Middle East in World War II, where he was seriously injured and not able to work when he returned home.

Edie lived at Mona Vale for 46 years. Being a widow at 40 and because she did not drive, she focused on her children and the neighbourhood, bringing up her family alone. She was a good mum. She also spent time at the local football club and the RSL Club, where she enjoyed playing the poker machines. She enjoyed knitting, raffles, and is interested in everything about the Royal Family. Edie loves animals and always had cats and dogs as pets.

Watching TV, sweeping and listening to Johnny Farnham's 'Sadie' are now some of Edie's favourite activities. She relates particularly well to the pets, enjoying bathing the hostel dog. She relates extremely well to small children and babies, so she enjoys talking to the baby doll her daughter Jill brought for her.

Integrated services and support for veterans

Happiness has far-reaching effects on health and well-being and is an important element of best practice in veterans' aged care. Happiness starts with 'feeling good' about oneself and enjoying life and wanting the feeling to continue. Unhappiness is 'feeling bad' and wishing things were different (Layard 2005). Happiness allows us to adapt to the inevitable changes associated with long life. Over the normal lifespan many aspects of one's life change, including some loss of hearing and sight; reduced mental and physical agility; and the loss of family and friends. Some people find happiness in relationships, or in doing good for others, in creating beautiful or useful things, or in reflecting on the meaning of life – but whatever the approach anyone takes, the health benefits of having a purpose in life are reflected in an ability to be happy. Making healthy psychosocial adjustments to changes related to living longer enables people to flourish in each stage of life.

Conclusion

In order to provide integrated services and supports for veterans in aged care, all of the issues canvassed above need to be resolved in ways that enable people to participate in both veteran and general community activities. Artificial segregation of people on the basis of their health status is not advised, as it prevents widespread participation by both active and less active veterans in the various ex-service and general civic events. Those who are cognitively compromised and those with physical difficulties can come together with members of the general community for a range of opportunities where all can experience the connection to each other that arises from their shared history.

Integrated aged care services for veterans are possible if aged care environments are set up and managed in ways that enable people to be happy in their own way or style, regardless of their physical and/or mental status. For veterans, in whatever society they may be living, special acknowledgement of their culture and values, in addition to the general aged care service approaches, increases their opportunities to be happy and fulfilled.

CHAPTER 15

On the Road to Emmaus: Ageing Religious Sisters, A Group with Specific Spiritual and Cultural Needs

Gabrielle Brian

Introduction

Each of the writers in this book has made a unique contribution towards the creation of a multifaceted mosaic, highlighting the spiritual and cultural needs of diverse communities of ageing members.

Just as it is generally acknowledged that particular ethnic and religious groups have specific cultural and spiritual needs, so, too, within mainstream cultures subgroups exist with their own specific needs; for example, veterans, and the topic of this chapter: ageing religious sisters, members of religious congregations.

In August 2008 I had the privilege of working with a group of Catholic religious sisters as part of their three weeks' 'mini-sabbatical', an initiative of the sisters to provide opportunities for renewal within their own environment. The chosen topic was 'Ageing and Spirituality'. As a group for whom the Bible provides nourishment and meaning in life, they examined this topic through the lens of the Journey to Emmaus (Luke 24:13–35). '*Off to Emmaus – white hair, wisdom, wit and worthiness*' was the theme for their gathering. Anstey (2008, p.108) has written about the role of Scripture in the spiritual development of older people, referring to religious communities in the broad sense of the word: 'This does not exclude other narrative resources, but recognises that for those elderly who identify themselves as belonging to religious communities the sacred texts are qualitatively distinct contributors in the formation of self-as-narrative.'

The experience of the 'mini-sabbatical' has formed the foundation of further reflection on the needs of the wider group of ageing religious sisters. In this chapter, as an observer and pastoral carer, I consider lessons that can be learnt from this particular group of older women, while acknowledging that the sisters hold a wealth of knowledge in regard to their own spiritual needs. Reflecting on the spiritual and cultural life of religious sisters may assist in providing spiritual support for sisters in residential care, while also raising awareness that there may be other, as yet unidentified groups with specific pastoral and spiritual care needs.

The quiet revolution

In the 40 years or so since the Second Vatican Council in the Catholic church, religious congregations have undergone a revolution as they responded to the invitation to begin a process of renewal based on the Gospel and the original inspiration and spirit, or 'charism', of their particular congregation, in the light of the needs of today's society: 'They lived through a time in which much of what they had learned and taken for granted in their early lives was transformed' (Matthews 2003, p.156). The majority of older religious sisters have seen incredible changes within their lifetime, as most congregations moved from a more monastic lifestyle to one which enables them to engage more actively with the broader community. There have traditionally been two streams within religious congregations: the contemplative or 'enclosed' orders and the 'apostolic' orders. Many congregations were established in the eighteenth and nineteenth centuries as apostolic orders, with a mission and vision to bring about change within their societies, often through education and health care, but over time many of these communities became more institutionalised and removed from the hurly-burly of 'secular' life. For many older religious sisters their early formative and training years would have been more geared to a contemplative regime, with long periods of prayer, silence, and a highly regulated lifestyle. Since the Second Vatican Council in the 1960s the emphasis has been on achieving a balance between work and prayer, with prayer and contemplation giving meaning and direction to apostolic activity.

On the road...

The sisters who gathered for the 'mini-sabbatical' were a wonderful, open, welcoming group of women and I treasure the memory of working with them. The venue, too, lent itself to prayer, reflection and renewal. Over the next two days we teased out the story of the journey to Emmaus, in the light of the journey into the later stages of life.

DAY ONE

Session One: The Emmaus story – intimacy and companionship.

Session Two: Images of God/images of ourselves.

Session Three: Telling our story.

DAY TWO

Session One: Hope and the mystery of suffering.

Session Two: Eucharist/spirituality.
               Life as a circle and living with change.

Session Three: Easter/ light from darkness.

Setting the scene: The Journey to Emmaus – Luke 24:13–35

The story begins after the death and resurrection of Jesus, as two dejected and disillusioned disciples leave the other disciples and set out for the town of Emmaus. Heads bowed, they share their misery and dashed hopes with each other as they trudge along.

'While they were talking and discussing, Jesus himself came near, but their eyes were kept from recognising him' (verses 15, 16).

Jesus gives them the opening, asking them what they have been discussing. This stops them in their tracks – they now have a listener with whom to share their story and the flood gates open: 'Are you the only stranger in Jerusalem who does not know the things that have taken place in these days?' (verse 18).

Jesus again invites them to pour out their story: 'What things?' he asks them (verse 19).

And the whole story comes rushing out: how they had put their hopes and expectations in this Jesus of Nazareth, but now he has been condemned to death and crucified. And to make matters even worse, if possible, now some women have visited his tomb and found the body missing. So, of course, not just being willing to accept the witness of the women, the men too have visited the tomb and found it just as the women had said.

Now Jesus enters the conversation and reminds them of the whole story of their tradition, namely that all the Old Testament prophecies pointed to this outcome: 'Was it not necessary that the Messiah should suffer these things and then enter into his glory?' (verse 26).

They have been so engrossed in conversation that they arrive at Emmaus before they realise it, and Jesus walks ahead as if going further. 'But they urged him strongly, saying, "Stay with us, because it is almost evening and the day is now nearly over." So he went in to stay with them' (verse 29).

The remarkable events of the day continue as, while sharing the meal, Jesus takes bread, blesses it, breaks it and shares it with them. Now, in amazement, they recognise the stranger in their midst, only to have him vanish from their sight.

'Were not our hearts burning within us, while he was talking to us on the road, while he was opening the scriptures to us?' (verse 32). How their gaze has moved through the events of this day – from eyes downcast, to recognising this stranger and now connecting with each other. Now it is time to face the other disciples with *their* new story:

'That same hour they got up and returned to Jerusalem; and they found the eleven and their companions gathered together. They were saying, "The Lord has risen indeed, and he has appeared to Simon!"' (verses 33, 34). Have they been upstaged, these two bearers of good news?

No, they have their own unique experience to share: 'Then they told what had happened on the road, and how he had been made known to them in the breaking of the bread' (verse 35).

As we moved into our consideration of the Emmaus journey, we looked at the intimacy of this scene, of Jesus walking with the two disciples as they trudged along the road to Emmaus and shared with him their disappointment that their dreams had been dashed.

Intimacy or isolation?

We considered our own need for intimacy as we age, intimacy being one of the tasks of ageing, including intimacy with God, companionship with others and being 'at home' with ourselves (Koenig 1994, pp.288–289). Intimacy may be a greater need as we age, and the loneliness often experienced by older people is not remedied by more activity, but by intimacy (Seeber 2000, p.150). I wondered about this need in older sisters, whether the modern structures of community living lend themselves to greater or less intimacy with others. These women have the gift of having travelled many years with like-minded women who share the same spirit and have similar values. How important it is, as well, to be open to new friendships as we age, to be open to new people God might bring into our lives, as well as treasuring life-long friends. It is recognised by Fleming (2002, p.115) that if residents make new friends soon after moving into an aged care facility, the settling in stage proceeds more smoothly, while those who lack engagement and involvement with others are at risk.

I am aware that some aged care facilities which house sisters provide them with dining areas separate from other residents. While this may be at the sisters' request and perhaps harks back to a time when many congregations had rules forbidding members to dine with people outside the congregation, even family members, I wonder if this limits opportunities to make new friends, as well as closing off possibilities for the other residents in befriending the sisters. Understanding some of the experiences of their early years in religious life will assist staff responsible for providing appropriate pastoral care. It is also worth recalling that the majority of older sisters will have experienced years of formation where they were warned of the dangers of 'particular friendships' and exclusive relationships, which were seen as detrimental to community living. While most will have grown through the experience of intimacy and close relationships, it may help to understand this feature of their early formation.

Recognising sacred places

As we took the time to reflect on our own life stories in the light of the Emmaus journey, we shared the sacred places where we meet God: with the gift of imagination, we might picture ourselves taking part in a Scriptural event, for example, sitting beside the well like the Samaritan woman (John 4:1–41), or at the entrance of Elijah's cave, waiting for God to pass by (1 Kings 19:13). Many people experience the presence of God in nature: the Celts spoke of 'thin places'; 'Indeed, we speak even today of some places being "thin places", meaning that the presence of the invisible and the spiritual in those places is almost palpable' (Silf 2001, p.9). The recognition of our own sacred places helps us appreciate something of the connection Indigenous peoples have with the land, a gift this particular congregation would value in having worked for many years with Australian Indigenous communities.

Other spiritual needs in ageing

Having reflected on the need for intimacy and the sacred places in our lives, we moved on to look at other spiritual needs in ageing, including those described by Koenig (1994, p.284). Although Koenig was referring to the needs of older frail people, these provided a backdrop for further discussion in the following sessions:

1. a need for meaning, purpose and hope

2. a need to transcend circumstances

3. a need for support in dealing with loss

4. a need for continuity

5. a need for validation and support of religious behaviours

6. a need to engage in religious behaviours

7. a need for personal dignity and sense of worthiness

8. a need for unconditional love

9. a need to express anger and doubt

10. a need to feel that God is on their side

11. a need to love and serve others

12. a need to be thankful

13. a need to forgive and be forgiven

14. a need to prepare for death and dying.

The participants were invited to consider whether these needs were being met in their own lives. To assist this reflection they were provided with quotations from Chittister's book (2008) about the challenges of ageing well and were invited to choose quotations which spoke to them personally. There was recognition that ageing well is a decision about how to grow into the later years of life: 'We are at the crossroads now, in the starkest kind of way. We are at the point in life where we must make the kinds of decisions that will determine the quality of our remaining years' (Chittister 2008, p.15).

'Imago Dei' – in the image of God

In the second session we considered the fact that the two disciples on the road to Emmaus failed to recognise Jesus. This led to reflection on our own images of God, and the connection between one's image of God and one's self-image and spirituality. The book of Genesis states that human beings are created 'in the image of God' (Chapter 1:27) and possess an intrinsic dignity. On the road to Emmaus Jesus gave the two forlorn disciples time, he respected and valued them, and he walked with them. Do people tend to believe their value is in what they do rather than in who they are? I shared the experience of meeting an elderly man, a new resident in an aged care facility. I later learnt he was in his mid-nineties at the time. He introduced himself as '"John Smith", the electrician'. I thought this was surely a rather elderly electrician and took a chance in asking him when he retired: 'In 1973' was his reply. It is worth considering the connection between self-identity, work and roles in life.

This movement of letting go of mid-life roles can be particularly challenging for those who have spent their lives working and caring for others, when they move out of 'active ministry'. Seeber examines the connection between 'vocation' and retirement: 'The principle of vocation as a life-long calling means that one may retire from a profession or job or series of jobs, but continue to seek ways of exercising the God-given talents he/she has to serve God through serving others' (1990, p.190). Religious sisters have the advantage of recognising in faith that their vocation of serving God through caring for others can continue throughout their lives, by virtue of their belief in the power of prayer. For many this can be seen as the transition from 'doing' to being and becoming, an opportunity to develop further the contemplative aspect of their lives. Melia (2008) noted this in her PhD research, 'Young in spirit, old in bones', pp.2–3:

> To study spiritual well-being in late life I listened to the life stories and spiritual narratives of forty Catholic religious women, ages 80–100. I learned how these women age gracefully. I watched how elder religious sisters, surrounded with positive role models, encourage others to remain engaged, practicing the 'ministry of prayer and presence'. I saw how their spiritual lives deepened through faith.

It is also important to recognise that this may not be the experience of every older religious sister. As with any other older person, or indeed at any stage of life, they may face a crisis of faith, where former certainties are shaken, and all that has formerly nourished them spiritually may no longer appear to do so. Clements (1990) has written about this possibility in later life, describing it as the 'stripping or shedding', 'the stage of life in which the adequacy of one's previous spirituality is tested mightily by the culture' (p.61). Then emptiness 'is now revealed in stark nakedness, no longer hidden by the social and cultural props that society has taken away' (p.62).

In regard to self-image and identity, religious sisters may not have the same social markers in their lives as other older women, particularly those related to children growing up, the birth of grandchildren, the signposts along the way that situate most women in their life's journey. In conducting spiritual assessments with older women, MacKinlay (2006) found that many responded to the question, 'Where do you find/What brings greatest meaning in your life?' with 'family', 'grandchildren'. This brings up the question of concept of generativity (Erikson, Erikson and Kivnick 1986, p.51), 'some kind of grandparenthood which must remain loyal to a defined and planned role for old age within an order of wisdom'. Generativity remains an important task for religious and single older women, and many find creative ways of continuing to give and be involved in the broader community, according to their strengths, interests and capabilities.

The ageing of the congregation as well as the ageing of its individual members must surely have an impact on how a community sees itself. Because of the declining numbers in religious congregations and the ageing of their members, the 'young' members of communities may be in their fifties or sixties, as noted by Raper (President's address, Catholic Religious Australia 2008):

> Our ageing and diminishing numbers tell an undeniable story of decline. In the 1970s, we recorded some 17,500 religious women, brothers and priests in the Australian Church, while today we count fewer than 8000, and the average age of religious women is in their seventies. We will soon be far fewer. Some communities have not received novices for years. For some their youngest members are in their fifties.

Self-image has an impact on the way people care for themselves at an individual and communal level. Those who value themselves for who they are rather than for what they do will be more likely to take proper care of themselves in a holistic way. David Snowdon (2001, p.170) has illustrated this:

> What I know for sure is that nutrition for healthy ageing is not just about eating certain foods or downing a certain number of milligrams of a prescribed number of vitamins each day. It also depends on where we eat, whom we eat with, and whether the meal nourishes our heart, mind, and soul as well as our body.

Meaning-making

The challenge to find meaning in life was considered, with the help of the insights of Viktor Frankl (1984), whose experience of life in concentration camps during World War II led him to ponder why and how some prisoners found a will to live among the daily horrors of life. He concluded that a human being's ultimate freedom is in being able to decide one's own attitude to life and its circumstances: 'everything can be taken from a man but one thing: the last of the human freedoms – to choose one's attitude in any given set of circumstances, to choose one's own way' (p.75).

Frankl wrote about 'the self-transcendence of human existence' pointing out that 'being human always points, and is directed, to something, or someone, other than oneself'; therefore 'self-actualisation is possible only as a side-effect of self-transcendence' (Frankl 1984, p.115).

According to Frankl, finding meaning in life is about finding purpose in life. In this sense, it is best understood by examining its opposite, meaninglessness. He explained that meaning in life can be discovered in three ways, 'first, by creating a work or doing a deed; secondly by experiencing something or encountering someone; and thirdly by the attitude we take toward unavoidable suffering' (p.133). He spoke of the importance of having a 'child', either physically or symbolically, something outside oneself to love and reach out to: 'A man who becomes conscious of the responsibility he bears toward a human being who affectionately waits for him, or to an unfinished work, will never be able to throw away his life. He knows the "why" of his existence, and will be able to bear almost any "how"' (p.88).

Frankl describes how the image of his wife and his love for her sustained him: 'nothing could touch the strength of my love, my thoughts, and the image of my beloved' (p.50). Also the desire to complete his manuscript, written on scraps of paper, gave him a purpose, a reason to survive and transcend life in the concentration camps.

Holding, telling the stories

To continue the story of the journey to Emmaus: 'While they were talking and discussing Jesus himself came near and went with them' (Luke 24:15). Reflecting on this scene and the outpouring of the two disciples led the group to think about the importance of story, and that one of the tasks of ageing is to make meaning of one's life's story. Noel Davis has provided a lovely image in his poem 'The Story Teller' (Davis 1991, p.98), which expresses God's love for each of us in our unique stories, inviting us to 'nestle into our Father God, who loves stories'.

It is also important to keep alive the stories of the community. How important this is in religious congregations today, that their stories and traditions are listened to, passed on and made relevant in today's world. With fewer members joining religious communities, congregations are making efforts to ensure that their stories are not lost – for example, by developing networks of associate members who share their spirit and charism.

We talked about the value of spiritual reminiscence and how remembering is different from regretting, being stuck in 'if only I had…' Sometimes we need to trust in God's forgiveness and remember that the choices we made have sown seeds for the future:

> It is through this self-acceptance and the acceptance of the past that we arrive at a broader conceptualisation of the meaning of life itself and of our own life in particular. Personal failures are matched with personal success, self-reproach gives way to a sense of self-esteem, and death can then be approached with calm serenity. (D'Apice 1989, p.166)

Just like it was for those two disciples, sometimes the only option is to walk through the downcast times. Jesus accepted that this was where they were in their lives and accompanied them through it, drawing them on to a larger vision. He gives them permission to tell their story: 'What things?' he asks them (Luke 24:19). Sometimes we, too, need to ask the right question to give others an opening to tell their story. Perhaps Jesus had a quiet smile in asking this question, being well aware of 'what things'! We talked about the transcending power of humour: 'Humour is knowledge with a soft smile' (Nouwen 1976, p.74).

As they told their story the disciples were gradually taking away layers of the experience, like the story of Jesus' healing of the blind man, who found his vision being restored in stages: 'I can see people, but they look like trees, walking…' (Mark 8:22–25).

'We had hoped…'

The disciples reached the depths of their disappointment – 'But we had hoped…' (verse 21). The meaning of hope and its place in later life was considered. What does the virtue of hope mean to this group of older women? The lifestyle to which they committed themselves decades ago has changed dramatically and the future is unsure. Many religious communities are 'reconfiguring' or restructuring, perhaps joining with other congregations who share a similar spirit. Some congregations have not received new members for many years. Many are trying new and creative ways to pass on their spirituality, charism and traditions. Processes are being put in place to ensure their ministries are continued. Often this entails finding the balance between wise, discerning trust in others to continue the work, and maintaining some involvement. Where does this leave the senior sisters who have worked 'in the heat of the day'? Cresp (2005, p.349) has written about the impact of these changes on her own congregation:

> As with all groups, each foundation of the Sisters of St Joseph as a body has gone through the organisational stages of enthusiastic beginnings, rapid growth demanding uniformity and decline with options for extinction or rebirth. The emotional impacts of these stages on the group are not to be discounted.

It could be expected that any group experiencing such dramatic change would be affected both on an individual level and communally, including the sisters who attended this 'mini-sabbatical'.

Some congregations, facing the reality of fewer and ageing members, have made major decisions in regard to the care of the sisters and the best use of the congregation's property. At times this has involved redesigning their larger buildings as aged care facilities. While this might make economic sense, at times it exacts an emotional toll on the older sisters, additional to the challenges most people experience in moving into an aged care facility, due to:

- an emotional attachment to what may have been the 'mother house' in earlier days

- the challenge of living with people from outside the congregation, both men and women, after years living solely with other religious sisters

- the challenge of maintaining a prayer life in community.

These challenges call for empathy and understanding on the part of those caring for the older sisters.

The two disciples had hoped, trusted, believed 'that he was the one to redeem Israel' (verse 21). Their hopes appear to be dashed by the crucifixion of Jesus. What does this say in regard to the spiritual development of older people? It could be seen as the stage of psychosocial development described by Erikson, that of integrity versus despair, the outcome of which is wisdom (Erikson *et al.* 1986). Frankl has painted a picture of the wise elder:

> What does it matter to him if he notices he is growing old? Rather than envying the young setting out on the journey of life he will think 'Instead of possibilities, I have realities in my past, not only the reality of work done and of love loved, but of sufferings bravely suffered. These sufferings are

even the things of which I am most proud, though these are things which cannot inspire envy. (Frankl 1984, p.125)

MacKinlay writes about the connection between wisdom and finding 'ultimate meaning' in life:

> From wisdom comes the ability to construct one's individual and final life meanings; the spirit grows, finding meaning in being, accepting the inevitable losses of life, and letting go of things that are no longer important. Meaning making in the later years becomes a critical aspect of effective ageing. And it is this search for the final meaning in life which is truly a component of the spiritual dimension. (MacKinlay 2001, p.153)

Discussions on the virtue of hope and the movement to wisdom in the context of ageing religious sisters led to a consideration of the spiritual tasks of ageing (MacKinlay 2001, p.42). The importance of being a hope-giver was discussed. How do we stay hope-filled and face our fears as we move into our later years? What might these fears be? Christine Bryden's words as she faced the future with a diagnosis of dementia might inspire others to face the future, whatever it might bring, with faith and trust:

> I know that as this disease progresses, I can live in the present, as Jesus lived in the present. I'll live for each day, not worrying about tomorrow, nor indeed about yesterday as my memories fade. With you walking alongside me as I walk this way with Christ, I can feel confident to believe in Julian of Norwich's uplifting words that she heard God say to her: 'I make all things well and I can make all things well, and I shall make all things well; and you will see for yourself that every kind of thing will be well.' (Bryden and MacKinlay 2002, p.75)

The end and the beginning

Koenig (1994, p.284) wrote about the 'need to prepare for death and dying' as a spiritual need in ageing. Jesus led the two disciples on the road to Emmaus to reflect on the mystery of suffering and death: 'Was it not necessary that the Messiah should suffer these things and then enter into his glory?' (Luke 24:26). It is in suffering that we see the 'defiant power of the human spirit' described by Frankl (Kimble and Ellor 2000, p.17). Suffering requires us to face the shadows in our own lives and in our communities. It usually implies loss or absence. It has been revealed since her death that even Mother Teresa suffered great spiritual desolation, in experiencing the absence of God (Livermore 2008, p.280).

In reflecting on death the sisters spent time with various writings, including 'A Blessing for Old Age' and 'A Blessing for Death' (O'Donohue

1997, pp.242, 278), as well as a reflection on death by Henri Nouwen, 'The Flying Rodleighs', where death is likened to the trapeze artist who lets go in trust, to be received in love by the 'Catcher' (Gagen 2001, p.37).

For religious sisters the death of one of their members brings sorrow and grief: often this is someone they have known most of their lives. As well as the personal loss there is also the added dimension of the diminishment of the congregation. Likewise, increasing frailty of the members is likely to be a source of grief. This is not a situation they would have 'hoped for' in entering the congregation, which would probably have been in the days when large numbers joined their communities. The call to transcendence is a communal call as well as an individual task: as one older sister shared with me, 'We (as a congregation) have become gentler.'

A new beginning

By the time the disciples reach Emmaus and the end of their journey they are able to reach out to the one who has been reaching out to them. They now have a relationship with him – it is no longer a matter of knowing 'about' Jesus of Nazareth. They invite him to stay with them (Luke 24:29). They have transcended their own limited understanding, needs and experience – that is, 'The wishes and needs of the self are transcended in favour of other people's needs and wishes' (Tornstam 2005, p.62).

Transcendence is certainly a spiritual process, linked with a developing sense of interiority and integrity (MacKinlay 2001, p.43). Those older people who are able to transcend their present difficulties may achieve a real sense of peace and acceptance that passes human understanding. Kimble has written, 'There appears to be an absence of symbols of transcendence in our society that would provide answers to the questions related to meaning of ageing and growing old' (Kimble 1990, p.113). In this group the stories of people who had displayed qualities of transcendence were shared. The stories of the community contain many examples of such people, people whose faith has strengthened them in transcending their disabilities and limitations.

The disciples now recognised Jesus: 'their eyes were opened' (Luke 24:31). They recognised him in the familiar actions of breaking and sharing the bread and blessing them (verse 30). Sharing the bread of Eucharist and the Scriptures are at the centre of the life of a religious community and nourish the faith of the individual and the community. Koenig has described the elements of a mature faith: keeping God at the centre of our ultimate concern, trusting completely in God, whatever the circumstances, and expressing our faith in loving action for others (Koenig 1994, pp.124–127).

The disciples now decide to set out on the return journey, a reminder of the spiral nature of human life. They come back to where they have started, but now with new insight, depth and experience. Often that can also be our experience – perhaps in later years we might have the opportunity to fulfil our early dreams, but in a different form. Nouwen's symbol, the wagon wheel, was a guide in further reflection on this theme:

> The wagon turns from ground to ground, but not without moving forward. Although we have only one life cycle to live, although it is only a small part of human history which we will cover, to do this gracefully is our greatest vocation. Indeed we go from dust to dust, we move up to go down, we grow to die, but the first dust does not have to be the same as the second, the going down can become the moving on, and death can be made into our final gift. (Nouwen 1976, pp.13–14)

'Choose life then...' (Deuteronomy 30:19)

The disciples continue their ministry, in returning to share their experience. Having offered hospitality to their guest, they reach out to the other disciples in sharing their story. Again the need to be generative, to encourage life in others, was discussed. Some of the challenges in ageing were highlighted, as well as the importance of resilience, flexibility and openness to change. As Chittister writes, changes happen anyway; our choice is in how we accept these changes (2008, p.46). Elsewhere she describes the options faced in ageing, in deciding what form life will take:

> Only one thing is necessary now: we must choose to begin a new kind of life, related to the past, of course, but free of strictures that bind us to it. We must see what we do in it as good. We must find it life-giving ourselves. We must be a gift to the world some way, somehow, for someone. It's those who go into this period washed-out, dried up, angry, hurt, humiliated, and resisting, for whom newness is a bane rather than a blessing. These people sit sullen or listless in a chair, not reviving themselves, not vivifying anyone else in life, either. They bring no joy to the world because they have no joy to give. They become grumpy old men, whining old women – *not* because that is what old age is about, but because they have chosen to be less than what they are meant to be. They have chosen to be less than what God has in mind for them these years – another kind of fullness of life, another kind of usefulness. (Chittister 2008, pp.48–49)

We shared ideas about the choices we face about how to age. Again Viktor Frankl (1984) offered inspiration, as well as Chittister (2008, p.15): 'We are at the crossroads now, in the starkest kind of way. We are at the point in life where we must make the kinds of decisions that will determine the quality of our remaining years.' MacKinlay (2001, p.62) also describes these choices: 'to face the reality of time, or to deny; to continue to grow spiritually, or to stagnate; the opportunity for developing spiritual integrity and hope, or for final despair. It is in each case a personal decision.'

The final session focused on Easter, the ultimate story of transcendence. 'The hope of resurrection lies at the heart of the way in which Christians embody the practices of growing old' (Hays and Hays 2003, p.15). This, they explain, is because the Resurrection 'shapes our understanding of ageing' in affirming God's fidelity to all creation and by proclaiming God's triumph over death, so that 'we are set free from fear, no longer paralysed or controlled by fear of ageing and dying'.

The participants brought to this session symbols of the experience of these two days. A quotation from Clarissa Pinkola Estes spoke of the Easter experience:

> There is great hope, for nothing can be destroyed. No good idea, no beautiful God's light illuming darkness can be done away with. The dousing is only momentary. All goodness comes back. Even from the grave, whether a real one or a psychic one. The ignition is always set for re-start and will often turn over and hum if there be but one small spark offered by a kind soul or a wise mind. Maybe repetitive and thoughtful and generous sparks before the ignition catches in all strength. But it will ignite again. (Estes 2008)

The spark of inspiration which has led women to embrace a vowed commitment in a religious congregation will continue to ignite, although the shape of religious life may appear different from that of previous generations. The contribution of religious sisters to the church in Australia and to Australian society in general cannot be overestimated, from the establishment of schools, hospitals, orphanages, to the support of people in rural and outback areas. At this time in history perhaps the most significant contribution they can make is to remind others of the spiritual tasks involved in ageing well. This is in keeping with research carried out by Ramsey and Blieszner into resilience in two groups of faith-filled older women in the United States of America and Germany:

> Just as each symphony creates a particular and special sound, so the marvellous, complex interweaving of the themes of personality, history, culture, and faith in each life story is unique. Yet if members of the (wider) religious community honor their older friends as the spiritual resources

they are, careful listening will allow them to recognise patterns of resiliency and to discover springs of strength more than sufficient for a lifetime of faithful living. (Ramsey and Blieszner 1999, p.140)

Conclusion

The story of the journey to Emmaus is a helpful framework in reflecting on the spiritual, cultural and pastoral needs of ageing religious sisters. Supporting these needs involves mutuality; it calls for an appreciation of the sisters' specific cultural and religious needs on the part of those involved in their care, and recognition on the part of the sisters of their continuing valuable contribution as spiritual elders, with gifts of 'wisdom, wit and worthiness'. Like the two disciples, they have a unique story to tell to all those fortunate enough to hear it.

CHAPTER 16

Promoting High Quality Care

Elizabeth Pringle

Introduction

Chapters of this book have examined aspects of ageing and spirituality across faiths and cultures and the types of care that may be offered. Care always takes place within a context. That context includes the buildings that house older people in need of care and it includes the environment in which care is delivered. The context of care also includes the standards that are used to monitor the kind and quality of care delivered to often vulnerable older people.

This chapter relates specifically to cultural and spiritual matters in residential aged care homes. Although this chapter is written within an Australian context, and is therefore focused on Australian Government subsidised residential aged care, the issues in relation to culture and spirituality are similar to the USA, Canada and the UK. In particular, it focuses on how the Australian accreditation body, the Aged Care Standards and Accreditation Agency Ltd (the Agency) fulfils its role in accrediting aged care homes and monitoring performance to ensure compliance with the Accreditation Standards. It outlines features of the Agency's role, the Accreditation Standards, and how they address culture and spirituality. Finally, it discusses some of the complexities relating to cultural and spiritual matters in residential aged care.

Residential aged care

For older people who require some form of assistance, Australia's aged care system provides two levels of supported care: residential aged care and community care (where services are coordinated for delivery in the person's home). These types of care are part of a broader system of health, income support, housing and community services. Aside from Medicare, Australia's universal health care system, most other support is income- or means-tested, depending on the level of income and assets of the care recipient, with some residents required to pay a daily fee to contribute to their care.

Australian residential aged care caters for older Australians who can no longer manage to live in their own homes. They receive accommodation, hospitality, personal and nursing care commensurate with their needs. The 'Report on the Operation of the Aged Care Act 1997 1 July 2007 to 30 June 2008' states that 208,079 people received permanent residential aged care in 2830 residential aged care homes run by 1547 approved providers. Sixty per cent of these homes are run by religious, charitable and community-based organisations. Thirty-three per cent are run by for-profit commercial enterprises, and 7 per cent are run by state and local governments. In 2007–2008 the Australian Government spent over AUD$6 billion on residential aged care subsidies.

Accreditation is part of the broader regulatory framework for residential aged care. The regulatory framework consists of legislation that specifies arrangement for the delivery of aged care, including:

- approval for individuals to enter residential aged care and receive Australian Government subsidies

- approval of corporate bodies who can own and operate residential aged care homes

- the number and location of subsidised places

- the fees that can be charged and the subsidies received by providers

- quality outcomes, including accreditation

- quality of building standards, including fire safety

- entry contributions by residents (accommodation bonds) and prudential arrangements for the refund of bonds, and residents' rights.

Aged Care Standards and Accreditation Agency Ltd

The accreditation arrangements for aged care homes exist for the protection of residents' health, safety and well-being and the promotion of quality care. The Aged Care Standards and Accreditation Agency Ltd is appointed by the Department of Health and Ageing under the Aged Care Act 1997 as the accreditation body (Department of Health and Ageing 2008b).

The accreditation body's functions are defined by the *Accreditation Grant Principles 1999* as:

- managing the residential aged care accreditation process using the Accreditation Standards

- promoting high quality care and assisting the industry to improve service quality by identifying best practice, and providing information, education and training to the industry

- assessing and strategically managing services working towards accreditation

- liaising with the Department of Health and Ageing about services that do not comply with the Accreditation Standards.

The Agency is paid a grant according to the Accreditation Grant Principles 1999. It also receives income from accreditation fees payable by homes and sales of education services. It is a company wholly owned by the Australian Government. The Agency is an company limited by guarantee, and subject to the:

- Corporations Act 2001

- Commonwealth Authorities and Companies Act 1997

- Aged Care Principles (made under subsection 96–1 (1) of the Aged Care Act 1997):

  - The Accountability Principles 1998 set out four requirements of approved providers. First, it outlines the consent to access that approved providers must give to a representative. Second, it defines the responsibilities of approved providers to ensure staff and volunteers meet requirements relating to police checks and statutory declarations. Third, it details requirements on approved providers relating to reporting assaults to the police or the Secretary (Head of the Department of Health and Ageing). Fourth, it sets out requirements on approved providers relating to alleged or suspected assaults.

  - Accreditation Grant Principles 1999 set out the framework to be followed by the Agency for the accreditation of aged care services and the conditions of the accreditation grant.

  - Quality of Care Principles 1997 set out the responsibilities of approved providers to provide quality care according to the Accreditation Standards and other requirements.

The Agency fulfils its functions using processes set down in legislation and is required to carry out regular supervision of accredited services to monitor their performance against the Accreditation Standards. Managing accreditation involves:

- assessment of homes' performance against the Accreditation Standards

- granting or refusing accreditation, based on performance

- deciding on the period of accreditation of individual homes

- monitoring the performance of accredited homes

- monitoring and assisting with improvements to address deficiencies

- assisting with continuous improvement

- providing information and education to assist the industry to improve.

Features of accreditation and regulation

The Agency has the responsibility under legislation to grant accreditation for a period of time, monitor ongoing compliance through support visits (announced and unannounced), and to vary or revoke the accreditation status of a home where there is a failure of a home to comply with the Accreditation Standards. The Agency has the power to recommend sanctions. However, only the Secretary of the Department of Health and Ageing has the power to apply sanctions or revoke an approved provider's status to operate aged care.

The Agency also provides an extensive industry education programme. The purpose of education is to disseminate examples of better practice and to assist the industry to improve its practice and monitor quality against the Accreditation Standards. The Agency provides education through conferences, seminars, courses and self-directed learning packages across Australia.

The main elements of the accreditation process are:

- self-assessment by the residential aged care home

- submission of an application for accreditation

- assessment by a team of registered quality assessors – desk and site audits

- decision made about accreditation by an authorised decision-maker from the Agency (not part of the assessment team) regarding compliance and period of the accreditation

- issuing of an accreditation certificate

- publication of the decision

- monitoring of ongoing compliance and continuous improvement through support contacts and review audits

- re-application for accreditation prior to expiry of the residential aged care home's existing period of accreditation.

Accreditation is not a one-off event. Once a residential aged care home is accredited, the approved provider is required to maintain compliance with the legislated standards of care for residents, and to undertake continuous improvement. Each home receives at least one unannounced visit each year. When an existing home applies for a further period of accreditation, an assessment team is appointed by the Agency to conduct a full audit of the home's performance against the Accreditation Standards.

The assessment team follows up on information supplied in the residential aged care home's application and assesses compliance with the Accreditation Standards by:

- verifying information provided in the self-assessment concerning compliance with the Accreditation Standards

- reviewing aspects of the residential aged care home's quality management system, which demonstrates compliance and continuous improvement for residents

- observing the environment and what occurs at the residential aged care home, including staff–resident interactions and general care for residents

- interviewing residents and their representatives, management, staff and other relevant people, such as visiting doctors and pharmacists

- reviewing records and other documents, such as care plans and education records

- considering other information provided to the team or observed while on site.

Accreditation Standards

The Accreditation Standards (Commonwealth of Australia 2007, Aged Care Principles, Quality of Care Principles 1997) (Department of Health and Ageing 2008a) outline the expected standard of quality of care and quality of life to be provided to residents in residential aged care. Forty-four expected outcomes are contained within the Accreditation Standards.

The four Accreditation Standards relate to:

- management systems, staffing and organisation development
- health and personal care
- resident lifestyle
- physical environment and safe systems.

Whilst the Accreditation Standards (Department of Health and Ageing 2008a) set out the expected outcomes that are to be achieved, they do not prescribe how they are to be achieved. This reflects the diversity of residential aged care homes and the needs and preferences of their residents. Therefore, although all homes must demonstrate that they meet the Accreditation Standards, how they meet these will vary from home to home. Homes must also demonstrate that they actively pursue continuous improvement in relation to each Standard.

Standard 3 and 'Expected Outcome 3.8 Cultural and spiritual life'

The overarching principle for Standard 3 is that:

> Residents retain their personal, civic, legal and consumer rights, and are assisted to achieve active control of their lives within the residential care service and in the community.

The expected outcomes within this Standard describe the various elements of the management, delivery and improvement of residents' lifestyle. Therefore, when a home is assessed, it needs to demonstrate how it meets its responsibilities to residents in relation to emotional support, independence, privacy and dignity, leisure interests and activities, cultural and spiritual life, choice and decision-making, and security of tenure and residents' rights.

In June 2008 the Minister for Ageing, the Hon. Justine Elliot MP, released the report: *Evaluation of the Impact of Accreditation on the Delivery of Quality of Care and Quality of Life to Residents in Australian Government Subsidised Residential Aged Care Homes – Final Report.* The report made comments about the need to review the Accreditation Standards. Upon releasing the report Minister

Elliot announced (Elliot 2008) that she was keen to work with stakeholders to consider the report, and in particular to strengthen the accreditation and monitoring processes. The review process commenced late 2008.

Currently 'Standard 3: Expected Outcome 3.8 Cultural and spiritual life' requires that:

> Individual interests, customs, beliefs, and cultural and ethnic backgrounds are valued and fostered.

In the context of the current Accreditation Standards and a possible review, this chapter will focus on the wording of the current expected outcome; however, it should be noted that many of the comments relate to broad principles. Therefore, assuming that any revised Accreditation Standards include reference to cultural and spiritual matters, these principles are likely to remain relevant.

'Expected Outcome 3.8 Cultural and spiritual life' includes three key words: *individual*, *valued* and *fostered*. The word *individual* recognises that cultural and spiritual aspects are highly individualised, and hence homes have to cater for the needs of individuals, not groups. The word *valued* reflects the way in which the home must show respect and honour in regard to each resident's culture and spirituality. The third key word, *fostered*, indicates that homes are not only to recognise and value the culture and spirituality of residents, but also to demonstrate how they encourage further growth and development.

The 'iceberg' model of culture is widely used in the public domain to depict how the visible or tangible aspects are relatively small compared to the invisible and intangible aspects. The model (Figure 16.1) has been adapted from the Ethnic Communities Council of NSW and NSW Community Options (2006) Participant Materials. The iceberg shows how aspects of a person normally visible on the surface are often simplistically used as markers of culture and spiritual life. However, there are very important non-visible aspects that also need to be explored, identified and understood. Culture and spirituality are highly individualised aspects of a person, and need to be understood in the context of the individual. Only considering the more obvious, visible aspects of a person can be misleading and lead to stereotyping. For example, if we identify someone as being of a particular ethnicity, based on their name and appearance, we may make assumptions about their religion, attitudes and preferences, all of which may be correct, entirely wrong or a combination of both. The key point is that that making assumptions and inferences based on generalisations is not helpful in understanding the uniqueness of each person.

The challenge in aged care is to discover what lies 'below the waterline' for each individual, so that individualised care and lifestyle plans can be developed to reflect each person's needs and preferences. Each person brings their own unique family culture, practices and beliefs to a community, and these influence their behaviour and religious awareness; culture affects music, food, clothing, identity, roots – it is what makes each person unique.

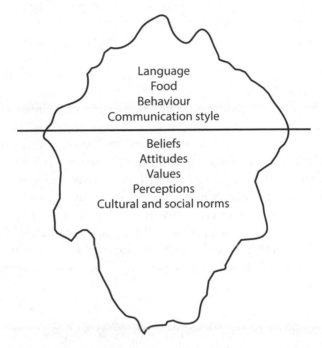

Figure 16.1 The iceberg model of culture (adapted from Ethnic Communities Council of NSW and NSW Community Options 2006 Particpant Materials)

Demonstrating compliance

In forming a view about compliance with 'Expected Outcome 3.8 Cultural and spiritual life', there are four key results that an assessor would consider:

- resident satisfaction
- systems and processes that are effective in identifying specific needs and providing appropriate support
- staff awareness
- evidence of accessing external resources.

The Results and Processes Guide (Aged Care Standards and Accreditation Agency Ltd 2008) states that 'Expected Outcome 3.8 Cultural and spiritual life' should focus on 'results for residents'. This means that a home must be able to show how management 'demonstrates its processes, systems and external relations are effective in valuing and fostering each individual resident's interests, customs, beliefs and cultural and ethnic backgrounds'. However, even if management *demonstrates* what superficially could be observed as effective management processes and systems, compliance can only be understood in the context of what the actual results are for the residents.

RESIDENT SATISFACTION

To ascertain resident satisfaction, an assessor conducts interviews with residents and/or their representatives to confirm that they are satisfied that the home values and fosters residents' individual interests, customs, beliefs and cultural and ethnic backgrounds. The key aspect here is that the residents'/representatives' level of satisfaction in relation to these matters is paramount. The advantage of this is that assessment of compliance is not determined against a set of externally imposed cultural or spiritual values that may or may not be acceptable to the resident population. Rather, it is measured according to the values and expectations of each resident. Their level of satisfaction is highly influenced by their background and expectations.

SYSTEMS AND PROCESSES

To ascertain if a home has effective systems and processes in place to identify specific needs and provide support, an assessor considers *how* the home assesses and internally communicates residents' individual interests, customs, beliefs and cultural and ethnic backgrounds. They would consider how this is then reflected in the care and services provided. For example, how is consultation with residents' representatives or others (for example, spiritual or cultural advisors) managed? What consideration is there of past and current cultural religious, spiritual and ethnic practices? This should include cultural aspects that are not necessarily related to ethnicity or country of origin. For example, some customs and religions may affect a resident's attitude to, and willingness for, some medical interventions. What processes are in place to identify support required for each resident's ongoing cultural and ethnic needs? Perhaps they have particular needs for language assistance, or food and drink preferences.

STAFF AWARENESS

Even if a home has thoroughly assessed a resident's cultural and spiritual needs, and determined what support is required to value and foster the resident's individual needs, unless there are processes for communicating this to staff, it is highly unlikely to be effective. Staff awareness and communication of residents' needs and preferences involves accurate assessment and recording of these in relevant documents such as care plans and resident assessments. However, it would also include how staff handovers occur, and how resident needs are communicated to all relevant staff (such as food services, cleaning, laundry and maintenance) so that residents' needs can be accommodated across the care and lifestyle spectrum.

EVIDENCE OF ACCESSING EXTERNAL RESOURCES

While each home is expected to meet the individual cultural and spiritual needs of residents, it is recognised that these are specialist areas and often require reference to, or input from, external resources. For example, to make a meaningful contribution, a resident may need access to appropriate cultural service or support staff, such as interpreters. A resident may wish to have an external person attend and participate in activities, as indicated in the plan. For example, when a resident has decisions to make about treatment options regarding a health condition, they may wish family members to be involved.

In addition to the four results stated on page 235, there are four key processes that an assessor would consider when forming a view about compliance:

- assessment of residents' needs

- planning

- implementation

- review.

ASSESSMENT OF RESIDENTS' NEEDS

At the heart of effective care and lifestyle is sound assessment of needs. Unless thorough assessments are undertaken by appropriately skilled staff, the home will not be in a position to develop individual care and lifestyle plans that reflect the needs and preferences of residents. Assessment of a resident's care and lifestyle needs must be holistic and contextual to the individual, taking into account their culture and spirituality.

PLANNING

After effective assessment, homes must reflect this information in appropriate plans, so that all relevant staff and health professionals can use it to provide individualised care. For example, care plans should describe a resident's specific needs and preferences for observance of particular significant religious days or times, and how this may impact on food preparation and consumption.

IMPLEMENTATION

After assessment and planning, the most important phase is that of implementation. Here the assessor is looking to see evidence of how the plans are executed. For example, for a resident who has expressed interest in attending cultural or spiritual activities, how are staff supporting and encouraging him or her to do so, and how do they interact with the resident?

Around culture and spirituality, this could be applied in numerous ways, including how staff dress the resident according to his or her preferences. For example, it may include assisting a resident to put on personal items such as a crucifix that may have significance.

REVIEW

This involves the residents, their assessed needs and whether the home has strategies in place to cater for changes in the residents' health and physical abilities so that they can still meaningfully participate in cultural and spiritual activities. For example, a person may have had a long association with a cultural club or faith-based organisation, but due to frailty can no longer attend gatherings, meetings and other activities. The assessor may consider how the home continues to support and facilitate continuing involvement, for example, by encouraging club visitors, arranging for the club newsletter to be sent, or facilitating the club members to have meetings in the home.

Links with other expected outcomes

When the 'Expected Outcome 3.8 Cultural and spiritual life' is assessed, it should be noted that this is inextricably linked to holistic care. Care should be provided in the context of recognising the whole person and their unique needs; hence assessment considers links to related expected outcomes.

Standard One expected outcomes

Standard One, 'Expected Outcome 1.8 Information systems', requires management and staff to have access to accurate and appropriate information to help them fulfil their various roles in relation to management, care provision, resident lifestyle and the environment. This expected outcome has a critical link to cultural and spiritual life because, unless there are adequate communications throughout the home, a resident's needs and preferences cannot be implemented if not made known to relevant staff. This is particularly pertinent where staff and/or residents may not all speak the same language, or have other communication barriers; literally and metaphorically. Translation, use of interpreters, use of graphics and use of shared terminology are all important tools to apply when sharing information. 'Expected Outcome 1.8 Information systems' is also about recording the information so that it can be used in planning and can be accessed by all relevant staff.

Standard Two expected outcomes

Components of 'Expected Outcome 3.8 Cultural and spiritual life' affect the performance of all expected outcomes relating to health and personal care, especially Expected Outcomes '2.9 Palliative care' and '2.10 Nutrition and hydration'.

'2.9 Palliative care' has very obvious links to '3.8 Cultural and spiritual life'. It could involve identification, assessment and treatment of physical pain, as well as providing comfort and support to meet psychological, cultural, spiritual and social needs. Palliative care has broad application regarding preferences, and for residents needing palliation, it becomes more important. Preferences might concern practical, but often very important matters, such as which people a resident wants to have with them in their final stages of life. It could encompass particular spiritual or religious rites, symbols, music, photos or other items that have meaning and bring comfort to a resident at this time.

'Expected Outcome 2.10 Nutrition and hydration' has obvious and subtle links to culture and spirituality. Residents may wish to observe religious and cultural practices such as fasting, eating or abstaining from particular foods on particular days, eating food prepared according to specific practices, timing of meals with other religious events, and self-denial of foods for a period. It is essential that a thorough assessment be conducted of each individual resident so that assumptions are not made according to ethnic or religious affiliation. Within any population there is likely to be a broad variation of adherence to religious and cultural codes, ranging from those who strictly observe all practices, to those who do some and those who do none, but still identify themselves with a particular group.

It is important that residents are supported to make choices and have those choices respectfully carried out by the home.

Standard Three expected outcomes

Cultural and spiritual considerations are inherent in all expected outcomes of Standard Three:

- 3.4 Emotional support

- 3.5 Independence

- 3.6 Privacy and dignity

- 3.7 Leisure interests and activities

- 3.9 Choice and decision-making.

Other expected outcomes under Standard 3 include the provision of emotional support on entry and throughout the resident's stay at a home. Standard 3 also includes choice and decision-making, which enables residents to exercise choice and control over their lifestyle, and assists them to achieve maximum independence, maintain friendships and participate in the life of the community both within and outside the residential care home. It may impact on how a resident prefers to be dressed. For instance, the assessment process should identify if there are any cultural or religious practices the resident wishes to observe, such as covering the head and wearing clothes of particular colours and styles. It should be culturally appropriate, with choice and decision-making taking into account ethnic (including language) backgrounds. Residents should have access to appropriate community groups as requested, and, if possible, emotional support should be relevant to the cultural and other beliefs of the resident. Aspects of 'Expected outcome 3.8 Cultural and spiritual life' are also encompassed in the Charter of residents' rights and responsibilities.

Standard Four expected outcomes

'EXPECTED OUTCOME 4.8 CATERING, CLEANING AND LAUNDRY SERVICES'

The home should have systems in place to ensure that residents are provided with meals appropriate to their cultural backgrounds, as previously discussed. In relation to cleaning and laundry, particularly where it involves entering a resident's room, it is important for staff to be sensitive to cultural and spiritual preferences. For example, a person may have a preferred prayer time, and during this period they do not wish to be disturbed. They may also have culturally defined standards about cleanliness that should be understood.

Key factors relating to culture and spirituality

There are a number of key factors to consider in relation to culture and spirituality. These are complex matters that challenge aged care providers for various reasons.

There has been considerable debate over recent times regarding the terms 'quality of life' and 'quality of care'. *Evaluation of the Impact of Accreditation on the Delivery of Quality of Care and Quality of Life to Residents in Australian Government Subsidised Residential Aged Care Homes – Final Report* (Commonwealth of Australia, Department of Health and Ageing 2008, p.49) has considered views of stakeholders and a literature review, and proposed the following definitions:

'Quality of care' is the degree to which acceptable standards are met or exceeded in relation to:

- physical, personal, psychological, spiritual and socio-cultural care and support

- medication, nursing and allied health care; and

- physical facilities.

'Quality of life' is the degree to which:

- an individual resident's overall well-being (including level of social activity, physical activity and health status) meets their personal expectations, the expectations of their carers or the expectations of the community; or

- a group of residents' overall well-being meets the expectations of the community.

These definitions highlight the importance of considering a person's health as a subset of factors contributing to their overall well-being. A resident may receive 'best practice' pain management in palliation; however, if this is approached without due consideration of the whole person and their preferences, the resident may not perceive this as quality of life. Regardless of the technical definitions of quality of care and quality of life, how the *resident* defines these will drive their expectations, and this may change according to their needs at various stages. For example, an individual with declining health and mobility may place more importance on quality of care, and for them this may define quality of life. Another person in the same physical state may transcend these limitations and focus on quality of life through spiritual beliefs, relationships or other meaning.

Providers have to manage the balance of meeting individual needs within a community setting. The Accreditation Standards includes some expected outcomes that relate to meeting individual needs and preferences of residents. This can be challenging to achieve when individual cultural or spiritual needs and preferences are diverse and extensive. For example, if a home has residents from a number of quite different cultures or religions, residents' needs and preferences may need to be negotiated and compromises made to accommodate what is reasonably possible.

Choice versus risk is another area that should be considered in the context of quality of life. A risk-averse culture can overtly or subtly impact on resident choice. When care is provided within a medical paradigm, there is fear of litigation and a paternalistic approach to residents; well-meaning decisions can be made that are contrary to a resident's choice. For example, a resident may wish to observe their spiritual practice by fasting; however, the person may have particular health conditions that are exacerbated by low intake of food and water. Should the home actively discourage the resident from their choice to fast? Or should they explain the risks and consequences to the resident and family/carer and allow the resident to make an informed decision that is respected and supported? In situations such as this, consultation between the resident, family, the resident's religious advisor and aged care facility staff will be important.

Conclusion

This chapter has outlined how cultural and spiritual care is assessed in Australian residential aged care homes. It has highlighted the fact that cultural and spiritual needs are far more complex than just celebrating important cultural days and organising visiting clergy to provide pastoral care. Addressing cultural and spiritual needs involves a deep understanding and thorough assessment of each person's needs and preferences. Quality of care and quality of life can only truly be achieved when they are provided in a way that recognises the unique physical, emotional, psychological, social, cultural and spiritual needs of each person.

CHAPTER 17

The Search Conference Process in Ageing and Spiritual and Pastoral Care: Directions for the Future

Elizabeth MacKinlay[1]

At the end of the 2006 national conference of the Centre for Ageing and Pastoral Studies (CAPS) (see MacKinlay 2008), there was a high level of excitement among the participants, and recognition from within the group that spiritual and pastoral care are important human needs. It was recognised that frail older people and those with disabilities, particularly those with dementia, need support to achieve their highest possible levels of well-being. There seemed to be a consensus from the participants that they needed to find a way forward that could lead to better care and education and research in the area of ageing and spirituality. However, the conference structure had not allowed a setting in which this could occur. In planning for the 2008 national conference, the planning committee carefully considered the feedback from the earlier conference and searched for a means of taking the issues raised at the 2006 conference forward, to make a difference in the community. This chapter recounts the story of the search conference that formed the second half of the 2008 national conference.

The theme of the 2008 national conference itself opened up new areas of concern about Western societies that are ageing and have become more diverse in culture and faiths over recent decades. For the majority of pastoral carers, many coming from a Christian background, there were few resources to inform them of the kind of care and spiritual needs of people from faiths other than their own. The search conference deliberately set out to provide

---

1   This chapter is based on the work of the search conference participants at the CAPS national conference 2008, as a whole, and it is acknowledged that without their contribution, this chapter could not have been written.

an opportunity to examine and grapple with the issues that emerged from the national conference.

The later part of the conference incorporated a participative planning process where the conference members had an opportunity to work together developing key strategies for the future of ageing and spirituality in multicultural societies. The search process is a powerful way of enabling a collective experience to be consolidated into resolutions by consensus of all participants. The search conference process recognises and incorporates contributions from each individual in the conference as it builds upon both the content of presentations made in the conference, and the experience of individual participants. The conference planning committee aimed to use this search process to provide new insights and directions in the field of ageing, spiritual and pastoral care which could be communicated widely beyond the conference.

The process of a search conference

The search conference process seemed, to the planning committee, to provide an appropriate setting to facilitate open discussion and direction for future development of this growing field of practice and study. Rehm *et al.* (2002) define a search conference as '…a participative planning event that enables people to create a plan for the most desirable future of their community or organization, a plan they carry out themselves' (p.3). The authors highlight the use of the word 'participative' within the search conference context (Rehm *et al.* 2002, p.5), emphasising that here it is not about a group of people giving input to an authority, or management; rather, in this context, 'participative' means that the participants actually create and carry out their own plan.

In advocating the use of search conferences to enable new understanding of issues, Tom Devane (Rehm *et al.* 2002, pp.xiii–xiv) highlights, first, the need for stakeholders to focus on common ground, then seeking to expand and develop actions to bring about an agreed and desirable future. The process enables group members to think and work collaboratively. They are enabled to recognise and capitalise on previously unrecognised trends and, further, the process motivates the group participants for implementing the outcomes. Against these benefits Devane contrasts the process of previous planning exercises, such as the traditional strengths, weaknesses, opportunities and threats (SWOT) analysis (Rehm *et al.* 2002, p.xiii). The problems he identified with traditional approaches were a tendency to extrapolate from the past, and a narrower focus on existing situations and problems. They 'do little if anything to ignite the passions of people in the organization who must implement the plan' (p.xiv). The traditional processes focus on solving current problems instead of looking for emerging trends. These points establish a rationale for the process that was used in this instance.

The characteristics of the search conference participants

According to Emery (1995) community conferences can be set up using any of three selection criteria; a geopolitical, professional or issue-related community. In this instance, the selection was on the basis of professional and issue-related community. The conference participants had some commonality of goals, as they had all registered to attend the conference. They came from different disciplines, although the majority of participants had a background in pastoral care and chaplaincy with older people, and some from different aged and health care disciplines. Most of the participants were from Australia, with New Zealanders making the next largest group. In total about 150 people participated in the search conference. It took place in a live-in environment, beginning on the first afternoon of the search process and continuing into the evening, and was completed the following afternoon. This is a little shorter than the time recommended by Rehm *et al.* (2002). The time-frame was set following much discussion that included costs and availability of the participants to attend for the extra time at the end of a national conference. All search conference participants had already spent an evening plus one-and-a-half days attending a conference on ageing and spirituality in multifaith and multicultural societies, immediately before entering into the search conference process.

The outcomes of the search conference

At the conclusion of the search conference there was agreement from the participants that the following six key themes provide new insights and directions related to spiritual and pastoral care in ageing, as outcomes from the national conference. The participants also agreed that these themes need to be worked on and communicated widely beyond the conference:

1. The need for developing social (including community) and professional recognition of the value of spiritual care.

2. The desirability of building a culture of holistic care and support which embraces diversity in faiths and cultures, and access and equity in the provision of pastoral care services for ageing people.

3. A requirement for education and training for pastoral carers with a theological and philosophical underpinning – coordinated and common standards – and issues of accreditation.

4. The establishment of a national peak body for spiritual care in aged care.

5. Provision of sustainable funding and resources.

6. Establishment of a quality research base with a theological and philosophical perspective, which is foundational to the practice of spiritual and pastoral care.

1. Developing social (including community) and professional recognition of the value of spiritual care

It was recognised by the participants that change will not occur unless and until there is recognition of the value of spiritual care. This is an important recognition, because the profession may want to push for change, but if the wider community fails to see the value of spiritual care, then political and policy changes will not eventuate. It is contended that it is of particular importance to recognise the place of spirituality in the lives of older people, particularly those who are disabled, frail and/or have dementia or other mental illnesses. In addition to those who are older and vulnerable, there is the wider canvas on which spirituality, spiritual growth and spiritual and pastoral care need to be painted. The issues of older adults facing changing roles and retirement and confronting life meaning are also part of this canvas on which the specific spirituality of later life is portrayed, and its variety of expressions, ranging from self-sufficiency to vulnerability, brings breadth and richness to the wider canvas of the whole of the lifespan. Understanding of the potential for spiritual growth and development in later life is a crucial component in the effective practice of spiritual and pastoral care with older people. This fact is under-recognized and therefore not adequately appreciated in either the wider community, or the professional community. There remains much work to be done.

THE MISSION STATEMENT SET BY THE SEARCH CONFERENCE FOR THIS THEME IS: To develop societal and professional recognition of the value of spiritual and pastoral care through:

•   raising consciousness of spiritual and pastoral care within our own organisations through education and practice

- gaining the support of all providers of spiritual and pastoral care for older people, in promoting the shared vision and understanding

- developing effective marketing strategies across all segments of the community.

2. Building a culture of holistic care and support which embraces diversity in faiths and cultures, and access and equity in the provision of pastoral care services for ageing people

There was strong recognition of the need to develop a culture of holistic care that includes spiritual and pastoral care. It was also clear, from the shared experiences of the participants, that this culture does not yet exist.

THE MISSION STATEMENT SET BY THE SEARCH CONFERENCE FOR THIS THEME IS:
To establish and maintain a culture of spiritual and pastoral care which integrates all aspects of a person's life journey and well-being through:

- *connecting phase:* go and meet the other key people we will work with – call a national forum (possibly the establishment of a peak body).

- *understanding phase:* audit what we have. What is society's understanding of pastoral care and spirituality?

- *action plan:* set goals, plan and implement. (Go for coffee and do it!)

3. Education and training for pastoral carers with a theological and philosophical underpinning – coordinated and common standards – and issues of accreditation

As for key issue number 2 above, education and training must not only be in general terms of pastoral and spiritual care, but must be focused on the growing body of knowledge about the particular spirituality journey and needs of older adults. It is now clear that this is a speciality area in its own right (Erikson *et al.* 1986; Killick and Allan 2001; Kimble and McFadden 2003; Kitwood 1997; Koenig *et al.* 2001; MacKinlay 2001, 2008; McFadden, Brennan and Patrick 2003; Moberg 2001; Moody 2005; Swinton 2001). It is noted that the key theme area that was identified from the conference is set in generic pastoral care terms, and not in terms of the older person's needs for specific 'spirituality of older persons'.

The voice missing from this conference was that of older people themselves. The voices of older people have been recognised in the research through the work of Goldsmith (2004) and MacKinlay (2001, 2006). These voices must be added to the voices of the practitioners. This is not a once only exercise, but must continue through the generations, as each cohort of older people will be different from the cohort that preceded it. At this point, it is certainly time to consider the ageing of the baby boomers.

Programmes developed to prepare practitioners will include certain skills that are needed in assessment and identification of needs, as well as in planning and implementation of care. Programmes will not only be about the specific and perhaps necessarily narrow framework of training, but, as well, leaders in spiritual and pastoral care need education that will equip them to address changing needs and priorities of spiritual care within church and societal settings. Leaders need advanced skills to be able to identify emerging issues and interact effectively at all levels of the field of ageing and aged care. This will require postgraduate preparation.

It is suggested that careful consideration needs to be given to the levels and types of education that are planned and provided for the different levels of practitioners. As well, it is noted that this is a multidisciplinary field and spiritual care concepts will need to be adopted and introduced into the education of other aged-care workers and health professionals – for example, nurses, social workers, psychologists, medical practitioners, life-skills coordinators and others.

THE MISSION STATEMENT SET BY THE SEARCH CONFERENCE FOR THIS THEME IS:

- to train spiritual and pastoral carers to nationally accredited minimum standards

- to develop agreed frameworks for training in spiritual care with theological and philosophical underpinning

- to develop an agreed set of competencies.

4. Establishing a national peak body for spiritual care in aged care

This was the fourth key theme area. It is suggested that while this is a vital aspect to consider, and undoubtedly of high priority, there is also another aspect to this: issues of spirituality in later life are not only about care. The majority of older adults remain living in the community until their needs for care no longer allow them to be cared for at home. Therefore, it is highly recommended that considerations for such a national body include ways of promoting spiritual growth, resilience and flourishing in later life, that will both increase quality of life for older adults and possibly even delay their entry into residential aged care. Therefore, it is argued, a strong focus of such a national body will be on positive ageing and the difference that spiritual well-being makes for older adults.

THE MISSION STATEMENT SET BY THE SEARCH CONFERENCE FOR THIS THEME IS: To unify, represent, promote and accredit spiritual/pastoral care providers in aged care throughout multifaith and multicultural Australia, grouped under the title 'The National Association for Spiritual Care with Older Persons' – and:

- to form a representative continuing committee from the search conference

- to draft initial terms of reference for the proposed National Association

- to call a meeting of representatives from state peak bodies and other stakeholders to work towards the creation of this National Association.

A task group was elected from the conference to pursue this issue further. A meeting to explore the way forward is planned.

5. Sustainable funding and resources

To provide quality spiritual care for older Australians of diverse faiths and cultures, sustainable funding and resources are needed.

In any new area of endeavour, it is initially difficult to attract resources and funding. To make real progress in this area, key theme area Number 1 (the need for developing social (including community) and professional recognition of the value of spiritual care) has to be successful. It is only then that spiritual care will be able to attract support and funding.

THE MISSION STATEMENT SET BY THE SEARCH CONFERENCE FOR THIS THEME IS:

- to develop a budget to initiate and sustain a peak body

- to communicate need to heads of faith groups, private business, philanthropic groups and appropriate government bodies

- to set up a tax-deductible charitable foundation connected to the peak body for the purpose of sustainable long-term funding.

6. Establishing a quality research base with a theological and philosophical perspective, which is foundational to the practice of spiritual and pastoral care

There was acknowledgement that the research must be conducted in collaboration with practitioners in the field of ageing and pastoral care. Again, it is emphasised that the voices of older people, including those who are frail and/or have dementia, must also be heard in the research process. The practitioners often drive initial research, as they occupy a more powerful position in the field; although people who work in aged care settings may not think their voices are heard, practitioners are more likely to be heard than those they care for (Goldsmith 2004; Kitwood 1997; MacKinlay 2006, 2008). Thus, the way forward is complex, and the voices both of aged-care personnel and of older people must be heard for research to be worthwhile and to advance practice. The term 'professional researchers' (see below) may seem strange to some readers. The consensus of the group was that the research should be conducted by people who were well qualified in research methodologies that are relevant to the field of enquiry, and that they should also have a strong knowledge and understanding of ageing and spirituality.

A sound body of knowledge is developing within the field of ageing and spiritual and pastoral care, with fine work on articulating the methods of enquiry being conducted by Swinton and Mowat (2006), McFadden *et al.* (2003) and others.

THE MISSION STATEMENT SET BY THE SEARCH CONFERENCE FOR THIS THEME IS:
To establish a quality research base with a theological and philosophical perspective, which is foundational to the practice of spiritual and pastoral care through:

- use of professional researchers, with a sound knowledge of spiritual and pastoral care within the ageing context

- providing opportunity for spiritual and pastoral care practitioners to participate in, and contribute to, the research process

- developing collaborative partnerships between the aged care industry, spiritual care providers, faith based groups, cultural organisations and research institutes.

It is noted by the author of this chapter that it is important to educate pastoral and spiritual care practitioners in the field of ageing to be discerning consumers of good research. Further, at least some of those working and studying in this field will take postgraduate studies to prepare them to doctoral level so that they may undertake relevant research and leadership. The leadership of this evolving field of practice and study must come from within the disciplines, rather than being driven by others from outside these specific disciplines of ageing. It is also noted that an important component of this rapidly developing area of study is its interdisciplinary nature. Effective team work is essential for developing best practice and care within this field of spiritual and pastoral care in ageing.

Critique and outcomes following the search conference

At the conclusion of the process, a task group was elected from the floor of the conference. This group of enthusiastic people set up a mailing list to stay in contact and to begin to examine how the issue could be taken forward. An invitation was extended to the group to report back at the next international conference on ageing and spirituality to be held in Auckland, New Zealand in September 2009. Initially this group began exchanging emails enthusiastically, with the desire to move forward. Barriers to development became apparent, with the acknowledgement that without funding and with lack of personnel it would be difficult to advance. It was also apparent that not all key players in this multidisciplinary field were part of the task group.

In subsequent emails the net was spread further, to identify key players in each state of Australia. The lack of people from other disciplines within the field of ageing and aged care was noted and an effort made to include representatives from these groups.

The time frame of the search process

This was compressed due to time and cost constraints. It is not known whether this detracted from the search process. Evaluations of the search process drew a mixed response with some critique from participants that there had not been a clear understanding of what this process would be like, even though the conference material contained a short but clear explanation of the process. It may have been that many of the conference participants had not experienced a process of this nature before.

Lack of participants from other disciplines of ageing that could be interested in spiritual care

This factor was a disappointment for the conference convener, who, as both nurse and priest, realised the important contribution that spiritual care has to make in nursing practice, as well as in other disciplines of care.

Conclusion

It is noted that a limitation of this search conference, when considering the topic of ageing and spiritual and pastoral care in multicultural and multifaith communities, is a lower than hoped-for number of representatives from faiths other than Christianity. The majority of conference delegates were pastoral carers and chaplains from aged care. These are the groups most deeply concerned for improving the quality of spiritual and pastoral care, but there are other voices that need to be heard as well. It is recognised that spiritual care is a growing concern for other disciplines working with older people; for example, nurses, medical practitioners, life-skills coordinators, diversional therapists, social workers, psychologists and other aged-care workers.

It cannot be known if the outcomes of the search conference might have been different, given a longer time frame for the process to develop, or wider representation of the groups of people who work with older adults; however, participants were engaged in the process and obviously felt a degree of ownership of the outcomes. However, it may be that if the search conference had been composed of a wider variety of people from different backgrounds, then the outcomes might have become more diverse and less focused. Acknowledging the limited time and diversity of participants as discussed above, the outcomes are summarised below.

Search conference outcomes in summary

First, the need for developing social (including community) and professional awareness of the value of spiritual care was recognised. Second, a culture of holistic care and support is needed, embracing diversity in faiths and cultures, and access and equity in the provision of pastoral care services for ageing people. It is recognised that education and training for pastoral carers with a theological and philosophical underpinning is an important requirement. This needs to be coordinated, have common standards and be accredited. To develop these standards and appropriate funding into the future, a national organisation for spiritual care in aged care is recommended. All of this can only be achieved in the context of establishing a quality research base with a theological and philosophical perspective, which is foundational to the practice of both spiritual and pastoral care.

Contributors

Dr Mohamad Abdalla is Associate Professor of Islamic Studies and is the founding director of the Griffith University Islamic Research Unit (GIRU), Brisbane, Queensland Node director of the Australian National Centre of Excellence for Islamic Studies, and Senior Research Fellow at the Key Centre for Ethics, Law, Justice and Governance. His most recent publication is *Islam and the Australian News Media* (Melbourne University Press 2010). He is regarded as one of Australia's most respected Muslim leaders, combining the roles of serious academic scholar, public intellectual and religious leader.

Subhana Barzaghi is a Zen Buddhist and Insight meditation teacher. She is the resident teacher and spiritual director of the Sydney Zen Centre and founder of Blue Gum Sangha, Sydney and the Kuan Yin Meditation Centre in Lismore. Subhana teaches regular intensive Zen meditation and Insight retreats throughout Australia, New Zealand and India. As an authorised religious marriage celebrant she enjoys assisting couples to create ceremonies from the heart. Subhana has been a psychotherapist for 20 years; she has a BA in Social Sciences, a Masters Degree in Applied Psychotherapy, and is a graduate of Hakomi Integrative Psychotherapy. She has a private practice in Mosman and leads a range of workshops, on death and dying, dreamwork, Zen and the arts, as well as workshops in the immeasurable qualities of heart and mind, loving-kindness, compassion, equanimity and joy. See www.subhana.com.au.

Purushottama Bilimoria is Professor of Philosophy and Comparative Studies at Deakin University in Australia, Senior Research Fellow, University of Melbourne, and Visiting Professor at State University of New York (Stony Brook), and Columbia University. His areas of specialist research and publications cover classical Indian philosophy and comparative ethics; continental thought; cross-cultural philosophy of religion, diaspora studies; bioethics; and constitutional justice in India. He is chief editor of *Sophia,* the journal of philosophy of religion (Springer). His most recent publication is *Indian Ethics I* (Ashgate 2007; Oxford University Press 2008). He is completing the manuscript for the second edition of *Hindu and Sikh Diaspora in Australia.*

Gabrielle Brian is an Academic Associate in the School of Theology, Charles Sturt University, and works in the Centre for Ageing and Pastoral Studies in Canberra. She has a Master of Arts (Ageing and Pastoral Studies). She was previously employed as Executive Officer – Mission Integration in a faith-based health service.

A significant aspect of her responsibility was to educate staff in finding relevant ways of translating in today's culture the values and ethos of the religious sisters who had formerly founded and developed these health care services. She worked for many years in pastoral care, in both parishes and residential aged care.

Jeffrey Cohen is a visiting senior fellow at the School of Public Health and Community Medicine, University of New South Wales. He is a senior lecturer for the Collaborative Centre for eHealth, the Graduate School of Information Technology and Mathematical Science at the University of Ballarat.

The Reverend Professor James Haire, AM, KSJ, MA, GradDipMiss, PhD, HonDD, HonDLitt, HonDUniv is Professor of Theology, Charles Sturt University (CSU), Canberra; Executive Director, Australian Centre for Christianity and Culture, CSU; Director, Public and Contextual Theology Strategic Research Centre, CSU; past president, National Council of Churches in Australia and the Uniting Church in Australia; and member of the Executive of the Christian Conference of Asia (CCA).

Dr Ann Harrington is a registered nurse with 33 years of clinical and teaching experience in health and higher education institutions in New South Wales and South Australia. She is a senior lecturer in the School of Nursing and Midwifery at Flinders University and currently teaches students in both the undergraduate and postgraduate programmes, with her research undertaken in the area of spirituality and/or palliative care. She has a PhD from Flinders University in South Australia. Her publications include book chapters and articles in palliative care and/or spirituality, qualitative research and infection control, as well as numerous conference presentations.

Associate Professor Rosalie Hudson, Honorary Senior Fellow, School of Nursing and Social Work, University of Melbourne, is a consultant/educator in aged care, palliative care and pastoral care with 12 years' experience as director of nursing of a nursing home, as well as clinical and administrative experience in hospice/palliative care. She has published widely on end-of-life issues, with a particular focus on ethics, in both nursing and theological journals. Her fourth co-authored book, *Palliative Care and Aged Care* was published in 2007 (Ausmed Publications). Rosalie is an academic associate with St. Marks Theological Centre, Charles Sturt University, Canberra, a sessional educator with Alzheimer's Australia (Victoria) and various theological colleges within the Melbourne College of Divinity.

Dr Rachael Kohn is the producer and presenter of 'The Spirit of Things' on ABC Radio National, which explores contemporary trends in religion. She is the author of *The New Believers: Re-imagining God* (HarperCollins 2003) and *Curious Obsessions in the History of Science and Spirituality* (ABC Books 2007). An academic in religious studies in Canada (McMaster University PhD 1985, MA 1977, Hon BA Concordia University, Montreal 1977), Dr Kohn has contributed many chapters to books, most recently 'Jews and Violence' in John T. Squires and William Emilson (eds) *Validating Violence, Violating Faith?* (ATF Press 2008).

Elizabeth MacKinlay, AM, is both a registered nurse and a priest in the Anglican Church and the Director of the Centre for Ageing and Pastoral Studies at St Mark's National Theological Centre, Canberra. She is a professor in the School of Theology, Charles Sturt University. Recently completed research includes an Australian Research Council project: *Finding Meaning in the Experience of Dementia: The Place of Spiritual Reminiscence Work.* Elizabeth was chair of the ACT Ministerial Advisory Council on Ageing, her term ending in 2008.

Dennis McDermott is a Koori psychologist and Associate Professor of Indigenous Health at Flinders University, Adelaide. He is also a poet. Dennis has a particular interest in Indigenous social, spiritual and emotional well-being, Indigenous health workforce and pedagogy, and the nexus of culture and context in service delivery, and he has published in a number of these areas. In 2005, he was made an Honorary Fellow – He Pūkenga Taiea of Te Mata o te Tau – of the Academy for Maori Research and Scholarship. Dennis was also awarded the 2006 Dr Ross Ingram Memorial Essay Prize by the *Medical Journal of Australia*.

Professor Tracey McDonald many years' experience in nursing, management, education, research and practice development validate her broad research base and scholarship profile, and allow her to be involved with policy issues arising from government legislation related to her fields of endeavour. Through professional conferences, non-government organisations and associations she has built up a network of scholars, policy makers and practitioners. She addressed the Shanghai International Symposium on caring for the elderly in 2006, and programme development in 2008. She is an invited member of the United Nations World Expert Group on Ageing (2007) and Social Integration (2008), and participated in the United Nations expert group on developing a convention on the rights of older persons. She is also an expert reviewer for the World Health Organisation World Alliance for Patient Safety.

Ikebal Mohammed Adam Patel is the President of Muslims Australia, the peak body articulating the interests of Australian Muslims. Muslims Australia manages seven Islamic schools including one of the largest Australian schools, of which Ikebal is the board chairman. Ikebal is the chair of the Australian Capital Territory Muslim Advisory Council and an Advisory Committee Member to the National Centre for Excellence in Islamic Education based at Melbourne University and also to the Griffith University Multi Faith Centre. He is a co-chairman of the National Dialogue between Australian Christians, Jews and Muslims. Ikebal has participated in many international conferences on interfaith dialogue as well as presenting papers at international conferences, including the Parliament of the World Religions.

Ann Peut is the former head of the Ageing and Aged Care Unit at the Australian Institute of Health and Welfare (AIHW) and an Adjunct Associate Professor at the University of Canberra. Ann has a Master of Arts (Sociology) and over 25 years of public sector experience in policy analysis, evaluation and research. She is a National Council member of the Australian Association of Gerontology. The AIHW's Ageing and Aged Care Unit publishes regular statistical reports about aged care in Australia, and produces the highly valued publication *Older Australia at a Glance*, now in its fourth edition.

Elizabeth Pringle has an interest in spiritual care of older people. She is a volunteer in a nursing home connecting with residents through worship services. Elizabeth holds a Bachelor of Adult Education, Master of Adult Education and a Master of Business Administration, and is currently working towards a Master of Arts in Ageing and Pastoral Studies at Charles Sturt University. Elizabeth has worked in aged care since 1998. Prior to this she held a variety of roles and consulted in the area of adult education and training. Her current role is General Manager, Education of the Aged Care Standards and Accreditation Agency Ltd.

Amy Rayner completed her Bachelor of Arts and Creative Arts at the University of Melbourne, with a major in Asian Philosophy. A student of Buddhism for over ten years, Amy has studied extensively in the Gelug Tradition, including completing Kopan Monastery's November Lam-Rim Course five times, receiving teachings from the Dalai Lama in Australia and India, and participating in meditation retreats. Amy is assistant to the editor of *Sophia*, the journal for philosophy of religion, and is overseeing the publications of *Indian Ethics II* (Springer 2010) and the *History of Indian Philosophy* (Routledge 2011).

Ingrid Seebus is a data analyst at the Australian Institute of Health and Welfare, which she joined in 2008. She has researched issues related to ageing since 2003. Her PhD in applied linguistics focused on elderly immigrant bilingualism and biculturalism.

Robyn Simmonds is a Registered Nurse who has over 20 years' experience in the aged care sector. Her ministry has been to support, encourage and assist frail, aged persons to reach their potential and recognise value in their lives, whilst providing for them a range of care and services to meet their needs. Robyn has qualifications in gerontology, aged care management, human resource management, cultural diversity, occupational health and safety. She is registered with the Aged Care Standards and Accreditation Agency as a quality assessor. Robyn is currently Director of Residential Care Services at St Basil's Homes.

Fr Nicholas Stavropoulos is CEO of St Basil's Homes, the aged care provider of the Greek Orthodox Archdiocese in NSW. He has a Bachelor of Arts, and a Masters in Education as well as a Graduate Diploma in Business. After a career in education, Nicholas was ordained to the clergy and eventually moved into aged care.

References

ABS (Australian Bureau of Statistics) (2003) *Deaths, 2002*. Cat. no. 3302.0. Canberra: ABS.

ABS (2004) *National Aboriginal and Torres Strait Islander Social Survey, 2002: Summary of findings*. Cat. no. 4714.0 2002. Canberra: ABS.

ABS (2006) *Australian Bureau of Statistics: 2006 Census*. Available at www.abs.gov.au/ausstats, accessed on 20 June 2009.

ABS (2007a) *Australian Demographic Statistics*. Cat. no. 3101.0. Canberra: ABS.

ABS (2007b) *Census of Population and Housing, Australia 2006*. Cat. no. 2068.0. Census tables. Canberra: ABS.

ABS (2007c) *General Social Survey 2006*. Expanded CURF, RADL. Findings based on use of ABS CURF data.

ABS (2008a) Discussion paper: 'Assessment of Methods for Developing Life Tables for Aboriginal and Torres Strait Islander Australians, 2006.' ABS cat. no. 3302.0.55.002. Canberra: ABS.

ABS (2008b) *Experimental Estimates of Aboriginal and Torres Strait Islander Australians, June 2006*. Cat. no. 3238.0.55.001. Canberra: ABS.

ABS (2008c) *Population by Age and Sex, Australia, 2006/2007*. Cat. no. 3235.0. Canberra: ABS.

ABS (2008d) *Population Characteristics, Aboriginal and Torres Strait Islander Australians, 2006: Summary of Findings*. Cat. no. 4713.0. Canberra: ABS.

ABS (2008e) *Yearbook Australia 2008*. Cat. no. 1301.0. Canberra: ABS.

ABS and AIHW (2008) *The Health and Welfare of Australia's Aboriginal and Torres Strait Islander Peoples, 2008*. ABS cat. no. 4704.0/AIHW cat. no. IHW 21. Canberra: ABS.

Aged Care Standards and Accreditation Agency Ltd. (2008) *Results and Processes Guide*. Parramatta, New South Wales. ISSN 1448-4986 (Print) 1448-6172 (Electronic). Available at www.accreditation.org.au, accessed on 30 November 2008.

AIHW (Australian Institute of Health and Welfare) (2004a) *Diversity among Older Australians in Capital Cities 1996-2011*. Bulletin no. 18. Cat. no. AUS 51. Canberra: AIHW.

AIHW (2004b) *Rural, Regional and Remote Health: A Guide to Remoteness Classifications*. Canberra: AIHW.

AIHW (2007a) *Australia's Welfare 2007*. Cat. no. AUS 93. Canberra: AIHW.

AIHW (2007b) *Older Australia at a Glance*. Fourth edition. Cat no. AGE 52. Canberra: AIHW.

AIHW (2007c) *Quality of Aboriginal and Torres Strait Islander Identification in Community Services Data Collection: Update on Eight Community Services Data Collections*. Cat no. HWI 95. Canberra: AIHW.

AIHW (2008a) *Aged Care Packages in the Community 2006–07: A Statistical Overview*. Cat no. AGE 57. Canberra: AIHW.

AIHW (2008b) *Residential Aged Care in Australia 2006–07: A Statistical Overview*. Cat no. AGE 56. Canberra: AIHW.

AIHW (2009) *International Group for Indigenous Health Measurement*. Cat. no. IHW 26. Canberra: AIHW.

AIHW: Benham, C., Gibson, D., Holmes, B. and Rowland, D. (2000) *Independence in Ageing: The Social and Financial Circumstances of Older Overseas-born Australians*. Cat. no. AGE 15. Canberra: AIHW.

Aitken, R. (1999) *Death: A Zen Buddhist Perspective, Diamond Sangha Hawaii*. (Unpublished article.)

Al-AlShaykh, S.A.M. (2000) *Al-Kutub al-Sita*. Riyadh: Darussalam [Arabic].

Anandarajah, G. and Hight, E. (2001) 'Spirituality and medical practice: Using the HOPE questions as a practical tool for spiritual assessment.' *American Family Physician 63*, 1, 81–88.

Anderson, E.B. (2003) *Worship and Christian Identity: Practicing Ourselves*. Minnesota, MN: The Liturgical Press Collegeville.

Australian Nursing and Midwifery Council Standards (ANMC) (2006) *National Competency Standards for the Registered Nurse, Enrolled Nurse, Registered Midwife, Nurse Practitioner*. Dickson, Australia: Australian Nursing and Midwifery Council.

Anstey, M. (2008) 'Scriptural Reminiscence and Narrative Gerontology: Jacob's Wresting with the Unknown (Genesis 32).' In E. MacKinlay (ed.) *Ageing, Disability and Spirituality: Addressing the Challenge of Disability in Later Life*. London: Jessica Kingsley Publishers.

Atchley, R. (2009) *Spirituality and Aging*. Baltimore, MD: The Johns Hopkins University Press.

At-Tirmidhi and Abu Dawud, Hadith no. 355 and no. 359: 'Revering the Scholars and Elders, Preferring Them to Others and Raising Their Status.' Available at www.witness-pioneer.org/vil/hadeeth/riyad/00/chap044.htm, accessed on 10 January 2009.

AustLii, Reconciliation and Social Justice Library, New South Wales, Victoria and Tasmania – *The Legacy of 'The Stolen Generations.* Available at www.austlii.edu.au/au/special/rsjproject/rsjlibrary/rciadic/regional/nsw-vic-tas/205. html, accessed on 10 February 2007.

Australian Association of Gerontology (2008) *Growing Old Well: A Life Cycle Approach for Aboriginal and Torres Strait Islander Peoples.* Randwick, NSW: University of New South Wales/Prince of Wales Medical Research Institute.

Babacan, H. and Obst, P. (1998) *Death, Dying and Religion: An Examination of Non-Christian Beliefs and Practices – A Guide for Health Care Professionals Including Those Working with HIV/AIDS.* Brisbane: ECCQ.

Baldacchino, D. and Draper, P. (2001) 'Spiritual coping strategies: A review of the nursing research literature.' *Journal of Advanced Nursing 34,* 6, 833–841.

Barnes, T., Smith, L., Yuejen Zhao and Guthridge, S. (2008) *A Comparative Analysis of Indirect Methodologies for Estimating Indigenous Life Expectancy.* Project commissioned by the National Advisory Group on Aboriginal and Torres Strait Islander Health Information and Data. Darwin: School for Social and Policy Research, Charles Darwin University.

Batson, P., Thorne, K. and Peak, J. (2002) 'Life-story work sees the person beyond the dementia.' *Journal of Dementia Care 10,* 3, 15–17.

Benner Carson, V. (2008) 'Spirituality – Identifying and Meeting Spiritual Needs.' In V. Benner Carson and H.G. Koenig (eds) *Spiritual Dimensions of Nursing Practice.* West Conshohcken, PA: Templeton Foundation Press.

Berkman, L.F., Glass, T., Brissette, I. and Seeman, T.E. (2000) 'From social integration to health: Durkheim in the new millennium.' *Journal of Social Science and Medicine 51,* 6, 843–857.

Bevans, S.B. (2004) *Models of Contextual Theology.* Maryknoll, NY: Orbis.

Bhat, P.N. Mari (2002) 'General growth balance method: A reformulation for populations open to migration.' *Population Studies 56,* 23–34.

Bonhoeffer, D. (1966) *Christology.* (J. Bowden, trans.) London: Collins.

Bonhoeffer, D. (1985) *Spiritual Care.* (J.C. Rochelle, trans.) Philadelphia, PA: Fortress Press.

Bouma, G. (2006) *Australian Soul: Religion and Spirituality in the Twenty-first Century.* Port Melbourne: Cambridge University Press.

Bowden, C. (2006) Chairperson, Kinchela Boys' Home Aboriginal Corporation, private communication, February.

Bown, J. and Williams, A. (1993) 'Spirituality and nursing: A review of the literature.' *Journal of Advances in Health and Nursing Care 2,* 4, 41–66.

Boyd, R.H.S. (1974) *India and the Latin Captivity of the Church: The Cultural Context of the Gospel.* (Monograph Supplement to the *Scottish Journal of Theology,* No. 3.) London: Cambridge University Press.

Bracken, P.J. and Petty, E. (eds) (1998) *Rethinking the Trauma of War.* London: Free Association Press.

Breggin, P. (2000) 'The NIMH multimodal study of treatment for Attention-Deficit/Hyperactivity Disorder: A critical analysis.' *International Journal of Risk and Safety in Medicine 13,* 15–22.

Breggin, P. (2003/2004) 'Suicidality, violence and mania caused by selective serotonin reuptake inhibitors (SSRIs): A review and analysis.' *International Journal of Risk and Safety in Medicine 16,* 31–49.

Broe, T. and Jackson Pulver, L.R. (2009) 'Ageing, Health and Dementia in Aboriginal People: A Life Cycle Approach.' Keynote presentation at 'Growing Old Well: A life cycle approach for Aboriginal and Torres Strait Islander Peoples', Australian Association of Gerontology, University of New South Wales/Prince of Wales Medical Research Institute, 15 August.

Broome, R. (2002) *In Search of Mulga Fred: Doing Aboriginal History.* Canberra: Australian Government National Centre for History Education. Available at www.hyperhistory.org/index.php?option=displaypageandItemid=573ando p=page, accessed on 5 November 2009.

Bryant, R.A, Sackville, T., Dang, S., Moulds, M. and Guthrie, R. (1999) 'Treating acute stress disorder: An evaluation of cognitive behavior therapy and supportive counseling techniques.' *The American Journal of Psychiatry 156,* 11, 1780–1786.

Bryden, C. MacKinlay, E. (2002) 'Dementia – A Spiritual Journey towards the Divine: A Personal View of Dementia.' In E. MacKinlay (ed.) *Mental Health and Spirituality in Later Life.* New York: Haworth Press.

Burgener, S. and Twigg, P. (2002) 'Relationships among caregiver factors and quality of life in care recipients with irreversible dementia.' *Alzheimer's Disease and Associated Disorders 16,* 88–102.

Burkhart, L. and Hogan, N. (2008) 'An experiential theory of spiritual care in nursing practice.' *Qualitative Health Research 18,* 7, 928–938.

Burnard, P. (1986) 'Picking up the pieces.' *Nursing Times 82,* 17, 37–39.

Burnard, P. (1987) 'Spiritual distress and the nursing response: Theoretical consideration and counselling skills.' *Journal of Advanced Nursing 12,* 3, 377–382.

Burton, J. (1990) *Conflict: Resolution and Prevention.* London: Macmillan Press.

Cady, J.F. (1964) *Southeast Asia: Its Historical Development.* New York, San Francisco, Toronto and London: McGraw-Hill Book Company.

Carlson, E.B. (2001) 'Psychometric study of a brief screen for PTSD: Assessing the impact of multiple traumatic events.' *National Library of Medicine Assessment 8*, 4, 431–441. Menlo Park, CA: Department of Veterans Affairs, Palo Alto Health Care System.

Carson, V., Soeken, K.L., Shanty, J. and Terry, L. (1990) 'Hope and spiritual well-being: Essentials for living with AIDS.' *Perspectives in Psychiatric Care 26*, 2, 28–34.

Chalmers, D. (2001) *City of the Dead. A History of the Necropolis, Springvale.* Melbourne: Hyland House.

Chittister, J. (2008) *The Gift of Years: Growing Older Gracefully.* New York: BlueBridge.

Chodkiewicz, M. (2009) 'Rūhāniyya.' In P. Bearman, Th. Bianquis, C. Bosworth, E. van Donzel, and Heinrichs, W. (eds) *Encyclopaedia of Islam.* Second edition Brill Online. Available at www.brillonline.nl/subscriber/entry?entry=islam_SIM-6323, accessed on 22 February 2009.

Chodron. T. (2001) *Spiritual Issues in Living and Dying.* Brisbane, QLD: Karuna Hospice Service Ltd.

Clarke, A., Hanson, E.J. and Ross, H. (2003) 'Seeing the person behind the patient: Enhancing the care of older people using a biographical approach' [Electronic Version]. *Journal of Clinical Nursing 12*, 697–706.

Clements, W. (1990) 'Spiritual Development in the Fourth Quarter of Life.' In J. Seeber (ed.) *Spiritual Maturity in the Later Years.* London: The Haworth Press.

Clipp, E.C. and Elder, G.H. (1996) 'The Aging Veteran of WWII: Psychiatric and Life Course Insights.' In P.E. Ruskin and J.A. Talbott (eds) *Aging and Posttraumatic Stress Disorder.* Washington, DC: American Psychiatric Association Press.

Cohen-Mansfield, J., Marx, M.S. and Werner, P. (1991) 'Agitation in elderly persons: An integrative report.' *Journal of the American Geriatric Society 39*, 8, 308–311.

Commonwealth of Australia (2007) *Aged Care Principles.* (Made under subsection 96–1 (1) of the Aged Care Act 1997) Reprint 6. Canberra: ACT. Copyright Commonwealth of Australia, reproduced by permission. Available at http://aodgp.gov.au/internet/main/publishing.nsf/Content/ageing-legislat-aca1997-prindex.htm, accessed on 27 March 2009.

Commonwealth of Australia (2009) *A Healthier Future for All Australians – Interim Report*, December 2008. National Health and Hospitals Reform Commission.

Commonwealth of Australia, Department of Health and Ageing (2008). *Evaluation of the Impact of Accreditation on the Delivery of Quality of Care and Quality of Life to Residents in Australian Government Subsidised Residential Aged Care Homes – Final Report.* Canberra, ACT. Copyright Commonwealth of Australia, reproduced by permission. Available at www.health.gov.au/internet/main/publishing.nsf/Content/ageing-iar-final-report.htm, accessed on 27 March 2009.

Cooper, C. and Hagan, P. (1999) 'The ageing Australian population and future health costs 1996–2051.' Department of Health and Aged Care. Occasional Papers: New Series No. 7. Canberra: AGPS.

Cotter, P., Anderson, I. and Smith, L.R. (2007) 'Indigenous Australians: Ageing without Longevity.' In A. Borowski, S. Encel, and E. Ozanne (eds) *Longevity and Social Change in Australia.* Sydney: University of New South Wales Press, pp. 65–69.

Cresp, RSJ, M. (2005) *In the Spirit of Joseph.* North Sydney: Sisters of St Joseph of the Sacred Heart.

Culliford, L. (2009) 'Teaching spirituality and health care to third-year medical students.' *The Clinical Teacher 6*, 22–27.

D'Apice, M. (1989) *Noon to Nightfall: A Journey through Midlife and Ageing.* Melbourne: Collins Dove.

Dalai Lama (2001) *Daily Advice from the Heart.* New Delhi: Harper Collins.

Dalby, P. (2006) 'Is there a process of spiritual change or development associated with ageing? A critical review of research.' *Aging and Mental Health 10*, 1, 4–12.

Danby, H. (1933) *The Mishnah* (translated from the Hebrew by H. Danby). 'The Fathers (Pirqê Abôth).' Oxford: Clarendon Press.

Danieli, Y. (1998) 'Introduction: History and Conceptual Foundation.' In Y. Danieli (ed.) *International Handbook of Multigenerational Legacies of Trauma.* New York: Plenum.

Davies, S. (2001) 'The long-term psychological effects of traumatic wartime experiences on older adults.' *Journal of Ageing and Mental Health 5*, 2, 99–103.

Davis, A. (2008) 'Recognizing Racism in the Era of Neo-liberalism.' Vice-Chancellor's Oration, Murdoch University, 2008. Available at www.abc.net.au/news/opinion/speeches/files/20080318_davis.pdf, accessed on 28 March 2009.

Davis, N. (1991) 'The Story-teller.' In *Heart Gone Walkabout: Poems, Prayers, Lines and Spaces.* Australia: Shekinah Creative Ministry Co-op.

Department of Health and Ageing (2008a) *Aged Care Principles.* Canberra: Office of Legislative Drafting and Publishing.

Department of Health and Ageing (2008b) *Report on the Operation of the Aged Care Act 1997 1 July 2007 to 30 June 2008.* Copyright Commonwealth of Australia, reproduced by permission. Canberra: ACT.

Department of Victorian Communities (2003) *Stolen Generations Taskforce: Report to Victorian Government.* Melbourne.

Derrickson, B.S. (1996) 'The spiritual work of the dying: A framework and case studies.' *The Hospice Journal 11*, 2, 11–30.

Dirkzwager, A., Bramsen, I. and Van der Ploeg, H. (2001) 'The longitudinal course of posttraumatic stress disorder symptoms among ageing military veterans.' *Journal of Nervous and Mental Disorders 189*, 12, 846–853.

Dodson, M. (1996) 'Aboriginal and Torres Strait Islander Social Justice Commissioner, Fourth Report.' *Human Rights and Equal Opportunity Commission.* Available at www.hreoc.gov.au/social_justice/sj_report/sjreport96.html, accessed on 27 June 2009.

DoHA (Commonwealth Department of Health and Ageing) (2008) Home and Community Care Programme Minimum Data Set 2006–07 Annual Bulletin. Canberra: Australian Government Department of Health and Ageing.

Donaldson, C., Tarrier, N. and Burns, A. (1997) 'The impact of the symptoms of dementia on caregivers.' *British Journal of Psychiatry 170*, 62–68.

Duckett, S. (2002) 'Rational care before rationed care.' *Internal Medicine Journal 32*, 533–534.

Department of Veterans' Affairs (DVA) (2009) *Veterans' Special Needs.* Australian Government, Canberra. Available at www.dva.gov.au/Pages/home.aspx, accessed on 17 April 2009.

Eaton, G. (1994) *Islam and the Destiny of Man.* Kuala Lumpur: Islamic Book Trust.

Edwards, B. (1995) 'Management of spiritual distress.' *Emergency Nurse 3*, 2, 23–25.

Efficace, F. and Marrone, R. (2002) 'Spiritual issues and quality of life assessment in cancer care.' *Death Studies 26*, 743–756.

Elliot, J. (2008) 'Minister releases accreditation report by previous government.' Media release 3 June 2008. Copyright Commonwealth of Australia, reproduced by permission. Available at www.health.gov.au/internet/ministers/publishing.nsf/Content/mr-yr08-je-je070.htm, accessed on 26 December 2008.

Ellis, J.B. and Smith, P.C. (1991) 'Spiritual well-being, social desirability and reasons for living: Is there a connection?' *The International Journal of Social Psychiatry 37*, 1, 57–63.

Ellison, C. (1983) 'Spiritual well-being: Conceptualization and measurement.' *Journal of Psychology and Theology 11*, 4, 330–340.

Emery, M. (1995) 'The power of community search conferences.' *Journal for Quality and Participation 18*, 7.

Erikson, J. (1997) *The Life Cycle Completed: Extended Version.* New York: W.W. Norton.

Erikson, E.H., Erikson, M. and Kivnick, H.Q. (1986) 'Ages and Stages.' In *Vital Involvement in Old Age: The Experience of Old Age in our Time.* New York: W.W. Norton.

Esler, P.F. (1994) *The First Christians in Their Social Worlds: Social-Scientific Approaches to New Testament Interpretation.* London and New York: Routledge.

Estes, C.P. (2008) 'Battle scars: women's souls cannot be killed'. *National Catholic Reporter 1*, 17. Available at http://ncronline.org/blogs/el-rio-debajo-del-rio/battlescars-women's-souls-cannot-be-killed, accessed on 28 January 2010.

Ethnic Communities Council of NSW and NSW Community Options 2006. Participant Materials Module 1: What is Cultural Competency? Available at www.eccnsw.org.au/assets/pdf/M1_Participant_Material.pdf, accessed on 26 December 2008.

Ferrucci, L., Mahallati, A., and Simonsick, E. (2006) 'Frailty and the foolishness of Eos.' *The Journals of Gerontology Series A: Biological Sciences and Medical Sciences 61*, 260–261.

Fleming, R. (2002) 'Depression and Spirituality in Australian Aged Care Homes.' In E. MacKinlay (ed.) *Mental Health and Spirituality in Later Life.* New York: Haworth Pastoral Press.

Fontana, A. and Rosenheck, R. (2004) 'Trauma, change and strength in religious faith and mental health service use among veterans treated for PTSD.' *Journal of Nervous and Mental Disease 192*, 9, 579–584.

Frankel, S., Ebrahim, S. and Davey Smith, G. (2000) 'The limits to the demand for health care.' *British Medical Journal 321*, 40–45.

Frankl, V.E. (1969) *The Will to Meaning: Foundations and Applications of Logotherapy.* New York: Plume.

Frankl, V.E. (1984) *Man's Search for Meaning; An Introduction to Logotherapy.* Third edition. New York: Simon and Schuster.

Gabb, D. and McDermott, D. (2008) 'What do Indigenous experiences and perspectives mean for transcultural mental health? In R. Ranzijn, K. McConnochie and W. Nolan (eds) Psychology and Indigenous Australians – Teaching, Practice, and Theory. Cambridge: Cambridge Scholars Publishing.

Gagen, P. (2001) (ed.) *Growing Older Gracefully: Sharing the Blessings.* Brisbane: Catholic Adult Education.

Garrard, K. and McDonald, T. (2007) 'An investigation of outcomes related to allied health programme participation in relation to safety in mentally confused older people.' Master of Clinical Nursing thesis. Sydney: ACU National.

Geertz, C. (1975) *The Interpretation of Cultures.* London: Hutchinson.

Gibson, D. (2007) 'Patterns of ageing and service use in a culturally diverse population.' Paper presented at the *Cultural Diversity in Ageing 2007 National Conference*, Melbourne, June 2007.

Gillespie, T. 'Older and wiser.' In *The Spirit of Things*, 16 November 2003. Available at www.abc.net.au/rn/spiritofthings, accessed on 12 January 2010.

Gillman, I. and Klimkeit, H.J. (2002) *Christians in Asia before 1500.* Ann Arbor, MI: The University of Michigan Press.

Goldsmith, M. (2004) In a Strange Land... People with Dementia and the Local Church. Southwell: 4M Publications.

Goleman, D. (1995) *Emotional Intelligence.* London: Bloomsbury.

Greeley, A.M. (1982) *Religion: A Secular Theory.* New York: The Free Press.

Groombridge, B. (2008) 'Age Shall Not Wither Them.' *The New Statesman*, 29 May 2008. Available at www.newstatesman. com/2008/05/age-neuberger-manifesto-care, accessed on 5 November 2009.

Guroian, V. (2000) 'O Death, Where Is Your Sting?' In C.E. Braaten and R.W. Jenson (eds) *Sin, Death and the Devil*. Grand Rapids, MI: William B. Eerdmans Publishing Company.

Haire, J. (1981) 'The Character and Theological Struggle of the Church in Halmahera, Indonesia, 1941–1979.' In *Studien zur interkulturellen Geschichte des Christentums, Band 26*. Frankfurt-am-Main und Bern: Lang.

Harrington, A. (2004) 'Hope rising out of despair: The spiritual journey of patients admitted to a hospice.' *Journal of Religious Gerontology 16*, 3/4, 123–45.

Harrington, A. (2006) 'The 'connection' health care providers make with dying patients.' *Journal of Religion Spirituality and Aging 18*, 2/3, 169–185.

Harrison, J. and Burnard, P. (1993) *Spirituality and Nursing Practice*. Aldershot: Ashgate Publishing.

Hart, D.B. (2003) *The Beauty of the Infinite: The Aesthetics of Christian Truth*. Grand Rapids, MI: William B. Eerdmans Publishing Company.

Hauerwas, S. (1986) *Suffering Presence: Theological Reflections on Medicine, the Mentally Handicapped, and The Church*. Notre Dame, IN: University of Notre Dame Press.

Hauerwas, S. (1988) *Christian Existence Today: Essays on Church, World, and Living in Between*. Grand Rapids, MI: Brazos Press.

Hauerwas, S. and Yordy, L. (2003).

Hawter, V.P. (1995) *The Spiritual Needs of the Dying: A Buddhist View*. Available at www.urbandharma.org/udharma7/dyingneeds.html, accessed on 24 May 2009.

Hayden, W. (1995). 'Right to make choices: Part of liberal humanism.' *The Age*, 23 June 1995.

Hays, R. and Hays, J. (2003) 'The Christian Practice of Growing Old'. In S. Hauerwas, C.B. Stoneking, K.G. Meador and D. Cloutier (eds) *Growing Old in Christ*. UK: Eerdmans.

Healey, J. (ed.) (2008) *Ageing – Issues in Society. Volume 277*. Thirroul, NSW: The Spinney Press.

Heavy Runner, I. and Marshall, K. (2003) 'Miracle survivors: Promoting resilience in Indian students.' *Tribal College Journal*. Minneapolis: 14:4. Available at www.cce.umn.edu/pdfs/NRRC/TJC03.pdf, accessed on 14 February 2009.

Heschel, A. (1987) *Insecurity of Freedom: Essays on Human Existence*. New York: Schocken.

Hochkins, K. and McDonald, T (2007) 'An investigation of outcomes related to allied health programme participation in relation to safety in mentally confused older people.' Master of Clinical Nursing thesis. Sydney: ACU National.

Hudson, R. (2000) 'Death and dying in a nursing home: Personhood, palliation and pastoral care.' *St Mark's Review 182*, 6–12.

Hudson, R. (2004) 'Ageing and the Trinity: Holey, Wholly, Holy?' In A. Jewell (ed.) *Ageing, Spirituality and Wellbeing*. London: Jessica Kingsley Publishers.

Hungelmann, J., Kenkel-Rossi, E., Klassen, L. and Stollenwerk, R. (1989) 'Development of the J.A.R.E.L. Spiritual Well-being Scale.' In R.M.C.-ü. Johnson (ed.) *Classification of Nursing Diagnoses: Proceedings of the Eighth Conference Held in St. Louis, MO, March 1988*. Philadelphia, PA: Lippincott.

Ibn Kathir Tafsir (2000) translated and abridged by a group of scholars under the supervision of Safiur-Rahman al-Mubarakpuri. Riyadh: Darussalam Publications, Volume 7.

Irion, P. (1988) 'Treatment of the relationship of hospice to the church, interpreting their work for one another.' In P. Irion (ed.) *Hospice and Ministry*. Nashville, TN: Abingdon Press.

Jackson Pulver, L.R. (2003) 'An argument on culture safety in health service delivery: Towards better health outcomes for Aboriginal peoples.' Unpublished PhD Thesis, University of Sydney, Faculty of Medicine. Available at http://ses.library.usyd.edu.au/handle/2123/609, accessed on 17 June 2009.

Jarrett, S. (2009) 'Violence the way of traditional life.' *The Australian*, 10 June. Available at www.theaustralian.news.com.au/story/0,25197,25611112-25192,00.html, accessed on 29 June 2009.

Jenson, R. (2003) *On Thinking the Human: Resolutions of Difficult Notions*. Grand Rapids, MI: William B. Eerdmans Publishing Company.

Jenson, R.W. (1995) *Essays in Ttheology of Culture*. Grand Rapids, MI: William B Eerdmans Publishing Company.

Jourard, S. (1971) *The Transparent Self (2nd edn)*. New York: Litton Educational Publishing.

Kabat-Zinn, J. (1990) *Full Catastrophe Living – How to Cope with Stress, Pain and Illness Using Mindfulness Meditation*. London: Piatkus.

Kamali, H. (2006) *An Introduction to Sharia*. Malaysia: Ilmiah Publishers.

Kearney, S. and Wilson, A. (2006) 'Raping children part of "men's business".' *The Australian*, 16 May. Available at www.theaustralian.news.com.au/story/0,20867,19149874-2702,00.html, accessed on 3 September 2006.

Keck, D. (1996). *Forgetting Whose We Are: Alzheimer's Disease and the Love of God*. Nashville, TN: Abingdon Press.

Keller, Nuh Ha Mim (1994) *Reliance of the Traveller: A Classic Manual of Islamic Sacred Law*. Lebanon: Sunna Books. (Original work published in 1991.)

Kendig, H., Browning, C.J. and Young, A.E. (2000) 'Impacts of illness and disability on the well-being of older people.' *Journal of Disability and Rehabilitation 22*, 1 and 2, 15–22.

Khadro, Y. (1997) *Spiritual Needs for a Buddhist at Death Time*. Windsor, QLD: Karuna Hospice Service,.

Killick, J. (1997). *You Are Words: Dementia Poems.* London: Journal of Dementia Care.

Killick, J. and Allan, K. (2001). *Communication and the Care of People with Dementia.* Buckingham: Open University Press.

Kimble, M. (1990) 'Aging and the Search for Meaning.' In J. Seeber (ed.) *Spiritual Maturity in the Later Years.* London: The Haworth Press.

Kimble, M. and Ellor, J. (2000) 'Logotherapy: An Overview.' In M.A. Kimble (ed.) *Viktor Frankl's Contribution to Spirituality and Ageing.* New York: Haworth Pastoral Press.

Kimble, M.A. and McFadden, S.H. (eds) (2003) *Aging, Spirituality and Religion: A Handbook.* Volume 2. Minneapolis, MN: Fortress Press.

King, P. (2004) *Quest for Life – A Handbook for People with Cancer and Life-threatening Illnesses.* Sydney: Random House.

Kirkwood, T.B.L. (2000) 'Evolution of aging: How genetic factors affect the end of life.' *Generations – Journal of The American Society on Aging 24,* 1.

Kirkwood, T.B.L. (2003) 'Aging with grace. The nun study and the science of old age: how we can all live longer, healthier and more vital lives.' *Ageing and Society 1,* 23, 255–256.

Kitagawa, J.M. (1992) *The Christian Tradition beyond European Captivity.* Philadelphia, PA: Trinity Press International.

Kitwood, T. (1997) *Dementia Reconsidered.* Buckingham: Open University Press.

Klostermaier, K.K. (1994) *A Survey of Hinduism.* New York: State University of New York Press.

Kobia, S. quoted in World Council of Churches News Release (2005) 'Restating the Ecumenical Vision Demands Conversion, Says Kobia.' Geneva, 15 February.

Koenig, H. (1994) *Aging and God: Spiritual Pathways to Mental Health in Midlife and Later Years.* New York: The Haworth Press.

Koenig, H.G. (2007) *Spirituality in Patient Care: Why, How, When and What.* Philadelphia, PA and London: Templeton Foundation Press.

Koenig, H.G. and Lawson, D.M. (2004) *Faith in the Future: Healthcare, Ageing, and the Role of Religion.* Philadelphia, PA: Templeton Foundation Press.

Koenig, H.G., McCullough, M.E. and Larson, D.B. (2001) *Handbook of Religion and Health.* New York: Oxford University Press.

Kohn, R. (2003) *The New Believers, Re-imagining God.* HarperCollins; Sydney.

Kohn, R. (2007) *Curious Obsessions in the History of Science and Spirituality.* Sydney: ABC Books.

Koshy, N. (2004) *A History of the Ecumenical Movement in Asia, Volume 1.* Hong Kong: World Student Christian Federation Asia-Pacific Region, Asia and Pacific Alliance of YMCAs, and Christian Conference of Asia.

Kozier, B.J., Erb, G., Berman, A.J. and Snyder, S. (2003) *Fundamentals of Nursing: Concepts, Process, and Practice.* (7th edn.) Englewood Cliffs, NJ: Prentice Hall.

Krieg, A. (2006) 'Aboriginal incarceration: Health and social impacts.' *Medical Journal of Australia 184,* 10, 534–536.

Kulka, R.A., Schlenger, W.E., Fairbank, J.I., Hough, R.L. *et al.* (1990) *Trauma and the Vietnam War Generation: Report of Findings from the National Vietnam Veterans' Readjustment Study.* New York: Brunner and Mazet Publishers.

Lathrop, G. (1993) *Holy Things: A Liturgical Theology.* Minneapolis, MN: Fortress Press.

Layard, R. (2005) *Happiness: Lessons from a New Science.* New York and London: Penguin.

Leimena, J. (1941) 'De Ontmoeting der Rassen in de Kerk.' *De Opwekker 86,* 626–642.

Leimena, J. (1968) 'The task of restoring fellowship within the Church and the Indonesian Nation.' *South East Asia Journal of Theology, 9,* 3.

Lennartsson, C. and Silverstein, M. (2001) 'Does engagement with life enhance survival of elderly people in Sweden? The role of social and leisure activities.' *Journal of Gerontology 56B,* 6, 335–342.

Levine, S. (1987) *Healing into Life and Death.* Bath: Gateway Books.

Lewis, A. (1982) 'God as Cripple: Disability, personhood and the reign of God.' *Pacific Theological Review 16,* 1, 13–18.

Link-Up NSW Aboriginal Corporation and Wilson, T.J. (1997) *In the Best Interests of the Child? Stolen Children: Aboriginal Pain/White Shame.* Aboriginal History Monograph 4. Canberra: Aboriginal History Incorporated, Australian National University.

Livermore, C. (2008) *Hope Endures: An Australian Sister's Story of Leaving Mother Teresa, Losing Faith, and her On-Going Search for Meaning.* Australia: William Heinemann.

Loader, W.R.G. (2002) *Jesus' Attitude towards the Law: A Study of the Gospels.* Grand Rapids, MN and Cambridge: Eerdmans.

Lossky, V. (1978) *Orthodox Theology: An Introduction.* Crestwood, NY: St. Vladimir's Seminary Press.

McCrindle Research (2008) *Bridging the Gap. An Employers' Guide to Managing and Retaining the New Generation of Apprentices and Trainees.* Available at www.mccrindle.com.au, accessed on 28 November 2008.

McDermott, D. (2003a) *Dorothy's Skin.* (Poetry collection.) University of Wollongong: Five Islands Press.

McDermott, D. (2003b) '"How do you get cured of spiritual sickness?" Discarding a "blacks behaving badly" model of Indigenous Australian violence in favour of shared responsibility and a "men's business" approach.' London: International Health Exchange.

McDermott, D. (2004a) 'Ghassan's Gran and My Mother: Strategic Whiteness among Aboriginal Australians and Immigrant "Others"'. Balayi: Culture, Law and Colonialism, University of Technology, Sydney.

McDermott, D. (2004b) '"Abo-Proof Fence": Can Poetry and Prose Ground a "Virtual" Australian Apartheid?' Ngara: 'Living in This Place Now.' 4th Australian Poetry Festival, Sydney, September. Wollongong: Five Islands Press.

McDermott, D. (2006) 'Unknown family at the taxi stand.' *Medical Journal of Australia 184*, 10, 519–520.

McDermott, D. and Gabb, D. (2008) 'How do you teach "Cultural Safety/Cultural Competence/Cultural Ease"'? Psychology and Indigenous Australians: Teaching, Practice and Theory. Second Annual Conference, University of South Australia.

McDermott, D., Minniecon, R., Jackson Pulver, L., Clifford, A., Blignault, I. and Guthrie, J. (2008). '"Bringing Them Home" – Kinchela Boys' Home Aboriginal Corporation Strategic Plan.' Sydney: World Vision Australia/Office of Aboriginal and Torres Strait Islander Health (OATSIH), Department of Health and Ageing/Muru Marri Indigenous Health Unit, University of New South Wales.

McDonald, T. (2006a) 'Nursing therapeutic interventions for elderly residents with Post-Traumatic Stress Disorder (PTSD) and symptoms of dementia.' Royal College of Nursing Australia, Annual Conference, Cairns, Queensland, July.

McDonald, T. (2006b) 'Does physical decline in the older person mean reduced quality of life?' La Trobe University Conference: *Evidence in Practice: Leading the Way in Aged Care.* Bundoora, Victoria, September.

McDonald, T. (2007) 'Are you there? Facilitating relationships between residents and staff through a positive connections strategy.' Hammond Care 4th National Conference on Depression in the Elderly: *Successful Aging: Countering Depression in Old Age.* Sydney, NSW, June.

McFadden, S.H., Brennan, M. and Patrick, J.H. (eds) (2003) *New Directions in the Study of Late Life Religiousness and Spirituality.* New York: Haworth Pastoral Press.

McFadyen, A. (1990) *The Call to Personhood: A Christian Theory of the Individual in Social Relationships.* Cambridge: Cambridge University Press.

McFague, S. (1987) *Models of God: Theology for an Ecological, Nuclear Age.* Philadelphia, PA: Fortress Press.

MacIntyre, A. (1999) *Dependent Rational Animals: Why Human Beings Need the Virtues.* Chicago, IL: Open Court.

McKeown, J., Clarke, A. and Repper, J. (2006) 'Life-story work in health and social care: systematic literature review.' [Electronic version.] *Journal of Advanced Nursing 55*, 237–247.

MacKinlay, E.B. (2001) *The Spiritual Dimension of Ageing.* London and Philadelphia, PA: Jessica Kingsley Publishers.

MacKinlay, E.B. (2006) *Spiritual Growth and Care in the Fourth Age of Life.* London and Philadelphia, PA: Jessica Kingsley Publishers.

MacKinlay, E.B. (2008) (ed.) *Ageing, Disability and Spirituality: Addressing the Challenge of Disability in Later Life.* London and Philadelphia, PA: Jessica Kingsley Publishers.

McSherry, W. (2000) *Making Sense of Spirituality in Nursing Practice – An Interactive Approach.* London: Churchill Livingstone (Harcourt).

Macquarie, J. (1977) *Principles of Christian Theology.* Second edition. London: SCM Press.

Malina, B.J. (1981) *The New Testament World: Insights from Cultural Anthropology.* Atlanta, GA. John Knox Press.

Malouf, D. (1978) *An Imaginary Life.* London: Chatto and Windus.

Martin, B. and King, D. (2008) *Who Cares for Older Australians? A Picture of the Residential and Community-Based Aged Care Workforce, 2007.* Adelaide: NILS.

Massey, K., Fitchett, G. and Roberts, P. (2004) 'Assessment and Diagnosis in Spiritual Care.' In K.L. Mauk and N.K. Schmidt (eds) *Spiritual Care in Nursing Practice.* Philadelphia, PA: Lippincott Williams and Wilkins.

Matthews, S. (2003) 'Aging and Change in a Religious Community.' In J. Gubrium and J. Holstein (eds) *Ways of Aging.* Oxford: Blackwell Publishing.

Meeks, W.A. (1983) *The First Urban Christians: The Social World of the Apostle Paul.* New Haven, CT: Yale University Press.

Meilaender, G. (2003) 'Why remember?' *First Things,* August/September, 20–24.

Melia, S.P. (2008) 'Young in Spirit, Old in Bones.' *Engaging Aging 3,* 2. Available at www.usccb.org/nrro/summer2008. pdf, accessed on 21 April 2009.

Meyerhoff, B. (1978) *Number Our Days.* (Film and book; focuses on elderly Jews in Venice Beach, California.) New York: Touchstone.

Meyerhoff, B. (1992) *Remembered Lives: The Work of Ritual, Storytelling, and Growing Older.* Ann Arbor, MI: University of Michigan Press.

Mickley, J.R., Soeken, K. and Belcher, A. (1992) 'Spiritual well-being, religiousness and hope among women with breast cancer.' *IMAGE: Journal of Nursing and Scholarship 24,* 4, 267–272.

Miller, W. (2009) CEO, Jawoyn Aboriginal Corporation. Private communication, June 2009.

Millison, M. and Dudley, J.R. (1992) 'Providing spiritual support: A job for all hospice professionals.' *The Hospice Journal 8,* 4, 49–66.

Miner-Williams, D. (2006) 'Putting a puzzle together: Making spirituality meaningful for nursing using an evolving theoretical framework.' *Journal of Clinical Nursing 15,* 7, 811–821.

Moberg, D.O. (ed.) (1979) *Spiritual Well-Being: Sociological Perspectives.* Lanham, MD: University Press of America.

Moberg, D.O. (ed.) (2001) *Aging and Spirituality: Spiritual Dimensions of Ageing. Theory, Research, Practice and Policy.* New York: Haworth Pastoral Press.

Moffett, S.H. (1992) *A History of Christianity in Asia. Vol 1.* San Francisco, CA: Harper.

Mol, D. (1985) 'Minjung Theologie, Zuid Koreaanse Bevrijdingstheologie in een geïndustrialiseerde Samenleving.' *Wending 1,* 21–22.

Moltmann-Wendel, E. (2003) 'Friendship – The forgotten category for faith and christian community.' In J. Moltmann and E. Moltmann-Wendel (eds) *Passion for God: Theology in Two Voices.* Louisville, KY: Westminster John Knox Press.

Moody, H.R. (2005) (ed.) *Religion, Spirituality and Aging: A Social Work Perspective.* New York: Haworth Pastoral Press.

Moon, C.H. (1983) 'Minjung Theology.' *Ching Feng 26,* 48–49.

Muhamad Ali (2003) *Teologi Pluralis-Multikultural: Menghargai Kemajemukan Menjalin Kebersamaan.* Jakarta: Penerbit Buku Kompas.

Mullen, P. (2000) *The Imaginary Time Bomb: Why an Ageing Population Is Not a Social Problem.* London: I.B. Tauris and Co.

Murad, Abdal-Hakim (undated) *Islamic Spirituality, the Forgotten Revolution – The Poverty of Fanaticism.* Available at www.masud.co.uk/ISLAM/ahm/fgtnrevo.htm, accessed on 19 February 2009.

Ñānamoli, Bhikkhu and Bodhi, Bhikkhu (1995) *The Middle Length Discourses of the Buddha: A New Translation of the Majjhima-Nikaaya.* (trans.) Boston, MA: Wisdom Publications.

Nasr, Seyyed Hussein (ed.) (1997) *Islamic Spirituality Manifestations.* New York: Crossroad. (Original work published c.1991.)

Neuberger, J. (2008) *Not Dead Yet.* London: HarperCollins.

Newell, P.F. (2008) 'Addressing You.' In *La Campanella,* a privately printed newsletter.

New Revised Standard Version Bible (1989) Nashville, TN: Thomas Nelson Inc.

Noon, B. (2003) 'Burning Bright.' In S. Benson and J. Killick (eds) *Creativity in Dementia Care Calendar 2004.* London: Hawker.

Nouwen, H. (1976) *Aging: The Fulfilment of Life.* New York: Image Books, Doubleday.

Oasim Mathar, H.M. (ed.) (2003) *Sejarah, Teologi dan Etika Agama.* Yogyakarta: Interfidei/Dian.

O'Brien, M.E. (1999) *Spirituality in Nursing: Standing on Holy Ground.* Sudbury, MA: Jones and Bartlett.

O'Donohue, J. (1997) *Anam Cara: Spiritual Wisdom from the Celtic World.* London: Transworld Publishers.

OECD (Organisation for Economic and Cooperation and Development) (2009) *Fact Book (2009)* (Economic, Environmental and Social Statistics). Paris: OECD.

ONS (Office for National Statistics) (2001) *Religion in the UK.* Census, April 2001. Available at www.statistics.gov.uk/cci/nugget.asp?id=293, accessed on 3 November 2009.

Osborn, E. (2001) *Irenaeus of Lyons.* Cambridge: Cambridge University Press.

Paloutzian, R.F. (2002) 'A time-tested tool: The SWB scale in nursing research.' *Journal of Christian Nursing 19,* 3, 16–19.

Paloutzian, R.F. and Ellison, C.W. (1982) 'Loneliness, Spiritual Well-being, and the Quality of Life.' In L.A. Peplau and D. Perman (eds) *Loneliness: A Source Book of Current Theory, Research and Therapy.* New York: John Wiley and Sons.

Pearson, L. (1973) *Popular Ethics in Ancient Greece.* Stanford, CA: Stanford University Press.

Perry, B. and McDermott, D. (2007) 'Koorie Children in Trauma/Trauma in Koorie Children: Deeper understanding for better responses.' Victorian Aboriginal Child Care Agency (VACCA), Melbourne, Victoria, 7 December.

Perry, B.D. (2001). 'The Neurodevelopmental Impact of Violence in Childhood.' In D. Schetky and E. Benedek (eds) *Textbook of Child and Adolescent Forensic Psychiatry.* Washington, DC: American Psychiatric Press.

Pert, C. (1997) *Molecules of Emotion.* New York: Scribner.

Po Ho Huang (2005) *From Galilee to Tainan: Towards a Theology of Chhut-thau-thin* (ATESEA Occasional Paper 15). Manila: Association for Theological Education in South East Asia.

Post, S. (2004). 'Alzheimer's and grace.' *First Things,* April, 12–14.

Price, A.F. and Mou-Lam, W. (trans.) (1985) *The Diamond Sutra and The Sutra of Hui Neng.* Boston, MA: Shambhala.

Productivity Commission (2005) *Economic Implications of an Ageing Australia.* Canberra: Australian Government.

Ramsey, J.L. and Blieszner, R. (1999) *Spiritual Resiliency in Older Women: Models of Strength through the Life Span.* Thousand Oaks, CA: Sage Publications.

Raper, M. (2008) 'Not in danger, only near to death: Religious institutions and church in transition.' (President's address.) *Catholic Religious Australia.* Available at www.catholicreligiousaustralia.org/en/34, accessed on 21 April 2009

Raphael, B. and Swan, P. (1997) (after Clayer and Divakaran-Brown, and McKendrick) 'The Mental Health of Aboriginal and Torres Strait Islander People.' *International Journal of Mental Health 26,* 3, 14–15.

Read, P. (1981) 'The stolen generations: the removal of Aboriginal children in New South Wales 1883 to 1969.' Occasional Paper No. 1. Sydney: NSW Ministry of Aboriginal Affairs.

Reed, P. (1992) 'An emerging paradigm for the investigation of spirituality in nursing.' *Research in Nursing and Health 15,* 349–357.

Rehm, R., Cebula, N., Ryan, F. and Large, M. (2002) *Futures that Work: Using Search Conferences to Revitalize Companies, Communities and Organizations.* Stroud: Hawthorne Press.

Relf, M.V. (1997) 'Illuminating meaning and transforming issues of spirituality in HIV disease and AIDS: An application of Parse's Theory of Human Becoming.' *Holistic Nursing Practice 12,* 1, 1–8.

Riemer, J. and Nathaniel, S. (eds) (1991) *So That Your Values Live On: Ethical Wills and How to Prepare Them.* Woodstock: Jewish Lights Publishing.

Rinpoche, S. (1992) *The Tibetan Book of Living and Dying.* London: Rider & Co.

Ritschl, D. (1967) *Memory and Hope: An Inquiry Concerning the Presence of Christ.* New York: The Macmillan Company.

Robertson-Gillam, K. (2008) 'The effectiveness of choir therapy to reduce depression and meet the spiritual needs of people with dementia.' Paper presented at *Ageing and Spirituality: A Diversity of Faiths and Cultures,* 4th National CAPS Conference, Canberra, 17–20 August.

Rodney, V. (2000) 'When nurses cry: Coping with occupational stress in Thailand.' *International Journal of Nursing 37,* 535–544.

Rowe, J. and Kahn, R. (1997) 'Successful aging.' *The Gerontologist 37,* 433–440.

Rundqvist, E.M. and Severinsson, E.I. (1999) 'Caring relationships with patients suffering from dementia. An interview study.' *Journal of Advanced Nursing 29,* 4, 800–807.

Salzberg, S. (1995) *Loving-kindness – The Revolutionary Art of Happiness.* Boston, MA: Shambhala Books.

Schachter Shalomi, Z. (1995) *From Aging to Sage-ing: A Profound New Vision for Growing Older.* New York: Warner Books.

Schachter Shalomi, Z. (2006) 'The Spirit of Things.' Available at www.abc.net.au/rn/spiritofthings, accessed on 16 September 2006.

Schmemann, A. (1979) *Church, World, Mission: Reflections on Orthodoxy in the West.* Crestwood, NY: St Vladimir's Seminary Press.

Schmemann, A. (2003) *O Death, Where Is Thy Sting?* Crestwood, NY: St Vladimir's Seminary Press.

Schoenbeck, S.L. (1994) '"Called to care"– addressing the spiritual needs of patients.' *Journal of Practical Nursing 44,* 3, 19–23.

Seeber, J. (1990) 'Ministry with Retired Professionals.' In J. Seeber (ed.) *Spiritual Maturity in the Later Years.* New York: The Haworth Press.

Seeber, J. (2000) 'Meaning in Long-Term Care Settings: Viktor Frankl's Contribution to Gerontology.' In M. Kimble (ed.) *Viktor Frankl's Contribution to Spirituality and Ageing.* New York: The Haworth Pastoral Press.

Sher, L. (2004) 'Recognizing post-traumatic stress disorder.' *QJM: An International Journal of Medicine 97,* 1–5.

Silf, M. (2001) *Sacred Spaces: Stations on a Celtic Way.* Peoria, IL: Paraclete Publications.

Simatupang, T.B. (1967) *Tugas Kristen dalam Revolusi.* Jakarta: Badan Penerbit Kristen.

Simatupang, T.B. (1973) *Keselamatan Masa Kini.* Jakarta: Badan Penerbit Kristen.

Singer, P. (1994) *Rethinking Life and Death: The Collapse of Our Traditional Ethics.* Melbourne: The Text Publishing Company.

Snowdon, D. (2001) *Aging with Grace: What the Nun Study Teaches Us about Leading Longer, Healthier and More Meaningful Lives.* New York: Bantam.

Song, Choan-Seng (C.S.) (1975) *Christian Mission in Reconstruction.* Madras: CLS.

Song, Choan-Seng (C.S.) (1979) *Third Eye Theology.* Maryknoll, NY: Orbis.

Song, Choan-Seng (C.S.) (1986) *Theology from the Womb of Asia.* Maryknoll, NY: Orbis.

Stein-Parbury, J. (2000) 'Nursing around the world: Australia.' *Online Journal of Issues in Nursing 5,* 2. Available at www.nursingworld.org/MainMenuCategories/ANAMarketplace/ANAPeriodicals/OJIN/TableofContents/Volume52000/No2May00/NursinginAustralia.aspx, accessed on 27 February 2009.

Stoll, R. (1989) 'The essence of spirituality.' In V. Benner Carson (ed.) *Spiritual Dimensions of Nursing Practice.* Philadelphia, PA: W.B. Saunders Co.

Strand, J.A. and Peacock, T.D. (2002) 'Nurturing Resilience and School Success in American Indian and Alaska Native Students.' In *ERIC Digest* ED471488, 2 (Educational Resources Information Center).

Straw, J. (2007) *Cyril Foster Lecture.* Oxford University, 25 January 2007. Available at www.jackstrawmp.org.uk/speeches_detail.asp?id_content=39, accessed on 4 November 2009.

Stubbs, G. (2007) CEO, Link-Up NSW Aboriginal Corporation. Private communication, March 2007.

Suh David Kwang-sun (1981) 'Minjung and Theology in Korea.' In Kim Yong Bok (ed.) *Minjung Theology: People as Subjects of History.* Singapore: Christian Conference of Asia.

Suh Nam Dong (1981) 'Towards a Theology of Han.' In Kim Yong Bok (ed.) *Minjung Theology: People as Subjects of History.* Singapore: Christian Conference of Asia.

Swinton, J. (2001) *Spirituality and Mental Health Care: Rediscovering a 'Forgotten' Dimension.* London and Philadelphia, PA: Jessica Kingsley Publishers.

Swinton, J. (2007) *Raging with Compassion: Pastoral Responses to the Problem of Evil.* Grand Rapids, MI: William B. Eerdmans.

Swinton, J. (2008) 'Remembering the Person: Theological Reflections on God, Personhood and Dementia.' In E. MacKinlay (ed.) *Ageing, Disability and Spirituality: Addressing the Challenge of Disability in Later Life*. London and Philadelphia, PA: Jessica Kingsley Publishers.

Swinton, J. and Mowat, H. (2006) *Practical Theology and Qualitative Research*. London: SCM Press.

Tanahashi, K. (ed.) (1985) *Moon in a Dewdrop: Writings of Zen Master Dogen*. San Francisco, CA: North Point Press.

Tarmiji Taher, H. (1997) *Aspiring for the Middle Path: Religious Harmony in Indonesia*. Jakarta: Center for the Study of Islam and Society (CENSIS).

The Holy Bible (1999) New Revised Standard Version: Catholic Edition. Nashville, TN: Oxford University Press.

Theissen, G. (1982) *The Social Setting of Pauline Christianity: Essays on Corinth*. (Edited and translated by John H. Schutz.) Philadelphia, PA: Fortress, 1982.

Theissen, G. (1992) *Social Reality and the Early Christians: Theology, Ethics and the World of the New Testament*. Edinburgh: T. and T. Clark.

Thielicke, H. (1960) *Theological Ethics (Vol. 1)*. Grand Rapids, MI: William B. Eerdmans Publishing Company.

Thomas, M.M. and Abrecht, P. (eds) (1967) *World Conference on Church and Society: Christians in the Technical and Social Revolutions of our Time*. Geneva: World Council of Churches.

Tornstam, L. (2005) *Gerotranscendence: A Developmental Theory of Positive Ageing*. New York: Springer Publishing Company.

Torrance, A. (1987) 'The self-relation, narcissism and the gospel of grace.' *Scottish Journal of Theology 40*, 481–510.

United Nations (2009) *Millennium Development Goals*. Available at www.un.org/millenniumgoals, accessed on 4 November 2009.

US Census Bureau (2009) *The 2009 Statistical Abstract: Christian Church Adherents, and Jewish Population, States*. Available at www.census.gov/compendia/statab/cats/population/religion.html, accessed on 3 November 2009.

VandeCreek, L. and Smith, D. (1992) 'Measuring the spiritual needs of hospital patients and their families.' *The Journal of Pastoral Care 46*, 1, 46–52.

Vanier, J. (1998) *Becoming Human*. Mahwah, NJ: Paulist Press.

Van Klinken, G. (2003) *Minorities, Modernity and the Emerging Nation: Christians in Indonesia, a Biographical Approach* (Verhandelingen van het Koninklijk Instituut voor Taal-, Land- en Volkenkunde, Volume 199). Leiden: KITLV Press.

Ven. Thich Nhat Hanh (1987) *Interbeing – Commentaries on the Tiep Hien Precepts*. Berkley, CA: Parallax Press.

Ven. Thich Nhat Hanh (1991) *Peace Is Every Step – The Path of Mindfulness in Everyday Life*. New York: Bantam Books.

Weaver, H.N. (1999) 'Indigenous people and the social work profession: Defining culturally competent services.' *Social Work 44*, 3, 217-225.

Wedderburn, A.J.M. (1988) *The Reason for Romans*. (Studies of the New Testament and Its World.) Edinburgh: T. and T. Clark.

Westerman, T. (2004) 'Engagement of Indigenous clients in mental health services: What role do cultural differences play?' *Australian e-Journal for the Advancement of Mental Health (AeJAMH) 3*, 3, 1–7.

Wickeri, P.L. (ed.) (2000) *The People of God among All God's Peoples: Frontiers in Christian Mission*. Hong Kong/London: Christian Conference of Asia and the Council for World Mission.

Widyatmadja, J.P. (2005) *Kebangsaan dan Globalisasi dalam Diplomasi*. Yogyakarta: Yayasan Bimbingan Kesejahteraan Sosial/Kanisius.

Williams, R. (2006) 'Christian identity and religious plurality.' *Current Dialogue 47*, 6–10.

Wilson, A. (2004) *Living Well: Aboriginal Women, Cultural Identity and Wellness*. Winnipeg: The Prairie Women's Health Centre of Excellence. Available at www.uwinnipeg.ca/admin/vh_external/pwhce/pdf/livingWell.pdf, accessed on 29 June 2009.

Wooding Baker, M., McLean Heitkemper, M. and Chenoweth, L. (2008) 'Older Adults.' In D. Brown, H. Edwards, M. McLean Heitkemper, S.R. Dirksen *et al.* (eds) *Lewis's Medical-Surgical Nursing. Assessment and Management of Clinical Problems*. Marrickville: Elsevier Australia.

Woods, B. (2008) 'Introduction.' In R. Woods and L. Clare (eds) *Handbook of the Clinical Psychology of Ageing* (2nd edn). West Sussex: John Wiley and Sons, Ltd.

Yewangoe, A.A. (1987) *Theologia Crucis in Asia: Asian Christian Views on Suffering in the Face of Overwhelming Poverty and Multifaceted Religiosity in Asia*. Amsterdam: Rodopi.

Zarabozo, Jamaal al-Din (2002) *Purification of the Self: Concepts, Process and Means*. USA: Al-Basheer Company for Publication and Translations.

Zizioulas, J. (1975) 'Human capacity and human incapacity: A theological exploration of personhood.' *Scottish Journal of Theology 28*, 401–448.

Zizioulas, J. (1985) *Being as Communion: Studies in Personhood and the Church*. London: Darton, Longman and Todd.

Zizioulas, J. (1991) 'On Being a Person. Towards an Ontology of Personhood.' In C. Schwöbel and C. Gunton (eds), *Persons, Divine and Human: King's College Essays in Theological Anthropology*. Edinburgh: T. and T. Clark.

Zopa, L.T. (2008) *How to Be Happy*. Somerville: Wisdom Publications.

Subject Index

Author Index